MESSIANIC FULFILLMENTS

MESSIANIC
FULFILLMENTS

Staging Indigenous Salvation in America

HAYES PETER MAURO

University of Nebraska Press

LINCOLN

Publication of this volume was assisted by the Virginia Faulkner
Fund, established in memory of Virginia Faulkner, editor in chief of
the University of Nebraska Press.

Library of Congress Cataloging-in-Publication Data
Names: Mauro, Hayes Peter, 1970– author.
Title: Messianic fulfillments: staging indigenous
salvation in America / Hayes Peter Mauro.
Description: Lincoln: University of Nebraska Press, [2019] |
Includes bibliographical references and index.
Identifiers: LCCN 2018044472
ISBN 9780803299955 (cloth: alk. paper)
ISBN 9781496216267 (epub)
ISBN 9781496216274 (mobi)
ISBN 9781496216281 (pdf)
Subjects: LCSH: Indians in art. | Art and religion—United States.
| Indians of North America—Cultural assimilation. | Indians,
Treatment of—United States.
Classification: LCC N8217.15 M38 2019 | DDC 700/.482—dc23
LC record available at https://lccn.loc.gov/2018044472

Set in Adobe Garamond Pro by E. Cuddy.

Contents

Illustrations

Acknowledgments

It is necessary and just to acknowledge several individuals and institutions that have assisted me in the timely completion of this manuscript. First, I would like to thank Matthew Bokovoy and Heather Stauffer at the University of Nebraska Press for their expertise in editing and preparing this manuscript and bringing it up to par for publication. I would also like to acknowledge the logistical and financial support of the CUNY Academy, which awarded me a prestigious fellowship supporting completion. In terms of funding, the Smithsonian Institution's very generous summer fellowship program allowed me to complete the bulk of research for this manuscript during an intensive stretch in the summer of 2015. I owe a debt of gratitude especially to Bill Truettner, Karen Lemmey, Eleanor Harvey, and Amelia Goerlitz. In addition, I would like to acknowledge Julius Rubin, one of the country's leading scholars on religious history in the United States. Professor Rubin's feedback was perhaps the single most important factor in the improvement and completion of this text. I would be remiss if I did not acknowledge the staff at the Hampton University Archives, the Smithsonian Archives, and the Cumberland County Historical Society, all of whom facilitated my work. Thank you all.

MESSIANIC FULFILLMENTS

Introduction

This book offers a critical art historical account of institutional processes of aesthetic and ontological assimilation in American history. My primary aim is to consider the use of imagery executed in a multitude of mediums by various evangelical Christian movements in the spiritual transformation of those deemed culturally or racially "subaltern"—especially Native Americans.[1]

This sense of "transformation" was informed by a positivistic belief in the ability to transform and thus uplift such groups and was enacted institutionally through a variety of educational projects. Its visual parallel and justification was in imagery consisting of a wide variety of mediums and styles. With Native Americans, the belief was that one could, through reeducation, transform the unevolved and destructive "blanket Indian" into a civilized American whose speech, behaviors, appearances, and ideological beliefs mimicked those of an ahistorical, idealized middle-class Anglo-American.[2] Not coincidentally, the depiction of the atavistic Native was a common and repetitive symbol in Euro-American art dating back to colonial times. As an aesthetic counterpoint, the famous "before-and-after" photographs (figs. 1, 2) made at Indian boarding schools, such as the Carlisle School in Pennsylvania, purported to display for the viewer a seemingly miraculous social and racial transformation, revealed in two apparently straightforward albumen prints published side by side in the school's official publications.

When taking into account both the *representational* and the *ritual* enactment of these racial, physiological, and spiritual transformations, it will become clear that the "deviant" Indian and the "normative" Anglo were polarizing constructs that were metaphorically staged in image and text and especially in material culture. Such staging, often seen in the images discussed within these pages, was intended as proof of the saving effects of Christian evangelical practices vis-à-vis the indigenous Other. Beyond this, the radical Protestant movements involved in this staging of salvation put out messages and metaphors often intended to be messianic, either by implication or through direct prescription. That is, they served as proof not only of the miraculous salvation of the Other(s) targeted for "salvation" but of the manifestation of the millennial imminence of the arrival of a new world, one infused by Christian charity and prosperity. The facilitation of this ideal new world was commonly seen as a "fulfillment" of theological covenants between Christ and the members of these various sects. This process is considered in great depth in the chapters herein.[3]

As discussed by scholars in previous studies, pseudosciences such as phrenology and craniology also played a central role in the perceived legitimacy of these widely consumed images. Upon reflection, what previous literature on this topic does not pursue thoroughly enough was not only the role of scientific discourse but its interrelationships with the well-known evangelical Christian movements that have been, at various times, popular in mainstream American culture. More specifically, I consider the visual cultures of such movements, including Puritanism, Quakerism, and Mormonism, each of which advocated a "millenarian" worldview in its own way.[4] In the final chapter I extend this consideration to the Gilded Age and the era of what historians call the Social Gospel, which was essentially a thinly veiled secularization of evangelical impulses inflected by the social Darwinian principle of total institutional immersion, then popular among social reformers.[5] By engaging in the conversion of spiritually defunct Others, many evangelical Christians in America believed, one was assuring one's own salvation through the fulfillment of the aforementioned covenant with Christ. Besides one's personal salvation, the upholding of covenants was important for the larger preparation of society in lieu of the perceived eschatological concern of Christ's return and final judgment. Each of these groups saw America as an ideal staging ground for this personal and collective salvation because of the "primitive" nature of the continent. It had an Edenic quality lacking in the corrupted confines of the Old World of Europe, and thus the search for the New Jerusalem could begin anew.

The historian Christopher Evans notes that some have interpreted the Social Gospel movement—despite its pseudoscientific conceptual underpinnings—as "liberal," in that it departed from earlier evangelical movements that sought primarily to save individual souls, without necessarily altering social or economic relations in this world. As Evans observes, this perception, held by Martin Luther King Jr. and others, has some historical viability. However, it overlooks the fact that even the "liberal" reformers of the Social Gospel era, while no doubt more ambitious in scope than their evangelical predecessors, often held Eurocentric and even white supremacist presumptions regarding race. The structural change sought was with an eye toward Anglicizing and proletarianizing racial and social subalterns, as their "capacities" were assumed to be limited. Thus while the movement did wish to integrate Native Americans and African Americans to a greater degree, it was via a cultural whitewashing intended to obliterate all traces of tribal or racial characteristics, while the promised economic benefits consisted mainly of subordinate economic occupations within the context of status quo market relations.[6]

These considerations have revealed to me a significant gap in the current literature on assimilation, as the concurrent and mutually reinforcing relationship between pseudoscience and evangelical Christianity in the uplifting of subaltern populations has not been adequately addressed, especially as pertaining to the visual representations of these "subalterns" by dominant cultural groups.[7] This is significant, as national leaders have commonly assumed that racial and spiritual characteristics have a necessary correlation, something presumably evident in both the psychic makeup and the physiology of various social and ethnic groups. This assumption has had historically wide-reaching consequences for indigenous populations and cultures. Further impacting this focus on a physiological-spiritual correlation is the politically popular idea that Americans more broadly do—or ought to—have some sort of unifying spirit, which at least in theory binds the nation's citizenry together. As such, by either implication or overt prescription, newer arrivals as well as the country's variously defined subaltern populations have been expected to fulfill the mandate of "becoming American" in this sense. And by "becoming American," any threat of social or spiritual dissolution of the body politic is thereby averted.

Such Americanizing projects must of course be viewed in the larger historical context of "race" as an emergent category in Western civilization during the Enlightenment. The overarching assumption often made by religious reformers and evangelists was that salvation and an "American" identity were attainable so long as variously defined Others would become Anglicized in their dress, speech, and behavior. In the context of European settler societies like the United States, this makes sense from a scholarly perspective, as many scholars have located the emergence of "race" as a sociobiological category during the Enlightenment, something constructed in response to the rise of colonial empires and industrial capitalism, and the consequently unprecedented level of exchange between Europeans and indigenous peoples globally.[8]

In this context and with respect to Native American populations, a proper "American" identity has commonly been seen in terms of dialectically related concepts. Thus advocates of assimilation and Americanization have generally favored Christianization over animism or other "pagan" cosmologies, market-based economic competition over communalism or tribalism, agrarian property ownership over nomadic hunting and gathering, and rigorous physical hygiene and mental discipline over the perceived sloth and squalor of indigenous life.[9] One may see this "proper" or "ideal" American identity as being shaped by encounters with these subaltern groups over time, and these dualities served to differentiate and hierarchize Anglo-American middle-class identity in relation to such Otherness. The images I discuss were often intended to convey an aesthetic reflection of these racial and cultural distinctions, inflected by an assumed spiritual significance.

The current project thus examines the role of radical religious movements in the fabrication of American identity and how artists influenced by or affiliated with such movements graphically depicted this idealized identity, as commonly projected onto the bodies and minds of racial and social Others. While these various religious movements differ significantly in terms of the specifics of their doctrines, they all ultimately advocate forms of Christian American triumphalism, which they assume is universally and unproblematically applicable to all peoples and all cultures. In this context, triumphalism may be taken to refer to the belief in the ultimate prevalence and success in the assimilation project and the "truth" of the doctrine to which it often refers: the preparation of souls for the Second Coming. This notion was openly and routinely discussed among reformers of various eras. For instance, the Carlisle School's founder, Richard Henry Pratt, commonly referred to the evangelically inspired boarding schools of the Gilded Age as foundational for the establishing of "Christ's Kingdom" in this world.[10]

This assumption becomes manifest in reformers' literature, art, and evangelical activities. Just as the practitioners of modern scientific empiricism have commonly assumed the universal applicability of their findings to all of nature and humanity, religionists have commonly made a similar assumption regarding their own versions of theological doctrine, no matter how idiosyncratic. A conceptual parallel between the racialized pseudoscientific depiction of the ideal American is present when considering these concurrent evangelical images. An overriding notion is that indigenous Americans, initially perceived as childlike, primitive, and/or heathen, were in desperate need of Christianization lest they be mired in perpetual sin and oblivion, a failure that would lead to their own damnation in the eyes of Christ, but also to the potential damnation of the very missionaries who believed themselves to be emissaries from Christ, enacting a perceived covenant with their god through the saving of heathen souls.

This covenant has its literary and cultural origin in the Abrahamic covenant with God as described in chapter 17 of the Book of Genesis in the King James version of the Bible, lending racial uplift the veneer of biblical sanction. There the patriarch Abraham (previously Abram) receives his new sacred name and exchanges vows with God, pledging to do the Lord's work on earth and in so doing multiply his followers. Through this covenant, God vows to make Abraham and his followers kings of all nations on earth, beginning with the promised land of Canaan. The Canaanite metaphor would be a central trope in Puritan theology, as the Massachusetts Bay Colony and its environs were commonly characterized as a modern Canaan, or "New Jerusalem," by Puritan leaders. Its inhabitants were "English Israelites" and as such were the new chosen people of Christ and needed to be held to a strict moral standard in their commercial dealings, the Puritan leader Cotton Mather wrote.[11] The Native thus required sanctification or banishment, and in either case it was believed that Christ's will was being executed.

Some Puritan leaders attempted to fulfill this covenant with Christ through direct action. Primary among these missionaries was John Eliot, who is discussed in greater length in the first chapter. Eliot established his famous "praying towns," in which he sought to convert thousands of Native Americans in the region through direct evangelism and the translation of the Bible into Algonquian languages.[12]

Beyond theology, pseudoscientific racial categories established by Anglo-American scientists during the Enlightenment served as an unwitting partner in the perception of the Native American as heathen and thus in need of salvation and Anglicization.

Native Americans, like other groups, could be lumped together in simplified categories based on spiritual deficiency and racial inferiority, indicated by "scientific" measurements of skull size and proportion. In turn, there were some in the scientific and evangelical communities who put forward what were ostensibly "empirical" claims that such physiological racial distinctions had a direct correlation with intellectual and moral capacities as well as a relative need for Christian salvation. I discuss these instances at length in this book. In fact some writers, such as the Puritans Richard Mather and Richard Baxter even drew overt parallels between then-current racial theory and biblical mandates in attempting to justify slavery or interracial warfare.[13]

Important to this discussion as well is a consideration of the *economics* of evangelical activity and racial pseudoscience. With this in mind, I here propose the term "market Christianity" to refer to a very specific historical iteration of Christian belief and practice, dating roughly from the Protestant Reformation in Europe in the sixteenth century to the height of industrialization in the late nineteenth and early twentieth centuries in the United States. By "market Christianity," I mean a brand of Christianity that historically coincides with the growth and evolution of capitalist economic modalities during this same period. This concept closely parallels that of "ascetic" capitalism, put forward by the sociologist Max Weber. It is a simultaneous iteration of faith and praxis that seeks to merge the dual concerns of salvation and profit. Weber argues for a "spirit" of capitalism specific to the rise of Protestant mercantilism in modern times, as outlined earlier. For him, and for my concerns in this study, such a spirit is unique to Protestant-dominated cultures during the eras of mercantile expansion and industrial development and played a critical role in legitimizing the conquest of the frontier and the assimilation of the continent's indigenous population.[14]

The practitioners of market Christianity were the newly empowered (mostly bourgeois) Protestant populations of Europe and its colonies, who rose in social, economic, and political stature during this era. These practitioners asserted their interpretation of Christian doctrine, especially biblical verse, in such a way as to accomplish psychic accommodation to the rapidly changing economic and technological worlds they inhabited. Market Christianity allowed for greater personal freedom in interpretation and practice, freeing the worshipper from the confines of Catholic and Anglican dogma and hierarchy. It was liberation theology for the mercantile bourgeoisie, a new form of faith that spoke to their specific needs over time.

In broad terms the well-known Reformation theology proffered by reformers like Martin Luther (1483–1546), John Calvin (1509–64), and their followers served to conveniently accommodate these same middle-class practitioners of the new faith to an increasingly intense engagement with market-based capitalism in its varying forms—many of which were morally questionable at the time, such as the slave trade, the obliteration of indigenous cultures, and the making of profit on interest. These newfangled mercantile practices may have been considered immoral or even heretical in previous eras in Europe. Therefore Weber's proposal, under Calvin's theological influence: that what emerges out of Protestant discourse in the sixteenth and seventeenth centuries is a new "spirit" of capitalism, which served to accommodate the changing exigencies of middle-class mercantilists during these centuries, both in Europe and the New World.[15]

While in broad terms Luther's theology, particularly his idea of the "calling," may be said to have "liberalized" Christian practice in the marketplace during the Reformation, Calvin's writings are more pertinent for my discussion. Indeed Weber derived his critique of the Protestant ethic from Calvin's writings, specifically Calvin's emphasis on "vocational aestheticism." This idea posits that one attains salvation through constant hard work on behalf of Christ. In this unceasing and self-cleansing work, one was to attain a closeness to *certitudo salutis*, a state of grace in the eyes of Christ. The practitioner could then in effect display fidelity to God's will and increase his or her likelihood of election in the next world by recapturing what Calvin termed the "first condition" of Adam before the Fall.[16] The "hard work" executed as a result was the accumulation of capital, which in itself could be a sign of the moderation, discipline, and self-control practiced by the wealthy. It was also the deployment of a portion of those accumulated resourccs in the effort of either obliterating or assimilating the unbelieving Other. By so doing, an act of Christian charity was accomplished, rendering the world a bit more prepared for the Second Coming.

In the context of mercantilism, such a religious practice as that proposed by Calvin and other Protestants had a high perceptual use value for its practitioners, as it sought to smooth over potential contradictions encountered in daily life under the mercantile system. Thus, in Marxist terms, it is tempting to see the Protestant faith historically as a "superstructural" or ideological implement used by many as a mechanism intended to facilitate the acceptance of mercantile values and practices in one's own life. More important for the discussion here, such a mechanism also facilitated the imposition of these values onto the bodies, minds, and cultures of various tribal Others who were encountered first in the North American imperial colonies of Great Britain and other European powers, and later in the western frontier of the United States. Through assimilation one was doing works on behalf of one's own *certitudo salutis* and was also building Christ's kingdom in this world by awakening the "calling" in the hearts and minds of those most in need: the uncivilized and heathen Other.[17] In this sense a Marxist-Weberian consideration of the uses of aesthetics in the upholding of mercantile relations within an ideologically Protestant culture lends an effective overarching methodological framework through which to critique such imagery.

The Marxist superstructural view of religion needs to be viewed here in the specific context(s) of evangelical Christian culture in America during the centuries mentioned. In *The Protestant Ethic*, Weber argues that viewing religion as a simple superstructural reflection of the "reality" of the economic base of market economies is problematic, as at times a society's religious ideals and material conditions diverge sharply. I believe that Weber is correct in this cautionary note. In the case of American evangelism and mercantile practices both in the colonies and later in the expanding nation, evangelical Protestantism did not so much function as an unproblematic mirror reflection of the material (economic) conditions of the American marketplace. As I have alluded, more often religious ideologies of varying sorts served to *accommodate* its practitioners to those material cultural realities, usually by *sanctifying* market-driven behaviors.[18]

Many American thinkers, from Puritan leaders onward, posited their own moral imperatives that sought to ease the tension between their constant hunt for mercantile wealth and their need for otherworldly salvation. The evangelizing of the nation's Others was yet another way of *proving* the righteousness of these two practices. For example, in his text Weber cites the writings of the famed American intellectual and politician Benjamin Franklin (1706–1790) as embodying such a desire. Weber argues that Franklin was an early example of a thinker who attempted to moralize the practice of monetary gain as a valid ethical end and in his writings attempted to persuade the reader of the virtues of its practice. Franklin characterizes monetary gain as an outgrowth of one's diligence, guided by his ten famous virtues. Through this diligence, one could not only make a profit but could use that profit for the benefit of the community in acts of charity. This notion dovetails with the motivations often expressed by Christian reformers who wished to "uplift" the savage through evangelization and the inculcation of a Protestant-style work ethic.[19] Weber's critical views of race relations and religion in America were informed by an extended trip he took to the country in 1904, during which he met and spoke with both evangelical and Native American leaders. This trip would lead to his writing and publication of *The Protestant Ethic*. I explore this contextualization in chapter 4, as it directly responds to the cultural politics of Gilded Age America.

Despite evidence presented by Weber and others of the ongoing historical inequities perpetrated against Native Americans by both governmental and "voluntary" institutions, as time passed many of the more committed evangelicals professed the idea and practice of Christian salvation through radical projects of social engagement with variously defined Others in the country, an activity that allowed them to define themselves as "saved." Through such intensive spiritual engagement, in the form of preaching, evangelism, conversion rituals, and even full-blown educational projects, it was thought that the cherished salvation mandated by biblical verse could be accomplished. And again, by engaging in these acts of salvation, the charity advocated in biblical verse would be enacted, thereby leading to a fulfilled covenant with Christ. Conveniently such projects of salvation, especially in the era of the Social Gospel of the Gilded Age, concurrently promoted the proletarianization of those to be saved. This in turn was thought to assure their social docility. This idea would be represented in the visual imagery and text rendered by various Protestant movements and would be most systematically actualized in Indian policy and the appearance of Christian boarding schools during the Gilded Age.

Proletarianization looked favorable when compared to slavery or reservation life, both of which were increasingly seen as distasteful or even outright immoral by some Christian leaders, especially Quakers and northern evangelicals before and after the Civil War. Other Christian leaders sought justification for slavery's abolition in biblical verse. A distaste for slavery is perhaps unsurprising in this context, as such an objection served both Protestant ethics and mercantile and industrial necessity, wage labor being seen increasingly as a better alternative.

As we shall see, though, not all Christians agreed. There were other committed Christians, in both the North and the South, who either turned a blind eye to the plight of slaves or actively advocated slavery as a sort of "merciful" paternalistic outcome for those enslaved. While the theological justification of slavery was deployed by some Puritan thinkers as early as the seventeenth century, nineteenth-century antebellum pseudoscientists, including Samuel Morton, George Gliddon, and Josiah Nott, viewed slavery as an acceptable burden to be borne by Anglo-America, as it guaranteed that a "scientifically" inferior race—African Americans—would be "taken care of" by the slave-owning class. Such caretaking of course had a use value for pro-slavery evangelicals who fancied that the system was humane, as the scientifically and spiritually inferior races could hardly be expected to care for themselves.[20] It was thus that enslavement could be sold as a form of ethical caretaking.

The upshot of all of this thought for my discussion is that evangelicals commonly assumed that racial and social Others of all stripes were in need of quick salvation, as time was growing short and the end of this world was nigh. To save these poor souls, one had to engage in an aggressive campaign of publicity and spiritual transformation, lest they be left behind in the coming golden age, a displeasure to God.[21] Conveniently, pseudoscientific doctrine, intentionally or not, could easily fuel evangelical flames, as it posited—from supposedly empirical investigations of skulls, bones, and other physiological traits—that African Americans, Native Americans, and others had lower "capacities" than Anglo-American populations. Many evangelicals assumed it was their moral obligation to uplift or save members of these groups, through a variety of means, as all humanity was potentially threatened by damnation.[22]

A primary means of so doing was by hiring visual artists to fabricate images that would signify the evangelical agenda for and activity toward racial Others (figs. 1, 2). Throughout this period we see the fabrication of imagery that juxtaposes the supposedly "degenerate" state of Others with an idealized state of civilized spiritual fulfillment. The truth value of such images, while clearly suspect to modern eyes, was so widely assumed at this time that for the most part they remained relatively uncontroversial during and after the time of their making.

While visualizing the racial or spiritual Other was of concern throughout American history, such an institutional practice became most pressing during the era of the Social Gospel of the late nineteenth and early twentieth centuries in America. The rise of industrial capitalism, as opposed to the earlier pre-industrial mercantile capitalism practiced by the Puritans and others, drove a new demand for a massive number of new laborers. These new laborers needed to be mentally and physically disciplined for the exigencies of the factory, the new workplace of the industrial world. As such, the boarding schools, being the institutional manifestations of the Social Gospel philosophy, were expected to produce these workers from the ranks of the growing masses of subaltern Others—not only Native Americans and African Americans but the newer waves of eastern and southern European immigrants.[23] The imagery and texts reproduced in school publications needed to demonstrate the students' proletarianization as well as their Christianization. However, this aesthetics of economic discipline was only a modernized version of earlier evangelical images in that both subsets display a form of what the cultural historian Ella Shohat has called "colonial didacticism."[24] Colonial didacticism is a visual and literary discourse that graphically depicts the "enlightening" of the Other via the intervention of the colonizer, who is of course represented as being morally, intellectually, and at times biologically superior.

A final consideration when viewing evangelical imagery in the context of American art history is the very historiographic quality of many of these images. As mentioned earlier, Weber cautions us in assigning a strictly "reflective" aesthetic relationship between the economic base of a civilization and its superstructural implements, such as its iconic imagery. This is important in consideration of the current subject matter, as many of these evangelical images are both retrospective and memorializing in conception, as well as transformative in intent. Thus some of the images considered here were executed by artists living decades or even centuries after the events and persons they purport to represent. For example, images and references to Puritanism, Quakerism, and Mormonism became fashionable in the United States at various points *after* the key events leading to the establishment of these movements took place. In some cases, decades or centuries had passed. Such historiographic disjunctions, while requiring scholarly reckoning, are essentially no different from the situation confronted by the "masters" of the Italian Renaissance centuries earlier when depicting biblical or classical scenes for their wealthy patrons in Florence and Rome.[25]

Such retrospective image-making is widespread in American evangelical cultures and serves to establish linkages with a tradition of narratives connecting later practitioners with the teachings of the founders of their respective movements. They play a critical epistemological role, both for practitioners of these faiths and for historians wishing to gain insights into the concepts and doctrines of these faiths. As John Winthrop, George Fox, Joseph Smith, and other "prophetic" figures sought to recapture what they saw as an authentic and primitive brand of Christian faith and practice independent of institutional constraints and histories, so the artists hired by their followers attempted to recapture an authentic sense of the spiritual and historical genesis of their respective movements, often driven by a need for empirical legitimacy as well as visual illustration and explication. It is important in this study and others like it that wish to understand the discourses of these movements in relation to cultural and spiritual Otherness to uncover the conditions under which such imagery was produced.

When we do examine the specific contexts in which these images were produced, we are reminded of the four basic functions of religious imagery, as outlined by David Morgan and Sally Promey in their book *The Visual Culture of American Religions*. Morgan and Promey's construct is helpful here, as it clarifies the conceptual and institutional structures under which such images are produced, and their principles may be applied to each of my four chapter topics. They claim that there are four overriding motivations or purposes for religious imagery. First, and most traditionally, it is intended to *communicate* between realms. In traditional medieval Christian icons, for instance, it is assumed that the image is a direct representation of the divine that communicates sacred ideas and doctrines directly to the worshipper, which the authors term a "ritualized exchange" between the deity and the viewer. Second, it establishes a *communion* of shared beliefs and experiences between a community of worshippers. Third, it creates and organizes *memory*, something akin to my earlier discussion. Fourth, it facilitates acts of *imagination* that serve as the meaning-making rituals of shared religious experience.[26]

When examining the visual imagery of the various Christian movements discussed here—Puritanism, Quakerism, Mormonism, and those of the more secular Social Gospel—we quickly see that these images are distinctly *modern* in medium and style and also in conceptual arrangement. The traditional function of the classically iconic images of the Middle Ages does not literally apply here. As I alluded to earlier, the function of modern American Christian images is more often in line with what Morgan and Promey would call communion, memory, and imagination. It is not assumed that the images were literal icons offering revelation of the Divine, but rather were most often historiographic, empirical, didactic, or binding in function. And as such, the overriding assumption on the part of the artists and their patrons was that a particular *posterity* was being "spoken to" by such images, and that these images had the power to influence behavior and perception, especially in the nineteenth century and beyond.[27] In other words, these modernized visions of Christian narratives and values were intended from the outset for a worldly audience, very often one either contemporary with the artist or patron or one assumed to be generations down the line. But in all cases the images are evangelical in the sense that they were directed at the minds of those who required conversion by naturalizing ideology and thus serving as a conceptual glue that binds the material and the spiritual, past and present, the prophet and the practitioner. This issue is taken up in greater depth throughout the text.

To sum up, then, chapter 1 considers the visual culture of the Puritans. Puritanism has often been seen as a foundational ideology for subsequent American culture and history, and as such the consideration of Puritan aesthetics is important conceptually for subsequent chapters. Chapter 1 examines portraiture in relation to Puritan theology, specifically the Calvinist doctrine of worldly success as a sign of God's favor. In contrast to this, I then consider the perception and depiction of various Others, especially Native Americans and the social deviants within their own society, persons accused of demonic possession. Such text and imagery resulted from inherited racist preconceptions of non-European peoples and from often negative encounters between the Puritans and these "deviant" groups, encounters seen by Cotton Mather and other Puritan intellectuals as threatening the very foundation of their New Jerusalem. And as we shall see, any aggression by the Puritan leaders in the pursuance of territorial conquest or monetary gain was consistently theologized by Puritan writers as being initiated by divine sanction.

In chapter 2 I consider Quaker history and theology as outlined by its founder, George Fox. The Quaker version of the New Jerusalem was the province of Pennsylvania, named after Fox's protégé William Penn, who founded the colony in the 1650s. The founding myth of Quakerism is Penn's subsequent treaty with the indigenous Lenape Indians, an event depicted by the Quaker artist Benjamin West almost a century later. I examine this foundational image in relation to the Quaker self-conception and trace its genealogy forward to the work of Edward Hicks, who sought to metaphorically recapture the supposed "golden age" of Penn's arrival in the wake of the Quaker schism of 1827. I look at Hicks's work, and his concern with racial harmony and natural history, in relation to the work of the Quaker scientist and naturalist Samuel Morton, who attempted to popularize pseudoscientific racial hierarchies in America during this era.

Chapter 3 focuses on the visual culture of Mormonism, founded by the charismatic theologian and entrepreneur Joseph Smith.

Issues of spiritual and racial identity collide at the core of Mormon doctrine. In his famous text *The Book of Mormon*—believed by his followers to be the translated word of previous divine prophets—Smith asserts that God willed that those lacking faith would be visually stigmatized with a sort of "mark of Ham." Specifically the faithless could be identified by having darker skin than the ancestors of the righteous. The use of color therefore becomes important in Mormon imagery, as Mormon exemplars—along with Jesus—are often depicted as genetically endowed Nordic superheroes.

Finally, chapter 4 considers the Social Gospel of the Gilded Age. I take a close look at images produced at the Carlisle Indian School and the Hampton Institute. Both institutions were evangelical in conception, in the sense that their founders wished to "improve" their students through Christianization and proletarianization. The images made at both schools emphasize a merging of Christian evangelical and social Darwinian evolution as seen in the subaltern students. This transformation was characterized as "miraculous" by school officials, and the images produced were vital in securing political and financial support for each institution.

I

Puritanism and Fidelity

In discussing religious radicalism in America, it is helpful to consider the ideas and motivations of some of the earliest European settlers in the New World, all of whom brought with them varying forms of Christian faith and practice. This chapter therefore examines the colonial era, paying particular attention to Puritan visual culture and comparing the imagery produced in this culture to some of that executed in other early colonial cultures, specifically New France. In both colonial contexts, Christianity played a central role in stabilizing and hierarchizing the social body. The Puritans are important because of their chronological place in American history, but also because the concepts espoused in their theology would prove central to American conceptions of race, class, and salvation well beyond the colonial period and find echoes in later millenarian Christian movements in America.

When considering Puritan theology, one must of course place it in its proper historical context in order to understand the power it had for its adherents. Likewise the status of images within Puritan society must be weighed to understand how Puritans communicated their specific sense of proper social order. Thus I examine the origins of Puritan thought, Puritans' perception of the Massachusetts Bay Colony as the fulfillment of biblical prophecy, the role of portraiture in fulfillment of their "errand," as well as visual images and textual references that depict the "Others" of Puritan society: Native Americans and the demonically possessed. I also discuss the centrality of retrospective perceptions and interpretations of the Puritans in American visual culture, as seen in images of them executed during the Second Great Awakening of the nineteenth century.

Puritanism, like all Protestant sects, has its conceptual origins in the Protestant Reformation in Europe, which unfolded during the fifteenth and sixteenth centuries. Central to the formulation of this new Christian faith and practice are the writings of John Calvin (1509–64) and Martin Luther (1483–1546).

Luther was a German Catholic priest who rebelled against the authority of the Catholic Church with the publication of his tract "Disputation on the Power and Efficacy of Indulgence," more popularly known as "The Ninety-Five Theses," in 1517. Luther's theses were a succinct statement against what he saw as the various corrupted practices of the Catholic Church, most notably the selling of indulgences. In the Middle Ages an "indulgence" was a guarantee from the Church of eternal salvation in exchange for some sort of material—usually monetary—contribution. In the first of his "Theses," Luther theologically critiques indulgences by claiming that one's entire life ought to be given to repentance, and as such a simple material donation is insufficient for attaining immediate salvation. Luther's writings and teachings eventually led to his formal excommunication from the Church in 1521. As a professor of philosophy and the study of biblical verse at a university in Germany, he was an expert in the interpretation of Holy Scripture. As such, he taught that Christian believers were sanctified through their own reading of the Bible and their faith alone, a doctrine known in Latin as *sola fide*, or "justification by faith." At the time this was a radically antiauthoritarian viewpoint, as Luther privileged the faith of the individual believer over adherence to Church tradition and deference to its ecclesiastical hierarchy. Luther also attempted to revise other aspects of Christian doctrine, such as his unconventional views of consubstantiation, *theologia crucis*, and the Two Kingdoms theory.[1] Essentially he acknowledged the existence of earthly things, such as authority, power, and secular rule, but saw them as subordinate to the will of God. From this perspective, the perceived arrogance of Catholicism and the subsequent corruption of the Church led him to reject its legitimacy.

Luther provides us with a convenient starting point for a discussion of radical Protestantism in Europe, but a far larger impact would be had in America by the followers of John Calvin. Calvin's teachings dovetail with those of Luther and were more immediately incorporated into Puritan theology. Calvin was a French Protestant theologian, who, like Luther, broke from the Catholic Church in the sixteenth century. His influence was arguably more wide-reaching than even Luther's as his writings were read in several countries at the time, including most of northern Europe. Anglican dissenters, who left England in the 1550s when the Catholic queen Mary ascended to the throne, encountered Calvin's writings while in exile on the continent, and then translated them and brought them back to England five years later, when a Protestant monarchy was restored with Elizabeth. This brief period, known as the Marian Exile, is commonly seen as the historical origin of a coherent Puritan theological movement; it was conceived in resistance to the teachings of the Church of England, which under Elizabeth sought a compromise position with English Catholics.[2]

Calvin's central concepts, as I discussed in the introduction, include *certitudo salutis*, or the attainment of a state of grace in Christ. To attain certainty of one's salvation, Calvin taught, faith alone was not sufficient. One had to engage in works throughout one's life, and in so doing proved to God that one's will was in accordance with his via the performance of acts that would please him. In this emphasis on works, Calvin's theology not only departs from Luther's *sola fide* but forms the foundation of the Puritan work ethic as outlined by Max Weber.[3] Calvin valued reason above all other human faculties, although he saw it as potentially in conflict with evangelical theology, which would demand that reason be subordinated to divine revelation through faith and the reading of scripture. While he was skeptical of the ability of human consciousness to grasp ultimate truths, Calvin is known for advocating a sense of naturalism in his theology, which states that humans share a universal "religious instinct" that allows them to discern evidence of God's existence within aspects of the natural world.[4] This latter point is crucial in understanding Puritan justifications for the production and consumption of images.

The art historian Wayne Craven offers a helpful discussion of Calvin's teachings in relation to Puritan art. Craven argues that in his religious tract *The Institutes of the Christian Religion*, Calvin adopts a surprisingly liberal view of pleasure in earthly existence. He saw no necessary problem with pleasure, provided it was indulged with moderation. In fact he encouraged his followers to actively engage in worldly activities, especially mercantile activities. This is because he saw worldly prosperity as a "natural" sign of God's favor, a view in keeping with his theological naturalism. In this formulation we have the seeds of the famous "Puritan work ethic."[5]

Craven extends this discussion to state that in his *Institutes*, Calvin differs from the Catholics in his view of the proper content and function of images. Calvin rejects sacred subject matter, seeing it as depleting God by making *overt* reference to that which is beyond human consciousness. He likens idol-worshipping Catholics to ancient pagans in their attraction to images of the divine. He argues against such a position by referencing scripture in the *Institutes*: "In the Law, accordingly, after God had claimed the glory of divinity for himself alone, when he comes to show what kind of worship he approves and rejects, he immediately adds, 'Thou shalt not make unto thee any graven image, or any likeness of any thing that is in heaven above, or in the earth beneath, or in the water under the earth' (Exod. 20:4)."[6]

Instead Calvin favors secular subjects done in a naturalistic manner, as such subjects are best suited to *indirect* references to the divine within the day-to-day. In this context, God's graces could be indirectly and thus humbly displayed via the appearance of the portrait's subject or through the domestic happiness of a family, as seen in the famous Freake portraits (figs. 3, 4).[7] In portraits such as these we see the merging of mercantile sensibility with Christian theology in a way perhaps unanticipated by Calvin.

In addition to the teachings of Calvin, Craven sees middle-class English mercantile culture of the era as influential on the stylistic appearance of Puritan portraits in the seventeenth century in the colonies. Craven cites the work of Weber as forging a key intellectual link between the concurrent rise of mercantile capitalism and Protestant theology in Europe. As discussed in the introduction, Weber sees the skills needed in mercantilism—hard work, initiative, personal responsibility, individualism, pragmatism, and so forth—as also setting the groundwork for the more practical bent in the theology of Lutheranism and Calvinism. Concurrently these are also foundational values in the formation of bourgeois identity during the modern era. The Puritans, constituting a largely middle-class movement set against the aristocratic prerogatives of both Catholic and Anglican authority, thereby identified with the merchant class in England from which they derived and whose values they largely shared. It is in this context that the concept of market Christianity is operative. In this sense, the seemingly straightforward quality of Puritan imagery is unsurprising and may be related to both English and Dutch Calvinist portraiture in Europe during this period.[8] In Puritan imagery we therefore see the combination of bourgeois empiricist and Protestant theological perceptions.

Puritan theology is complex and is heavily influenced by the writings of Calvin. Its ideas were expressed most famously in the learned and imagistic language used by its leaders, most notably John Winthrop (1587–1649), Cotton Mather (1663–1728), and others. Beyond the influence of Calvin, it is noteworthy that the structure of Puritan writing, as seen especially in the work of Winthrop and his theological opponent John Cotton (1584–1652), bears a rationalist influence, at least in terms of the structuring of the arguments. For example, upon reading their texts, one may see that both men write in a structure similar to the dissident

French philosopher René Descartes in his *Meditations*. In that famous work, Descartes sets up a series of "objections" that he had received from other thinkers upon the publication of his earlier work, the *Discourses*. He then writes out his philosophical "meditations" in hypothetical response to these objections. Similarly both Winthrop and Cotton, when trying to appeal to their followers, write out a series of hypothetical questions and then respond to these questions in an effort to dispel spiritual doubt, as their responses are commonly grounded in either biblical verse or historical analysis. Such similarities are perhaps unsurprising. While the three thinkers clearly had broad philosophical and theological differences, all three nonetheless wished to modernize Christian doctrine by giving it a rationalized basis and by freeing Christian faith and practice from the traditional controls of aristocratic Catholic or Anglican authoritarianism.[9]

Conversely Descartes wrote that the faculty of thought, or the *cogito*, was the quality that differentiated humans from lower animals. This faculty, although conceived by him as a rationalist trope governed by reason, was given to man as a "pure intellect" by God. Thus the rationalist Descartes had a grounding in Christian metaphysics, which was to be the foundation of his system, in a manner similar to the Puritan thinkers of his era. In both cases, and despite their very real doctrinal differences, Descartes and the Puritans tacitly recognized the new need for the use of a rationalist and empirical *method* in the forwarding of Christian thought during the post-Reformation era, as each desired to establish a Christian faith and practice beyond the confines of ecclesiastical traditions in Europe. This was an era in which all claims on truth, be they scientific or theological, were subject to a heightened empirical scrutiny unknown to medieval thinkers. It was no longer sufficient to simply quote the Bible or cite the supposed occurrence of miracles in the abstract; one was now obligated to "scientize" Christian truths via the logical methods of the emerging Enlightenment.[10]

Winthrop wrote and first delivered his famous sermon "A Model of Christian Charity" while traveling to the colony from

England aboard the ship *Arbella* in 1630. Winthrop was trained as an attorney and thus was not a member of the ecclesiastical class, but a layman. Nevertheless the Protestant doctrine of *sola fide*, as outlined by Luther, permitted even laypersons to assume roles of spiritual leadership within congregations. With this doctrine, it was asserted, any individual could attain forgiveness and salvation through the act of faith alone. While mainstream Puritan leaders did reject the similar doctrine of antinomianism and insisted upon works (in addition to faith) as a prerequisite for salvation, Luther's concept nevertheless opened doors, broadly speaking. Thus laymen such as Winthrop could be taken seriously as legitimate representatives of Christian learning. Such a modern, individualistic view of faith and practice flew in the face of older Catholic ecclesiastical hierarchies. The Catholic idea that faith could be arrived at only through deference to ecclesiastical authority was derided by Protestant critics as "popery."[11]

Another factor propelling Winthrop in his sermonizing was the Protestant practice of the "spiritual" miracle. In contrast to Catholic interpretations of miracles, Protestant theologians tended to believe that miracles consisted in the use of faith to teach oneself and others about the path to salvation. As the Puritans were a premillennial Protestant sect and believed in the *future* coming of Christ, this task was tantamount. By saving "dead souls," or those who had lost their way, Winthrop and others could do Christ's work in this world by sermonizing, and thereby bridging the work-faith gap. This was in stark contrast to the medieval Catholic conception of the miracle, which was seen as a *literal* event that occurred in a time and place and thus needed to be historicized and proven. For Protestants, such a notion was characteristic of the deceptions of popery; they saw miracles as immediately accessible to any faithful individual, and as such miracles could directly and positively change the lives of others in the community with a view to the coming world.[12]

With this in mind, Winthrop delivered his sermon to his fellow passengers aboard the ship. In it he famously idealized the new colony as a "city on a hill," a place that could potentially serve as a beacon of divine light for the rest of the world for generations to come. However, the hopeful vision he lays out in the sermon is tempered by the insertion of Puritan doctrine and its potential applications in the context of social realities in the colony: "God Almighty in his most holy and wise providence hath so disposed of the condition of mankind, as in all times some must be rich, some poor, some high and eminent in power and dignity, others mean and in subjection."[13]

In his sociospiritual model, Winthrop here deftly and concisely lays out the "human condition" in Puritan terms: the inevitable distinctions between individuals and social classes are the doing of "holy and wise providence" rather than something produced and exacerbated by mercantile or economic conditions and practices. As a foil to these inequitable conditions, Winthrop and other Puritans perceived such difficulties as a de facto test given to them by God, something intended to separate the charitable from the selfish. One was obligated as a saintly leader of a congregation to engage in acts of charity, which served to both offset socioeconomic distinctions and defuse potential social upheaval within the colony. In explaining God's reasons for this social model, Winthrop says it so "that he might have the more occasion to manifest the work of his spirit: first upon the wicked in moderating and restraining them, so that the rich and mighty should not eat up the poor, nor the poor and despised rise up against their superiors and shake off their yoke; secondly in the regenerate, in exercising his graces in them, as in the great ones, their love, mercy, gentleness, temperance, etc.; in the poor and inferior sort, their faith, patience, obedience, etc."[14]

As embodied in this quote, Winthrop's conception of the colony is not so much revolutionary as quite conservative in terms of social and economic relations between the "regenerate" and the "poor and inferior." It is through the charity of the wealthy that society remains peaceable, and these works of charity are seen by Winthrop and other Puritan writers as an enactment of divine will in this world. In engaging in them, one can better save oneself and possibly others. In fact Winthrop makes this explicit in his writings, such as his essay "Reasons to Be Considered." He sees the new colony, and reasons for its establishment, as a fulfillment and extension of the Abrahamic covenant discussed in chapter 1 of the Book of Genesis. As he wrote, "The whole earth is the Lord's garden and he hath given it to the sons of men, with a general condition, Genesis 1:28, *Increase and multiply, replenish the earth and subdue it.*"[15]

For his part, Mather published his epic history of Puritanism in America in 1702. The tome, titled *Magnalia Christi Americana* (*The Glorious Works of Christ in America*), attempts a systematic account of the works and lives of the Puritans from early settlement through the end of the seventeenth century. Mather's perspective differs significantly from Winthrop's. The hopeful vision offered by Winthrop in his sermon had necessarily been tempered by the harsh historical realities of the intervening decades two generations later. As such, Mather is giving us a summation of the Puritan vision and history in the wake of the Antinomian Controversy, the Salem witch trials, the Pequot War, the 1660 Restoration, and King Philip's War, each of which had a significant impact on the colony and its self-perception. Nevertheless it seems to be Mather's intent in his history to rectify the millennial vision of a New Jerusalem with the material realities of life in the colonies, and he tends to fall on the side of his fellow Puritan intellectuals, still wishing to idealize a sense of hopefulness for the colony's future.

Two aspects of Mather's history strike one immediately when considering Puritan relations with both the American land and its indigenous inhabitants. His opening paragraph in the introduction to the text is illuminating: "I write the *Wonders* of the CHRISTIAN RELIGION, flying from depravations of *Europe*, to the *American Strand*: and, assisted by the Holy Author of the *Religion*, I do, with all conscience of *Truth*, required therein by Him, who is the *Truth* itself, report the *wonderful displays* of His infinite Power,

Wisdom, Goodness, and Faithfulness, wherewith His Divine Providence hath *irradiated* an *Indian Wilderness*."[16]

Like Winthrop, Mather attributes the settlement and subsequent history of New England to divine providence. And like his predecessor, he perceives the new land as a sort of "primitive" space into which the Puritans gloriously fled in order to escape the "deprivations of Europe," in this context a reference to both Roman Catholicism and the Church of England. In this new space it is "divine providence" that is required to enlighten the "Indian Wilderness," a phrase of central concern here.

Mather then delves into greater historical and cultural detail about the Puritan errand in the New World. He states that the main reason for Protestants coming to America was so that they could pursue an uncorrupted practice of Christianity free of "Popery." In his view, the "First Reformation" was incomplete and needed to be superseded, and the Church of England failed to accomplish this. Thus true Christians had to leave Europe altogether to practice a version of Christianity in line with the true laws of Christ. While Puritans wanted initially to be part of the Anglican Church, they were driven off by misled leaders. This action obstructed a true "Evangelical Reformation," precipitating the "exile" of the Puritans in the "horrible wilderness" of America. Significantly Mather goes on to claim that Protestant churches must return to what he repeatedly calls the "first Ages" of Christianity that existed prior to Catholic corruption.[17]

Mather's discourse here is instructive. For Puritans, and indeed for many other radical Christian movements in the nation's history, one sees a particular desire for a *restoration* to what they perceived to be the "true" conditions of Christian faith and practice prior to the supposed corruption of the religion by Roman influences in the early Middle Ages. In this sense the Puritans, as Mather indicates, wanted more than mere reformation; they wanted a pre-Roman, purified basic form of the faith, and they perceived the New World of America as an untouched space in which to enact Christ's will by establishing a spiritual utopia. Interestingly this notion of the "primitive" church being restored historically and in a sense conceptually parallels the Puritan views of the "primitive" Others they encountered.

These views indicate that, as Winthrop states in the description of his model for Puritan society, the leaders of the movement were idealistic and yet had no illusions about the very real differences that existed between themselves and these various Others. Otherness in Puritan terms could mean Others without, such as Native Americans and African Americans, or Others within, such as the "mean" classes to which Winthrop refers directly. Even more famously, Mather and other Puritan intellectuals would introduce another group of Others in their writings: the demonically possessed. In all such cases, these various groups were construed as spiritually lacking, and this lacking was conveyed in their writings as well as in the various aesthetic presentations seen in Puritan culture.

In fact, in his writings Mather envisioned a social order in the colony that was parallel to his desire for spiritual sanctification. He tended to label all perceived social and even racial types as in need of "benedictions" of various sorts, a process he describes in a series of diary-like entries he wrote, collected, and published as the "Reserved Memorials." For instance, he claims that when in a public place such as a street corner, he would "bless thousands of persons, who never knew that I did it."[18] The purpose of these secret benedictions was an effort on his part to maintain the spiritual fabric of the colony, in the face of its increasingly diversified population, one that was diversifying socially, economically, and racially in the late seventeenth and early eighteenth centuries. Thus Mather had special benedictions, each one corresponding to a typology assigned to the individuals he encountered in public spaces. For a "young Gentlewoman," he applied the benediction "*Lord*, make 'em *wise Virgins*, as the *polish'd Stones of thy Temple*." His views on race are expressed even more graphically in his benediction for "A *Negro*": "*Lord, wash* that poor Soul *white* in the *Blood* of thy Son."[19]

Mather's views on race were informed by both theology and the fashionable scientific trends of his lifetime, as I will discuss later in this chapter. Chromatic metaphors standing in for spiritual purity or defilement were readily used by him and many other Christian leaders in their writings and in their imagery throughout the nation's history, as we shall see. For now, it is important to note that Mather's sense of the colonial social structure was one held together by spiritual "whiteness," with all people therein having a preordained or proper place sanctioned by Christ. His seemingly magnanimous benedictions were thus a silent effort on his part that paralleled his public lamentations over the breakdown of order in the colony during the period following the revocation of the colony's original royal charter.

While the Puritans are known primarily for their textual production, some wealthy Puritans hired painters to execute portraits. In these portraits, such as those of the Freake family, we commonly see the articulated Puritan self, whose body is rational, intact, and blessed by Christ, all of which is signified in the facial expression, clothing, physical bearing, and surroundings of each subject. Looking at these images, it is as if Winthrop's ideal metaphor of the "body of Christ" is visualized therein. Referring to specific biblical excerpts from Ephesians 4:16, I John 4:8, and I Corinthians 12:22 and 27, he wrote in "A Model of Christian Charity": "Love is as absolutely necessary to the being of the Body of Christ, as the sinews and other ligaments of a natural body are to the being of that body."[20]

The original excerpts from the Bible as quoted by Winthrop make no mention of specific organic bodily parts such as "sinews and ligaments," these metaphors being his own insertion for his sermon. The *biological* body, an inheritance from modern empiricism and the scientific method, thus becomes a central metaphor for grace or lack thereof in Puritan literature and art. The body imbued by Christ's love has strength and coherence, that love being likened to the structure holding together healthy physical bodies. The assumption on Winthrop's part that these two systems of thought, one ancient and theological and the other modern and empirical, can be seamlessly combined in an argument reveals the distinctly *modern* character of much Puritan thought. As Sacvan Bercovitch has noted repeatedly, it was the Puritans above all others who wished to effect an ideal merging of metaphysics with materialism, seeing their material attainment as an earthly sign of God's good grace.[21]

Paralleling Winthrop's biological metaphors, Mather infused his history with millennial significance, as if the colony were predestined by God's will. In a later sermon, "Theopolis Americana," he speaks of America as having streets "paved in gold," a direct reference to the apocalyptic visions set forth in Revelation 21:21 in the King James Bible.[22] Like Winthrop he perceived the new colony as a sort of New Jerusalem, a place where Christian charity and fellowship could potentially be redeemed in lieu of the perceived corruption of European Christendom. In that sense both attempted, through complex and varied rhetorical metaphors, to establish the colony as a *fulfillment* of biblical prophecy for modern times. The "mission" undertaken in the New World may therefore be seen as an effort to prove the legitimacy of their perceived divine calling through a material manifestation. As Mather puts it in "Theopolis Americana":

> *Come hither, and I will show you* an admirable Spectacle! 'Tis an Heavenly CITY, *descending out of Heaven, from* GOD. There is an Heavenly CITY, which the Great GOD, has *Prepared* for them, to whom *He will be a God*: A CITY to be inhabited by an *Innumerable Company of Angels*, and by the *Spirits of Just Men made Perfect* by a Resurrection from the Dead, with JESUS *the Mediator of the New Covenant* shining upon them: A CITY; where *God shall dwell with men, God Himself shall be with them*, and we shall *Inherit all things*.[23]

Mather here defines New England in terms of divine providence, as a glorious gift bestowed upon humanity by Christ. As such, it was of paramount importance that his listeners be exhorted not to abuse such a gift. Mather's perception of the new society is heavily influenced by Martin Luther's formulation of the Two Kingdoms. Both saw this world as having been sent to man by God so that they might enact the divine will through secular laws. With this gift came responsibility, as Mather continues:

> The *Business* of the CITY shall be managed by the *Golden* Rule. The *Things* that use to be done in the *Market-Place* shall be done without *Corruption*. There shall be no *Base* Dealing in it. It is added, It is *as it were Transparent Globe*: That is, The Dealing shall be so *Honest* that it shall bear to be *Look'd* into; it shall be so *Sincere* that men shall be willing to have their very Hearts *Look'd into*. There shall be no *False-Dealing*: All shall be done with all possible *Integrity*.[24]

While Puritans, coming under the influence of Calvin, saw prosperity in business as a sign of divine favor, greed and ostentation were a constant problem, and spiritual leaders like Mather attempted to continually regulate the habits of their adherents through such sermonizing. In a parallel vein, one sees concurrent lofty spiritual and material ideals represented in Puritan images of the New World. The Freake portraits (figs. 3, 4) and the self-portrait of the Puritan artist and businessman Thomas Smith (fig. 5) attempt to display the Puritan self, fully actualized and shown as materially triumphant, a sign of Christ's favor. And yet as we shall see, Smith also renders a vision of that "self" as mortal and vulnerable, a nod to humility in the face of Christ's beneficence.

The Freake portraits are important for a number of reasons, especially because they represent not only their literal subjects but a historical moment in New England, when mercantile sensibility was overtaking the colony's original doctrinaire religious sensibility. Such portraits come about after 1660 due to the increasing economic viability of the patrons. Such evolving economic conditions, and not an aversion to images, dictated the presence or absence of portraits at various times.[25]

Puritan portraits such as these were done for the home and were intended to be displayed for family members and invited guests only. They celebrate marital domesticity, familial lineage, and social position. Family contentment, such as that seen here, was endorsed in scripture and also in Calvin's writings. The material prosperity shown in Freake's portrait, for instance, was acceptable, as it indicated that John Freake, who owned multiple businesses, had worked hard at God's calling for him, and thus affluence was his reward.[26]

In closely examining these portraits, Craven argues that the fine quality of the metals and textiles in the Freake portraits suggests affluence and mobility, as many of these materials—including lace, taffeta, silver, and velvet—needed to be imported from abroad at great expense. Importantly, the hair styles and coloring of the clothing show prosperity and confirm the couple as members of the mercantile class, as opposed to the ministerial class or the working class. This insistence on class confirmation is an indication of the increasing influence of mercantile values in New England at this point; the differences between the merchants and ministers were not matters of prohibition versus allowance but of degree. The debate was about where the line ought to be drawn between respectable prosperity and ostentation. These lines were constantly being negotiated by individuals and the society in which they lived, as merchants tended to respect Calvinistic calls for moderation (but not prohibition), and ministers allowed for display to some degree, as it indicated a consistent successful following of Christ's calling. Such negotiation was often a political and legal issue, as the General Court, the legal governing body of Massachusetts Bay, always had trouble regulating mercantile attire despite trying to do so repeatedly.[27]

Perhaps most important when considering the Freake portraits and other Puritan images is that they are not garbled attempts at emulating the European Baroque style that existed concurrently across the ocean. The images rather are partaking in a separate tradition that is more oriented toward middle-class consumption and as such is less sensual than the continental Baroque styles. Craven refers to this comparatively flattened, linear style as not only middle class but "subcourtly," indicative of the Elizabethan-Jacobean tradition in Britain as well as the Netherlands.[28]

The self-portrait of Thomas Smith (fig. 5) seems to rest at a crossroads both aesthetically and culturally. When compared to the Freake portraits or other, earlier Puritan images, Smith's self-portrait takes on a greater sense of dimension and more assertively incorporates familiar Baroque-era visual tropes within the composition, including the window leading to a distant background and the red drapery on the upper right. With his body set amid these accoutrements, Smith rests his hand on top of a skull, which serves as an important symbol in Puritan art, as it is intended to remind viewers of their own mortality and impending judgment at the hands of God, a visual symbol also commonly seen in Puritan tombstone carving from this era. Nevertheless the prosperous Smith—his prosperity signaled by the drapery, the fine furniture in the room, and his full head of hair—inhabits a space with clear perspectival recession. This spatial recession exceeds the comparatively flattened formula used by the anonymous limner who executed the Freake portraits. The table on which the skull and a piece of paper rest clearly recedes toward the window in the rear of the room, and in turn the window lets out onto a seascape in which a naval battle rages.

While Smith is clearly concerned with indicating his earthly prosperity, and thus divine favor, he is equally concerned with themes that interested his contemporary Mather during this post-Restoration era in the colony. Smith indicates his humility in the face of God by the presence of the *memento mori* of the skull, and even paints a brief poem onto the paper lying on the table. The famous poem is written in Early Modern English:

Why why should I the world be minding
Therein a World of Evils Finding.
Then Farwell World: Farewell thy Jarres
Thy Joies thy Toies thy wiles thy Warrs
Truth Sounds Retreat: I am not sorye.

Puritanism and Fidelity

The Eternall Drawes to him my heart
By Faith (which can thy Force Subvert)
To Crowne me (after Grace) with Glory.
   T.S.

Smith thus indicates his awareness of his own vulnerability at the hands of God and his willingness to relinquish his existence at any time deemed appropriate by the creator. In this sense, his self-portrait is not to be read as sheer mercantile vanity but as a document indicating his existential balance. He is both prosperous and humble, materially engaged and unattached. As a final touch, Smith renders a sea battle happening outside the window. The battle is most commonly interpreted as not happening in the "present" moment that has Smith sitting in his room, but rather as a scene from his past. As a young man, Smith worked as a merchant marine and was aboard a ship that was involved in a battle off the Barbary Coast of North Africa. The naval convoy of which Smith was a part consisted of British and Dutch ships, and the enemy ships, as well as the fort on the shore, bear Islamic flags, perhaps that of the Ottoman Empire. Thus Smith indicates his dual role as merchant and faithful Christian and also as defender of the faith against the "heathen" forces of Islam.[29]

In contrast to these portraits, which seem to desire a balance between sanctification and mercantile display, the secular and the sacred, Puritan imagery gives us the inverse of the triumphant Puritan self in the figure of the unarticulated indigenous Other. In what is perhaps the first Puritan image to depict an indigenous body, we see an opposite of the well-composed, sanctified bodies praised by Winthrop. In 1629 Puritans in England set up a trading company known as the Massachusetts Bay Company (MBC). The establishment of the MBC was financed by wealthy donors in England, and it was intended to oversee trade between the colonies and the Crown.[30] Its foundational document was the charter, which established a structure of governance for the company and also stated the concurrent evangelical aims of this mercantile endeavor.

The charter discusses the ultimate aim of the rules and structures established therein: "Whereby our said People, Inhabitants there, may be soe religiously peaceable, and civilly governed, as their good Life and orderlie Conversation, maie wynn and incite the Natives of Country, to the Knowledge and Obedience of the onlie true God and Savior of Mankinde, and the Christian Fayth, which in our Royall Intention, and the Adventurers free Profession, is the principall Ende of this Plantation."[31]

The authors of the charter wished the entire governing structure and the laws of the MBC to serve evangelical ends, for the salvation of both colonists and Natives alike. This lofty ideal would come into question as the seventeenth century wore on and historical and economic pressures began to secularize and diversify the Puritan colonies.

Interestingly the seal used to illustrate the MBC charter depicts an Edenic and primitive-looking indigenous American uttering the words, "Come over and help us" (fig. 6). The central image is set within a roundel frame that contains a Latin phrase that in English translates as "Seal of the government and society of Massachusetts Bay in New England." The Native figure in the seal is depicted in terms common in early European encounter and settlement images of indigenous peoples. He stands welcoming and seemingly helpless, arms open, looking at the viewer.

It is thought that the seal was manufactured in England and was originally made of silver. According to entries in the *Records of Massachusetts*, a copy of the charter was sent to the colony via ship to John Endicott and was transported by a Samuel Sharpe, who may have been involved in manufacturing the original seal. Under the charter, Endicott would be appointed an original member of the Council, the governing body of the colony, and would serve as an assistant to Winthrop. Multiple entries in the *Record* indicate that the seal impression was transported in 1629. One entry is an inventory for a ship headed to the colony, and another is a letter written to Endicott indicating the importance and meaning of the charter. The entries date to March and April 1629. The inventory mentions a "patent under seale," a reference to the charter with the seal impression upon it. This was sent on Endicott's ship with other, more common provisions for the colonists.[32]

The Endicott letter, sent to him by the governor and deputy governor of the MBC, further explicates the presence of the seal:

> Since yor depture, wee haue, for the further strengthening of or graunt
>
> from the councell at Plymoth, obtayned a confirmacon of it from his maty [i.e., majesty] by his tres pattents, undr the broad seale of England, by wch said tres pattents
>
> wee are incorporated into a body pollitique, wth ample power to goune [i.e., govern] & rule all his mats [i.e., majesty's] subjects that reside wthin the limitts of our plantacon, as by the duplicate thereof under the broad seale, wch we have delivered to Mr. Sharpe to bee deliued to yow, doth fully appeare.[33]

The anachronistic typography, orthography, grammar, and syntax of this passage render it difficult for a modern English-speaking reader. Essentially it references the seal of the MBC and its political significance for the new colony. While the charter was legitimized under the "broad seal" of England, a reference to either the king's privy seal or the more general Great Seal of Parliament, the letter goes on to specify, "We have caused a common seal to be made, which we have sent by Mr. Sharpe." This reference seems to indicate the presence of the specific MBC seal, created expressly for the Company. The presence of the Company seal, bearing the image of the Native American, is further indicated by an addendum to this letter: "The aforewritten is, for the most part, the copy of our general letter sent to you together with our patent, under the broad seal and the company's seal in silver, by Mr. Samuel Sharpe."[34]

The engraver—perhaps the aforementioned Samuel Sharpe—has given the figure a "voice" by inserting the bubble emitting from its mouth, thereby projecting a will and consciousness favorable to the Puritans. The figure holds a bow and arrow, props that would become a staple in depictions of Indians for centuries and that indicate the figure's lack of civilization, as he apparently needs to rely on hunting and gathering rather than the more civilized forms of animal domestication and agriculture in order to survive. The bow and arrow also commonly signify the implied belligerence of the indigenous warrior, although here they are held uselessly to the side, with the arrow pointing down, indicating submissiveness. Further, the figure is in an open and ambiguous landscape, with no settlement or other sign of civilization in sight. Finally, the figure is dressed in a skirt of foliage, akin to how European Christian artists depicted Adam and Eve after the Fall. Thus the Indian is not only unsophisticated, uncivilized, naïve, and in need of help but also spiritually defunct. This last point would be recognizable to contemporary Puritan viewers and would serve as a reminder to them of their obligations as charitable Christians, and also of the "principall Ende of this Plantation." Such assumed obligations are in keeping with a more general sense of the Puritan covenant with Christ, as highlighted by Mather in his *Magnalia* when characterizing the divine colony.

In addition to having these Edenic and biblical connotations, the rendering of the figure also seems to have been influenced by classical and medieval European concepts. It is slightly muscled, and the open-arm stance is vaguely reminiscent of the famous orant pose in the early medieval period in Christian art, which was intended to signify a prayerful figure openly praising Christ in an enthusiastic posture. Given this possible influence, the figure could communicate to the contemporary Puritan viewer a version of Indians that foreshadowed their supposed future enlightenment at the hands of Puritan missionaries. As the orant was originally intended to convey a spiritual openness to Christ, this figure indicates an openness to the "help" to be brought to the wilderness by the Puritan settlers and missionaries.

This image sees parallels in other early depictions of Native peoples executed by European artists, for example in a famous engraving executed by the engraver Theodore Galle (1571–1633) in 1630 after a drawing by the artist Jan van der Straet. Galle's

Puritanism and Fidelity

image depicts the Italian explorer Amerigo Vespucci's arrival in the New World and was popular and widely distributed as an engraving, and thus was likely known to educated Puritans in England and possibly even the colonies. In addition to being a Flemish engraver, Galle was also a Protestant minister living in the Netherlands in the wake of the Reformation. His engraving would become a staple of European imperialist imagery both at the time and subsequently for scholars.[35]

The Galle image maintains this iconic status due to its explicit and graphic depiction of what the historian Michel de Certeau has termed the "discourses of mastery."[36] Galle neatly summarizes in one image the ideological and technological implements that were taken by European explorers at the time to constitute their superiority over the Native: Christianity, science, and armaments. These are shown in the cross being held by Vespucci, the nautical astrolabe in his other hand, and the sword he bears at his waist.

Similar to the Puritan depiction of the Native American on the MBC seal, the figure in Galle's engraving is apparently in need of assistance. While in the Puritan image we see the Native being given a voice—miraculously in English—in the Galle engraving we have a Latin caption along the bottom that narrates the scene for the viewer. In English it reads, "Americus rediscovers America; he called her once and thenceforth she was always awake." Thus the slumbering allegorical female figure is given consciousness by Vespucci's arrival, as some Puritans would attempt to bring spiritual consciousness to the Natives within their midst. While the two figures differ in gender—one male, the other female—both are shown as veritably helpless and in need of some sort of awakening. Both don the Edenic skirt of foliage around their waists, and both are in compliant physical positions in relation to the viewer: the Native with arms outstretched in what appears to be a welcoming gesture and Galle's figure in a reclining position indicating her lack of preparedness for the encounter with Vespucci, who here is given the role of upright conqueror. It is also implied that both figures lack civilization. Galle goes even further, representing not only the "sloth" of the slumbering America, seen literally in the animal next to her, but also in the cannibalism shown in the background. Thus both figures appear to be in need of Christian and scientific enlightenment, a trope that smooths over the philosophical tensions inherent in Reformation theology between empiricism and metaphysics.

The MBC seal was significant for the Puritans, as it gave a visual reference to the supposed ultimate aim of the colony, which was evangelization. It was first used when the charter was drafted in 1629 and would remain in use until the MBC was disbanded in 1691. In fact the charter itself, in its opening lines, makes reference to the seal: "And further, That the said Governour and Companye, and their Successors, maie have forever one common Seale, to be used in all Causes and Occasions of the said Company, and the same Seale may altar, chaunge, breake, and newe make, from tyme to tyme, at their pleasures."[37]

This image was therefore iconic in the Puritan colonies and may be seen as a direct analog to Mather's famous claim that the Puritan "errand," as Bercovitch famously put it, was defined in the charitable enlightening of the dark wilderness and its unfortunate inhabitants, something Mather discusses at length in his *Magnalia*.[38] Thus, from an early date (1629), the Puritans would rhetorically and visually construct a duality between "saved" and "heathen" that would come to define Anglo-Indian relations into the twentieth century.

Returning to the Puritan portraits discussed earlier, and viewing them in direct relation to the other bodies depicted in early images of indigenous Americans, this dichotomy becomes all the more apparent, and as suggested it was indeed pressing for Puritan leaders, as the idea served their own political and theological ends. When viewing the Native as the aesthetically polarized opposite of the "sanctified" Puritan individual, it is helpful to consider the question in the context of larger theological debates going on within Puritanism during the seventeenth century. One need not look far to find texts rife with references to the "savagery" of the Native or to their perceived spiritual malaise. It was during this era that the Puritans were famously ensconced in the witch trials in Salem and other Puritan towns. At times we see references to Otherness made by Puritan writers that seem to dissolve distinctions among any persons deemed problematic by them, be they Indians, Catholics, or those accused of witchcraft within their midst.

Cotton Mather, assuming the role of Puritan scholar par excellence, prided himself on the empirical basis for his historical writings, and, as has been noted, he indeed went through great pains to include primary source data in his biographies and histories of Puritan leaders.[39] Despite this, Mather exhibited at times a surprising level of interest in the dark arts of witchcraft, demonic possession, and devil worship. He wrote extensively on the topic, perhaps most notably in his essay *The Wonders of the Invisible World*. As we shall see, in designating the world of demonic possession "invisible," Mather was in fact constructing a dichotomized racial theory regarding the nature of Native Americans in contradistinction to the "lightness" and thus "visibility" of the Puritan soul. In this fascinating text, published in 1692, during the witch trial controversies, Mather invokes the ongoing presence of Satan in the colony in stark terms:

> The New Englanders are a people of God settled in those which were once the devil's territories; and it may easily be supposed that the devil was exceedingly disturbed when he perceived such a people here accomplishing the promise of old made unto our blessed Jesus, *That he should have the utmost parts of the earth for his possession.* . . . The devil, thus irritated, immediately tried all sorts of methods to overturn this poor plantation. . . . I believe that never were more satanical devices used for the unsettling of any people under the sun than what have been employed for the extirpation of the vine which God has here planted, casting out the heathen.[40]

Mather here reiterates the notion of New England as a God-given New Jerusalem for the Puritans to inhabit and civilize. It is significant that he perceives the territory on which the colony rested as previously being the "devil's territories." The Puritan errand consisted in the Christianization of this previously heathen territory, and by extension its native inhabitants. This evangelical process, according to Mather, derives from the de facto covenant made between God and the Puritans (his erstwhile chosen people): they were miraculously given the land on which to build their new utopia, and in turn they were obligated to make the land wholly Christian. Mather then describes in more specific terms the obstacle facing the Puritans at the moment: "Wherefore the devil is now making one attempt more upon us; an attempt more difficult, more surprising, more snarled with unintelligible circumstances than any that we have hitherto encountered; an attempt so critical that if we get through we shall soon enjoy halcyon days with all the vultures of hell trodden under our feet. He has wanted his incarnate legions to persecute us, as the people of God have in the other hemisphere been persecuted."[41]

Importantly, Mather saw the travails of the colony as paralleling the efforts of Satan in the "other hemisphere," namely, in Europe. The devil's work here thus was tantamount to the persecutions conducted by the Anglican Church as well as those undertaken by the Catholics in Europe against the "true believers." This sense of transatlantic persecution, of "us against the world," is a dichotomy set up by Mather in the introduction of his *Magnalia*, among other writings. Of course the "legions" Mather perceives attempting to subvert New England are embodied in those suspected or accused of witchcraft:

> And we have now with horror seen the discovery of such a witchcraft! An army of devils is horribly broke in upon the place which is . . . the first born of our English settlements. And the houses of the good people there are filled with the doleful shrieks of their children . . . tormented by invisible hands with tortures altogether preternatural. . . . The terrible plague of evil angels hath made its progress into some other places where other persons in a like manner have been diabolically handled.[42]

Puritanism and Fidelity

In the 1680s and 1690s, especially during the height of the witch trials, Mather became something of a resident expert on things supernatural in the colony. His views on the matter tended at times to be extreme and were even seen as such by some of his Puritan contemporaries, as his views on the question differed significantly from those of his respected father, Increase Mather. Increase urged caution in the accusation and persecution of alleged "demonic" activities.[43] Despite this, Cotton threw caution to the wind, as he was apparently a true believer in the existence of witchcraft and possession, both within the colony and beyond.

Specifically in his writings on witchcraft, Cotton Mather emphasizes what he saw as the dual threat of Satan to the well-being of the colony. As the earlier excerpts indicate, he saw it as a threat *within*, as certain persons (usually female) exhibited what were deemed "abnormal" behaviors that he and other advocates of the trials saw as the influence of Satan creeping into the heart of the city on the hill and as a metaphor for the "evils" of Old World corruption as perpetrated against the Puritans and other true believers back in Europe. Thus the threat was not only spiritual and moral but also potentially political, as moral backsliding could result in the failure of the colony and the triumph of the corrupted Christianity of the Anglican royalists and Catholic papists.

There was also a threat from *without*. This dimension brings the discussion of witchcraft into the discussion of Native Americans. In his text *Memorable Providences, Relating to Witchcrafts and Possessions* of 1689, Mather attempts, through anecdotal evidence, to establish a history of witchcraft practice in the colony and thus the need to ferret out potential perpetrators of these dark arts. In reference to his own motivations for writing the tract, he states the following in the introduction:

> It becomes the Embassadors of the L. Jesus to leave no stroke untouch't that may conduce to bring men from the power of Satan unto God; and for this cause it, that I have permitted the ensuing Histories to be published. They contain Things of undoubted

Certainty, and they suggest Things of Importance unconceivably. Indeed they are only one Head of Collections which in my little time of Observation I have made of Memorable Providences, with Reflections thereupon. . . . Go tell Mankind, that there are Devils and Witches; and that tho those night-birds least appear where the Day-light of the Gospel comes, yet New-Engl. has had Exemples of their Existence and Operation; and that no only the Wigwams of Indians, where the pagan Powaws often raise their masters, in the shapes of Bears and Snakes and Fires, but the House of Christians, where our God has had his constant Worship, have undergone the Annoyance of Evil spirits.[44]

In this text Mather makes the explicit perceptual linkage between the fallen "House of Christians" infected by the Satanic impulse, and the "pagan Powaws" in the "Wigwams of Indians." This excerpt is perhaps the key to understanding Mather's perception of Native peoples, and indeed the Puritan concept of wilderness more broadly. The wilderness, for them, was not only a place that lacked the implements of civilization, nor were the inhabitants of the wilderness simply naïve and uncivilized. They were savage in the sense of lacking civility and education, but also in the sense of being spiritually damned. Their darkness was thus multiple: not only intellectual and cultural but moral and spiritual.

Also important in considering Mather's perception of the supernatural elements supposedly present in the colony is that his perceptions were inflected by his views on race, and his views were impactful for both Native Americans and African Americans. As the scholar Ibram X. Kendi has noted, Mather's perception of that which is "demonic" was not merely a theological perception but was firmly grounded in then-current ideas about race and Otherness, both within the colony and beyond.

Kendi argues that Mather's views on race, as well as those of other Puritan leaders, including Richard Baxter, were influenced by biblical text. Specifically Kendi points to the first Book of Corinthians in the New Testament, traditionally thought to be written by the Apostle Paul of Tarsus in the first century. In it Paul legitimizes the practice of slavery in the ancient Roman world—perhaps a surprising concession to the Roman elite at the time—by claiming that the "natural" order on earth was a reflection of God's will. As such slavery becomes both naturalized and morally acceptable.[45]

Kendi goes on to state that Mather's views on race were further informed by his interpretation of chapter 9 of the Book of Genesis, where the author conveys the story of the patriarch Noah and his sons. Noah was designated by God to survive a cataclysmic flood in ancient times and to therefore become one of the progenitors of the human race. After the flood, and following a bout of drunkenness, Noah cursed his son Ham over a disagreement, and according to a popular interpretation of the story favored by Mather, as a result Ham's descendants were endowed with darker skin. Historians commonly refer to this as the "curse theory" of race, whereby racial difference is the result of theological and spiritual causes rather than environmental ones. In modern times, then, persons with darker skin were deemed spiritually deficient by some Christian clerics and in dire need of spiritual salvation.[46] Such a "mark" of spiritual and racial inferiority was central to Puritan writing and to the racial discourse of Mormonism two centuries later.

Further complicating Mather's perception of Native Americans were contemporary events and ideas in the colony in the seventeenth century. On the one hand, violence between the Puritan settlers and Native Americans in the region, most notably the Pequot War and King Philip's War, contributed to a negative view of Natives. Kendi points out that Puritans conflated Indians and African American slaves ideologically and also treated them interchangeably as indigenous prisoners of war; they were often enslaved and shipped to penal colonies in other reaches of the British Empire. Further, scientific ideas of the time contributed to Mather's perception of the "invisibility" of the damned, as codified in his writings on the topic of possession such as *The Wonders of the Invisible World*. Mather had read Isaac Newton's *Optiks*, a scientific tract that addresses vision and perception. According to Newton's thesis, white is the central and principal color on the color wheel, and all other colors represent a "deviation" from its perceived purity. By absorbing biblical texts and current scientific theory and interpreting current events, Mather construed an essential "evil" in the nature and aesthetic appearance of Native Americans that would inform his theological writings on them.[47]

When considering the racially inflected violence that occurred between Puritan settlers and the surrounding indigenous tribes, perhaps the most well-known visual representation of one such incident is an illustration for John Underhill's narrative account of the Pequot War, titled *Newes from America*, published in London in 1638 (fig. 7). This engraving was executed by an artist identified in the lower left corner of the image as "RH." The definitive identity of the artist is not currently known; however, it may be one Richard Hearne, the only engraver with those initials in London during the years the book was published.[48]

The text and this image work together to forward a narrative of the war that is infused with an apocalyptic tone. Underhill was a Puritan military leader who led the fight against the Pequots, an indigenous tribe native to Connecticut. While recent historians agree that the war was essentially an attempt at a land grab, Underhill and other Puritans at the time perceived it in theological terms, seeing the war's outcome as divinely prescribed.[49] Therefore this image, which has a descriptive cartographic appearance and details the British destruction of a Pequot town, must be viewed in this light as well. Underhill sets the tone early:

> I shall according to my promise begin with a true relation of the new *England* warres against the *Block-Islanders*, and that insolent and barbarous Nation, called the *Pequeats*, whom by the sword of the Lord, and a few feeble instruments, souldiers not accustomed to warre, were drove out of their Countrey, and slaine by the sword, to the number of fifteen hundred soules in the space of two monthes and lesse: so as their Countrey is fully subdued and

fallen into the hands of the English: And to the end that God's name might have the glory, and his people see his power, and magnifie his honour, for his great goodnesse.[50]

Underhill, who interestingly had antinomian sympathies and would later be driven out of the colony during the Antinomian Controversy, claims that the war was started by the Pequots, who, he alleges, murdered a Puritan merchant and sacked his ship for its supplies. As the "blood of an innocent" was spilled, Underhill states that Governor Henry Vane (also an antinomian) asked him to lead a retributive fight against the Pequots, given Underhill's prior military experience in Europe. Not only was this a war for the justice of a slain comrade, but according to Underhill, the Pequots were in need of a violent spiritual reckoning, as "the old Serpent according to his first malice stirred them up against the Church of Christ."[51] As the historian Alfred Cave has noted, Underhill and others saw the war as a cosmic struggle waged between Christ and Satan at ground level, between the "lightness" of the Puritan soul and the "darkness" of the Indian soul, something Mather likewise references in his writing.

When we look more closely at the engraving, it gives us a surprisingly frank depiction of the burning of a Pequot village, which was the turning point of the war. The composition is neatly concentric, which gives the bloody event a sense of rationality and closure. The engraver shows the numerical superiority of the Pequot, who symbolically surround the British forces in an outer ring set against a vast landscape. And yet the Puritans prevail due to their tactical and technological superiority, seen as God-given in this case. During this event, hundreds of Pequots were killed either through direct exposure to the flames or by being shot down upon exiting the burning village walls. While this may run the risk of striking the reader as a dishonorable treatment of an opponent, again it must be recalled that for the Puritans, this was a moral and spiritual war and thus the "Satanic" Pequot needed to be vanquished, as Christ would have wanted. As Underhill puts it in his text, "Wee could not but admire at the providence of God in it, that souldiers so unexpert in the use of their armes, should give so compleat a volley, as though the finger of God had touched both match and flint."[52]

The "darkness" of the Native, as both spiritual and physiological metaphor, may also be seen in surviving prints done in New England in the wake of the witch trials and Mather's writings. The date of these images indicates the lingering influence of Mather's ideas, even during an era of increasing diversification, secularization, and political change in the region. In prints from the eighteenth century there is a surprising persistence of an almost medieval hellfire iconography. An example of this is an image executed by Paul Revere in 1773 for a pamphlet titled *A Vision of Hell* written by a Presbyterian minister, Jacob Green, and published by John Boyle, on the eve of the Revolution (fig. 8).[53] The pamphlet recounts a vision of Hell Green claims to have experienced one day while praying and meditating. He wrote that it was brought about by his "musing upon the low state of religion and the progress of vice" and goes on to say that the illustration by Revere was based on this vision of the gates of Hell guarded by four imposing devils. The text of the pamphlet contains an extended conversation between variously named devils on how to subvert piety in the world and shame God. The presence of Green's writings demonstrates the persistence of Christian radicalism and evangelism even during the Revolutionary era.[54]

This image is surprising for multiple reasons. First, Revere is much better known for his silversmithing, most notably the Sons of Liberty bowl. As that piece was explicitly political in intent, it takes on a decidedly secular aesthetic, addressing the grievances against the Crown on the part of revolutionary leaders in Boston. Also, decades after Mather's paranoiac exhortations against the destructive power of the "invisible world" of Satanic possession, Revere treats us to the famous Hellmouth theme, as four dark-skinned demons sit gleefully at the entrance to Hell, represented as a fiery dragon's mouth. This image is a modernized instance of the Hellmouth trope originating in medieval Anglo-Saxon manuscripts, a grim reminder to the reader and viewer of the perils of a life of sensual indulgence.[55]

Although Revere's engraving does not reference Native Americans, there is clearly a lingering aesthetic and conceptual parallel in images of Natives from this same period in New England. In many we see figures that are primitivized and nearly always darkened. Figure 9 appeared in the popular *Bickerstaff's Boston almanack*, published annually by Boston printers Mein and Fleeming in 1767. The purpose of *Bickerstaff's* was to give the reader a smattering of Enlightenment-era knowledge regarding multiple aspects of the planet. Thus we find climatological and astrological charts, which would appeal to farmers, as well as factoids about various countries around the world. Interestingly, the almanac includes a "historical" calendar that dates a variety of well-known events, but on a biblically inspired timeline. In this calendar the Flood of Noah is the starting date, and all human events are dated chronologically from that time.[56]

This illustration appears midway through the text and is only one of two such illustrations in the entire document. Its appearance is curious, as it does not seem to relate to the information given in the text. It is accompanied by a brief story explaining the image; it tells of a young British officer who encountered two "Abenakee savages" during the French and Indian War. He was cornered by the two hatchet-wielding Natives, but his life was only spared by a tribal elder who miraculously intervened and saved his life, an unlikely event akin to the Pocahontas–John Smith narrative. According to the story, the elder took the injured officer in and nursed him back to health, and the two became friends. The two part when the officer returns to his regiment a few months later, but not before recognizing each other's humanity.[57]

Compositionally we see the familiar aesthetic duality of white colonist confronting darker-skinned Natives. Significantly the well-dressed, uniformed colonist is on the left of the composition and is more closely aligned with the cultivated fields. The darkened Natives, on the right, are more closely aligned with the untamed forest, a visual trope that would become more common in American art during the nineteenth century and serves as a metonymic stand-in for the civilized/savage dualism. The posture of the "peacemaking" Native figure in the front resembles that of the figure on the MBC seal from the previous century. Although he holds a bow, it is lowered and his gesture seems to be conciliatory, as he blocks out the more aggressive figures behind him, thereby sheltering the colonist. This image indicates a complex relationship between the soldier and the Natives and seems to acknowledge the various colonial conflicts between Natives and settlers but displays a resolution in the ingratiating pose of the leader coupled with the cultivated agrarian landscape in which they stand. In this sense the image confirms the conquest of the New World by military means as well as agrarian cultivation and Christian fellowship, albeit not explicitly stated in the text. The elder Native figure takes on didactic behaviors, as his idealized posture indicates a willingness for compromise and perhaps assimilation, in stark contrast to the bearing of his more "barbaric" companions. Such narratives would indeed imbue Christian missionaries with hope, despite the "darkness" of their indigenous charges.

Mather's thinking about witchcraft and things demonic was also heavily influenced by two English thinkers of the time, the philosopher Henry More and the theologian Joseph Glanvill. Glanvill and More coauthored a massive tome, originally published in 1681, titled *Saducismus Triumphatus*, or *Triumphant Sadducism*. The book's odd title appears to be a reference to the Sadducees of biblical times, a Jewish sect whose teachings revolved around theological skepticism. In his introduction, More seems to imply that modern skeptics of witchcraft are akin to the Sadducees, who disbelieved the teachings of Christ. Through their atheistic disbelief in all things metaphysical, these modern skeptics enable witchcraft and detract from Christ's teachings. The book's narrative thus attempts to prove the existence of the dark arts, which will enable readers to better combat them. The book's extensive and technical text was illustrated in various editions by the English engraver William Faithorne (1616–91), whose bizarre illustrations were apparently intended to lend a sense of empirical legitimacy to the supernatural subject matter. Faithorne renders a variety of supernatural scenes, in which common people are visited and tormented by angels and demons. The images are executed in a fairly naturalistic style, lending a sense of viability to the unlikely subject matter. The book is a strange but provocative combination of late medieval mysticism and superstition, but systematized in near encyclopedic form, an influence of the early Enlightenment. It is thus a merging of discourses from various eras, attempting to in effect "scientize" the supernatural. Mather even defers to Glanvill and More in his *Memorable Providences*, crediting them with being "Great Names" in the study of "Witchcraft and Possessions." He goes so far as to refer to his own work as a "little Book" that serves as a "Lackey" to the "more elaborate Essays of those learned men."[58]

One may certainly fault Mather with erring on the side of mysticism, or even fanaticism, in his view of witchcraft and the witch trials, to the detriment of a more empirical analysis based on the radically changing political and social conditions within the colony. It is not a coincidence that the hysteria surrounding witchcraft reached its peak in the late 1680s and early 1690s, in the wake of the revocation of the original MBC charter in 1684. This revocation, coming from the Crown, was a response to the growing population of and economic activity in the colony and indicated a need for greater imperial control. The original form of government established by the charter was dissolved by 1686 and was replaced by royally appointed governors. Thus the General Court, the original legal arbiter in the colony, ceased to function, and with it the previous judicial structures and to some degree social customs seem to have deteriorated. Such disconcerting political and legal changes, in addition to demographic changes, led to a widespread perception of social malaise on the part of hard-line theologians like Mather, as the older Puritan system gave way to greater secularization. In this context accusations of witchcraft would have their uses, as any form of social nonconformity could be explained in terms of the outmoded mandates of the older system, which nevertheless maintained quasi-legal sway within the changing colony. Thus social deviants within the communities and "savage" elements without could be lumped together under the "demonic" rubric. Religious fanaticism substituted for rational social analysis in this case.[59]

In hindsight the perceived deviance on the part of alleged witches may have been, at least to some degree, influenced by fears about these changes. That these fears quickly morphed into mass hysteria has subsequently been concluded by historians, but escaped many involved at the time. Mather seemed to anticipate such criticisms and thus took great pains to "document" his histories of witchcraft, thereby bolstering his view of those possessed as well as the heathen Indians with whom they shared the colony. Apparently the sense of Otherness Mather and his colleagues encountered was so great that it overrode their empirical grasp of the realities of the situation.

As we have seen, Mather's rhetoric fluctuates between high-falutin, honorific, and paranoid. He perceived the colony as a signpost of a coming world, yet riddled with corruption and degradation. Throughout the seventeenth century the realities of Puritan-Indian relations were indeed messy. While the original charter seal, in use until 1691, indicated a desire to enact Christian charity in relation to the Indian, periodic outbreaks of violence, including the Pequot War (1636–37) as well as King Philip's War (1675–76), greatly complicated evangelical outreach. Margaret Connell Szasz has argued that Puritan missionary work was not always consistently executed, often due to a lack of either will or financing.[60]

Nonetheless the activities and writings of John Eliot (1604–90) provide a direct example of one Puritan leader whose missionary work attempted to honor the MBC charter's ideals of establishing a sort of godly plantation in the New World. Eliot was a widely respected theologian in the colony and was well versed in the indigenous Algonquian language, going so far as to write a version of the Bible in a Latinized version of the Massachusett language, a dialect of Algonquian. This text has come to be known as Eliot's Bible. For decades Eliot attempted to evangelize Native Americans of various tribes in the area, and his indigenous followers were known as "praying indians."[61]

Eliot left behind valuable documentation of his perception of his evangelical activities among the natives of the colony. He wrote a series of letters on the topic, some of which have been collected and published; they offer conversion narratives intended to inspire other Christians as to the malleability of the indigenous population, despite doubts on the topic held by other Puritan leaders, including Increase and Cotton Mather. Significant for considerations of visuality, Eliot, like Mather, deploys a metaphor of sight at the start of one letter, written to his friend and fellow minister Robert Boyle, describing the indigenous population as "poor blind Indians of New England."[62] Eliot's view of the Native both parallels and inverts that of Mather, who viewed the spiritual life of the Native in demonic terms and as something that functioned nefariously in its "invisibility." Eliot attributes a complete lack of vision to the Native, thus his use of the term "blind." In both cases the Native is either spiritually and culturally obscured due to his heathen nature or is incapable of proper spiritual or cultural undertaking due to his alleged blindness. His is both unseen and unable to see, being rendered wholly inarticulate.

Eliot continues in his letter with a dramatic and moving description of a revival meeting attended by both church representatives and indigenous leaders: "In a day of Fasting and Prayer, they making confession of the Truth and Grace of Jesus Christ, did in that solemn Assembly enter into Covenant, to walk together in Faith and Order of Gospel; and were accepted and declared to be a Church of Jesus Christ. These *Indians* being of kin to our *Massachuset-Indians* who first prayed unto God, conversed with them, and received amongst them the light and love of the Truth."[63]

The covenant between God and man thought to be central to the establishment of the colony by John Winthrop and Cotton Mather is here extended, in an act of evangelical radicalism, to those most in need and least prepared for it. Such activity reinforced the perception of the colony as a miraculous fulfillment of this covenant, as well as the consummation of the Christian triumphalism I discussed in the introduction. This first step was critical, as Eliot later states that the converted Natives would then be tasked with converting others in their communities, as "the Lord should give them ability and opportunity" to do so.[64]

Aiding Eliot in his monumental task was the fact that he was well placed politically, as his efforts were mandated by the General Court in an ordinance in 1646. This court order was the result of a number of factors. The Pequot War had cost hundreds of Pequot lives. Disease outbreaks among various tribes during the early decades of English settlement also cost lives, and land was increasingly taken by settlers. This induced tribal leaders to greater compromise with the Puritans, and perhaps the colonial leaders sensed this. Beyond these political causes, Puritan doctrine likewise played a central role in the formation of this official policy. It was thought by many that the establishment of the colony was biblically mandated, an "errand in the wilderness," as outlined in the Book of Isaiah. This errand, while prophetically mandated, implied a covenant between the Puritans and God, something Eliot sought to actualize through his ideal Christian commonwealth.[65] The land was seen as a gift from God, and in return the Puritans felt obligated to not only cultivate the land but to bring Christianity to the inhabitants of that land. This motivation was apparently strong enough to induce the Court to appoint Eliot to the task, to which he adhered for nearly thirty years.[66]

In visual terms, Eliot's legacy was most famously characterized by a popular evangelical print of the early nineteenth century by the artist J. A. Gertel, reproduced by the engraver John Chester Buttre (1821–93) and published by Johnson, Fry, and Company of New York (fig. 10). At this point it is helpful to recall Morgan and Promey's analysis of religious imagery in America and key motivations for its making. While Gertel and Buttre lived roughly two centuries after Eliot, Puritanism nonetheless maintained a strong cultural foothold in the Anglo-American psyche during the nineteenth century. In this context images of bygone Puritan leaders would create and organize a cultural and spiritual memory for latter-day evangelists living during the Second Great Awakening, with such imagery establishing a tradition of evangelism in relation to subaltern populations.

Buttre owned a publishing firm and capitalized on his engravings by publishing three volumes of them in a series titled *The American Portrait Gallery* in the early 1880s, reissued after his death. This series contains engravings by Buttre and other luminaries in the graphic arts, including Asher B. Durand and John Sartain. The gallery Buttre amassed was intended to "present a series of biographical sketches . . . of those who stand forth to the world as emphatically the representatives of our country."[67] Apparently Eliot and his missionary work were seen as "emphatically representing the country."

Such published galleries were popular in the country throughout the nineteenth century, especially during the postbellum period. They represent an effort to establish a unified national identity in the wake of the Civil War and a more general interest in aesthetically classing together persons of perceived cultural and historical significance. Throughout much of Buttre's career, he specialized in bust-length portraits of notable Americans depicted in relaxed, seated postures. In figure 10 Buttre emphasizes Eliot's activism in Christianizing the Natives, and this distinction in format seems to indicate that he and the publishers saw Eliot as a special individual in the shaping of a national identity. As such, the complexities of Puritanism and Eliot's controversial nature are glazed over in favor of making him part of a lineage of great Americans. In this way Puritanism was established, both in art and literature, as an essentially American cultural and religious movement.

Images such as these, popular during the Second Great Awakening (c. 1800–1850s) and the Social Gospel era (c. 1860s–1900), tended to romanticize and glorify the evangelical activities of earlier eras. They became more common as lithography and engraving became more widely used in newspapers and magazines, which were at the time increasingly distributed on a national—rather than simply local—basis. In literature the culture of the Puritans was most famously romanticized by Nathanial Hawthorne in his novel *The Scarlet Letter*, and fascination with Anglo-America's Puritan past also captivated visual artists. In a compositional staple repeated in many such prints and paintings of the nineteenth century, we see in figure 10 the civilized Anglo-American evangelist set in contrast to the heathen Natives whom he addresses. This is important for the emerging Social Gospel, as the didactic and pedagogical function of Eliot's evangelism is emphasized by Buttre. This gives an indication of the modernized twist the image contains: it both looks back to an earlier era and in a sense looks forward to the Indian boarding schools of the Gilded Age. We see the animated, literate Eliot conveying sacred knowledge to the mute, still, and mostly compliant Natives, a trope that would become one of the centerpieces of boarding school imagery.

In figure 10 Eliot's animated preaching captures the attention of most of the natives, save the man on the lower left, who seems lost in introspection, perhaps brought on by the forcefulness of Eliot's theological argumentation. Eliot was extraordinary among Puritans in his efforts to evangelize the Massachusset tribe and was proficient in their language, allowing him greater access. While this aspect of the image may be taken as historically accurate, the landscape in which Eliot and his audience are placed is fanciful and seems to have been romanticized for effect, as no such dramatic mountain landscapes exist in this part of the country. While the members of the tribe are mostly docile, two of the men hold weapons, but in an unthreatening posture. Eliot's dramatic gesture, holding the Bible in his left hand and punctuating his argument with his right, seems to be aimed at the attentive but slightly skeptical chief directly in front of him.

As I mentioned, this compositional formula was repeated many times in varying contexts in American visual culture in the nineteenth century. Even before the popularization of Indian boarding school imagery, one sees it in other evangelical contexts, such as C. C. A. Christensen's depiction of the Mormon prophet Joseph Smith preaching to Indians (fig. 11), and even in secular contexts, such as the painter George Catlin's famous self-portrait among the Mandan. In Catlin's encounter with Otherness, his conveyance of artistic skill and knowledge replace the sacred aims of most evangelical imagery. Instead of a Bible, he amazes his indigenous audience with palette and brush.

Perhaps the most "modern" aspect of Buttre's retrospective take on Eliot's evangelism is that which seems so obvious as to be overlooked: the aesthetic style of the image. It is clearly executed in an academic, naturalistic manner typical of the nineteenth century in the United States and western Europe. This style differs significantly from the original Puritan style, which Wayne Craven has described as "Elizabethan-Jacobean" and indebted to middle-class British formulas popular in the sixteenth century.[68] In the Puritan formula the savage is never present in the same pictorial space with the sanctified Puritan body, as the two were thought to exist in differing spiritual realms. In contrast, Buttre places Eliot in the same pictorial space as the savage. Such overt equations, especially the depiction of evangelical acts in a naturalistic style, were prohibited by Puritan cultural conventions, which dictated a more indirect manner for depicting sanctification, per Calvin's dictates. The Puritan's sanctity was *implied* by its material absence; the simple presence of the coherent, articulated Puritan body in pictorial space with its earthly accoutrements was sufficient. The savage existed in the wilderness and as such had no business appearing in this space.

Native responses to Eliot's missionary efforts were varied and complex. While many Natives resisted, the historian Lee

Irwin notes that Eliot was successful in establishing a large number of "praying towns," indigenous settlements inhabited by converted Algonquians. He estimates that several thousand converted Algonquians lived in over one thousand villages spread out across the MBC and beyond. They practiced a version of Christianity based on Puritan teaching and familial relations. Becoming Christian altered Native gender roles, as women tended to become domesticated and men gravitated toward agricultural work. Further, many Algonquians were motivated politically. Becoming Christian meant a closer alliance with local Puritans and thus was a form of protection from intertribal warfare and plunder. Despite the moderate successes of Eliot's work, many Puritans, most notably Mather, persisted in seeing Natives as somehow allied with Satan. Or, as Mather wrote, they were "unregenerated men" and "diabolical heathens."[69]

While the Puritans, ever inflected by the teachings of Calvin, demurred from making overt references to either sacred icons or evangelical activity or other works of "charity," such was not the case in the Catholic-dominated colonies of nearby New France. A brief comparison is warranted, as the Puritans were self-consciously competing with French Jesuits in the sanctifying of the wilderness. Winthrop made clear reference to this agenda in his writing, seeing it as part of the covenant between the Puritans and Christ. He described the Massachusetts Bay Colony as a "bulwark against the Kingdom of Antichrist, which the Jesuits labor to rear up in those parts."[70]

The evangelical cultures of these different colonies warrants some consideration, as it reveals striking aesthetic differences in terms of the visualization of the sacred and the salvation of the Other. By examining one example of evangelical imagery from French Catholic colonial society, one gets a greater sense of the specificity and difference of the Puritan conception of faith as embodied in visual images. In New France, perhaps the most well-known example of evangelical imagery is to be seen in a painting by the artist and monk Frère Luc (fig. 12). Frère Luc painted this image for François de Laval, the first bishop appointed to the post in New France. Laval would go on to found the Seminaire de Quebec, a community of Catholic priests who oversaw spiritual training in the colony. Being a French Catholic, he would have had no cultural injunction against the use of naturalistic imagery in the conveyance of faith, as the Catholic Counter-Reformation of the sixteenth and seventeenth centuries actually encouraged the use of images and statues for pedagogical purposes.[71]

Thus in the image he commissioned from his colleague Frère Luc, we see a Native American, perhaps a member of the Huron tribe, kneeling before an allegorical figure representing imperial France. The pedagogical value of images is shown in how France holds up a painting for the Huron, and he in turn drops to his knee in awe and gratitude. It is as if the painted image has a literal parallel to the "actual" spiritual scene miraculously appearing in the sky above; France's left arm forms an *axis mundi* linking the two realms, aesthetic and mystical. In both the painting and the scene above, Luc renders the Trinity, the Virgin Mary, and accompanying saints. Aesthetic perception therefore becomes the portal through which the Native attains a state of grace. His seeming unproblematic acceptance of the new faith is further depicted in the huts in the background, which, while primitive in appearance, nevertheless bear crosses on top. He also has been cloaked in a luxurious garment bearing the *fleur-de-lis* pattern, the insignia of the French monarchy at the time. The beauty of the cloak likewise implies the material prosperity of New France and the transatlantic trade that would ensue. Thus the submission of the indigenous Other profits both the Church and the empire and implies not only his spiritual submission but his willingness to labor for the benefit of France.

It is helpful to view this image in the larger context of the geopolitical struggles then transpiring between the British and French empires. Beginning around this time, the expansion of both into the westward frontiers of North America increasingly brought them into conflict over territory and resources. As discussed earlier, many Puritan leaders during this era viewed natives through either pseudoscientific or theological lenses. Natives of varying tribes were perceptually conflated, commonly seen as less civilized and childlike at best, or actively Satanic at worst. Such views were in keeping with those of most British in Europe, who had highly mediated and thus inaccurate perceptions of Native Americans. Nevertheless, as time wore on, and the interests of the two empires began to collide, the British in both the colonies and back home increasingly felt the need to forge strategic alliances with indigenous tribes in an effort to outflank the French in control of territories and trade routes.[72]

Led by these concerns, Queen Anne invited leaders of the powerful Mohawk tribe to London on a diplomatic visit in 1710, hoping to establish a military alliance. The Mohawk alliance was critical, as they were the most powerful tribe of the even larger Iroquois Confederacy. Eventually four Mohawk leaders left for London representing the tribe. Importantly, the Mohawks had been partially converted to Christianity in the preceding years by the missionary work of the Society for the Propagation of the Gospel in Foreign Parts (SPG), an evangelical Anglican organization based in London. Their leaders were more inclined to negotiate with the British, as the SPG had "saved" their people from the clutches of the Jesuits also working in the area. Additionally they had enjoyed prosperous trading relations with the British for decades. Upon their arrival in London in 1710, the delegation was painted by the Dutch British portraitist John Verelst, himself a member of the Dutch Reformed Church.[73]

Verelst's portraits were commissioned by the queen, then reproduced by the engraver Jean Simon and widely published in Britain, becoming popular depictions of Native Americans. The most well-known is the portrait depicting the Mohawk leader the British dubbed "Hendrick" (fig. 13). As the historian Troy Bickham has noted, the formula of the portrait echoes common depictions of British nobles during this period. He is shown in an iconic posture, posed frontally and engaging the viewer directly.

　　　　　　　　　　　　　　　　　　Puritanism and Fidelity

He is in the foreground and seems to lord over the wilderness landscape behind, much as a British noble would be shown in the fore of his family's estate in a formal portrait. Further, Hendrick is accompanied by a wolf, his clan's totem, and bears a wampum belt, a sign of diplomatic goodwill. Verelst takes care to dignify Hendrick by particularizing his identity as a member of a specific tribe and clan and as a high-ranking leader authorized to negotiate. This contrasts with more common images of Natives in Britain, which opted for generalization and stereotype.[74]

Beyond this the image accomplishes something important for the British. Being so ennobled by Verelst, he is shown as independent and yet also in alliance with the British imperial agenda, in a manner different from that of the Huron kneeling before the allegorical figure of France in Frère Luc's image. Hendrick is dignified to a far greater degree, as he literally stands on his own two feet and engages the viewer as an equal. He is thus compliant with the alliance, but he is not cowed, as his fellow indigenous leader is by the popery and pomp of the Jesuits. His friendship is thus more genuine because it is of his choosing, something made possible by the magnanimous treatment given to him by the British. This is ironic, as many in both Britain and the colonies still commonly viewed Natives as biologically, culturally, or spiritually inferior. Nonetheless the veneer of friendship and diplomacy was important, as the British imperial administration was self-consciously competing with the French for the favor of these potential soldiers in their battles.[75]

While depictions of Natives varied widely throughout the colonial world, and as they respond to shifting exigencies and geopolitical alliances, one sees a consistent theme: imperial Christian triumphalism. This is implicit in the Hendrick portrait, as he and other Mohawk leaders had accepted the missionary teaching of the SPG. For the Puritans in particular, the *dispensation* of charity became a centerpiece of their errand in the wilderness, even if images of evangelical themes were prohibited. The tenuous status of the image—a tacit admission of the potential power it contains—was not only an ongoing negotiation between artists, patrons, and institutions in Puritan culture but would be a central debate in Quaker culture, as another radical Christian movement made its way to the New World in search of utopia. In Quakerism, as we shall see in the next chapter, discussions regarding images were similar to those in Puritan culture, which is unsurprising as Quakerism also had its roots in English Calvinism of the Reformation.

2

Quakerism, Skulls, and Sanctity

The "tenuous" status of graven images that was a central concern in Puritan theological debates—with the center ground sought by both the ecclesiastical and mercantile classes—proved to be nearly as controversial within the Quaker movement. This chapter considers images executed by the Quaker artists Benjamin West and Edward Hicks. As we will see, these works were done with motivations in keeping with Morgan and Promey's basic principles of religious art. West and Hicks wished to memorialize key events in the history of the Quaker movement, and they both sought to establish a communion among Quakers of their respective eras and with future generations. Further, they both offer aestheticized acts of imagination that depict rituals of kindness important for intergenerational continuity in the Society of Friends. Each thereby was seeking to bridge political and theological schisms within the Quaker community.

Beyond these aims, both artists depict encounters between Quaker exemplars and racial Others, which brings us to the central theme of this book. While both intended to proffer a perception of a benign colonial didacticism between Quaker leaders and Native Americans, the scientific contexts of the Enlightenment, with its newly systematized racial physical typologies, played a key role in impacting how many in the Quaker community saw Native Americans. This chapter is thus divided into two parts: the first addresses textual and visual depictions of Quaker-Indian exchanges as an example of the famous Quaker magnanimity; the second examines the overtly scientific racist discourse of the Quaker physician and craniologist Samuel Morton and his pro-slavery followers. This will serve as an interesting aesthetic and conceptual counterpoint to the more well-known "benign" intentions of Quaker discourse on race and religion, as seen in the work of West and Hicks. Along the way, it will be necessary to closely examine several aspects of Quaker culture and history: the early history and founding of Quakerism, the movement's theology, its attempts to establish a Christian utopia in Pennsylvania, its internal disputes and contradictions, its *actual* interactions with Native Americans, Quaker attitudes toward race, and finally the starkly contrasting agendas of the Enlightenment-era pseudosciences embraced by Morton and others.

During the English Reformation, dissidents of varying sorts cropped up around the kingdom, often in direct opposition to the perceived hegemony of the Anglican Church. Like the controversial Puritan movement, Quakerism under the auspices of its first leader, George Fox (1624–91), came to the forefront as a theological alternative to the imperial theology of Anglicanism. The term "Quakerism" was used by Fox in his famous *Autobiography*. He claimed that during his lifetime, he was continually harassed by authorities in England due to the nature of his teachings, which were seen as an affront to the spiritual and political authority of the Crown. He claimed "priesthood" for all adherents of his movement, assuming them to be individually capable of making their own spiritual decisions without the intervention of higher state or ecclesiastical authority. As such, he and his followers came to the attention of English authorities, and at one point Fox was brought up on charges of blasphemy. In describing this episode in his autobiographical narrative, Fox states that one of the presiding magistrates "was the first that called us Quakers, because I bade them tremble at the word of the Lord."[1] The term was originally intended as a mocking insult to Fox and his theology but was soon co-opted by his adherents and is used to this day.

Quakerism, Skulls, and Sanctity

A further interpretation of this epithet is provided by the historian Michel Foucault. In his study *Madness and Civilization*, Foucault provocatively associates Fox and his Quaker followers with the rise of the insane asylum and the scientific containment of insanity during the Enlightenment in England. Foucault states that Fox and some of his early followers were imprisoned in England and corporeally punished for their unconventional religious beliefs. He asserts that Fox and others were perceived as *irrational* in their forms of worship, which revolved around individual spontaneous spiritual testimony. The term "Quaker," as used by their persecutors, thus takes on a slightly more sinister connotation of a lack of reason. This concern with insanity and its containment and treatment would prove central to later Quaker culture in colonial America, as will be discussed later in this chapter.[2] Quaker theology was deeply interwoven with ideas about race and also insanity during the eighteenth and nineteenth centuries, and both themes are represented by West, Hicks, and Morton in their respective interpretations.

Fox, whose teachings proved as controversial as that of the Puritans who were his contemporaries, was raised in a Puritan household, the child of parents with Calvinist leanings. In his autobiography he describes his father, Christopher, as having "a Seed of God within him" and claims that friends and neighbors referred to his father as a "Righteous Christer."[3] Fox's Puritanical roots are evident throughout his autobiography, and a foundation of subsequent Quaker thinking may be seen in this quote, as he describes his early childhood spiritual state:

> When I came to eleven years of age I knew pureness and righteousness; for while a child I was taught how to walk to be kept pure. The Lord taught me to be faithful in all things, and to act faithfully two ways, viz., inwardly, to God, and outwardly, to man; and to keep to Yea and Nay in all things. For the Lord showed me that, though the people of the world have mouths full of deceit, and changeable affords, yet I was to keep to Yea and Nay in all

things; and that my words should lie few and savoury, seasoned with grace; and that I might not eat and drink to make myself wanton, but for health, using the creatures in their service, as servants in their places, to the glory of Him that created them.[4]

Fox attributes great spiritual wisdom to himself at a very young age, emphasizing his "purity" in the midst of a corrupted world. Indeed the preservation of a self purified of worldly malfeasance is a theme that runs through both Puritanism and Quakerism. Fox's emphasis on both "inner" and "outer" faith is perhaps the most important aspect of this quote for later Quaker thinking. The cultivation of what the Quaker preacher and visual artist Edward Hicks (1780–1849) would later call the "Inner Light" became the central focus of Quaker practice, and the trope "mind the Light" would be incorporated by Hicks in versions of his *Peaceable Kingdom* series. As Fox indicates here, the cultivation of this light was not a hypothetical endeavor but was something that every Quaker ought to seek to share with those in the external world.

Thus Fox tells the reader that the Lord had commanded him to live by "using the creatures in their service, as servants in their places, to the glory of Him that created them." The editor of Fox's autobiography, Rufus Jones, points out that by "creatures" Fox is referring to all things created by God. Like many Christians of his era, Fox assumed a universal applicability of his own views to all things in the world around him, presumably including other human beings. For Quakers, as for other Anglo-American Christian evangelicals, there was therefore a sacred covenant with Christ that obligated them to endow others with the Inner Light.

While Fox and his followers emphasized the "purism" of the Quaker project, it should also be noted that Quakerism, like Puritanism, was a cultural movement that not only revolved around a "reformed" practice of a perceived "authentic" or "primitive" brand of Christianity but also entailed an aggressively mercantile ethic. For example, the historian Gregory Evans Dowd observes that despite the overarching themes of Quaker theology, such

Quakerism, Skulls, and Sanctity

as peace, justice, tolerance, and equanimity, all of which were preached by Fox and his followers, Quaker merchants often altered prices on goods when trading with the Lenapes in Pennsylvania, assuming an ignorance of market principles on their part.

This market-driven treachery earned the scorn of some Lenape spiritual leaders, most notably Papoonon, a prominent Lenape prophet of the 1750s. Papoonon regularly spoke out against Quaker merchants and also his fellow tribesmen who he felt had become greedy through their contact with the Quakers. In other words, he rendered a sort of indigenous version of the Puritan "jeremiad," as Sacvan Bercovitch calls it. He bemoaned what he saw as his own people's loss of spiritual values and their newfangled preference for mercantile values.[5]

Interestingly, such a jeremiad, or narrative of regret and loss, was central to the writings of Cotton Mather, who criticized the materialism and worldliness of Puritans of his own generation, in contradistinction to the perceived values of the original settlers of New England decades earlier. From this perspective the lamentation of Papoonon and other indigenous prophets may be seen as eclectic internalization of both indigenous traditionalism and Anglo-American evangelism. Not all interactions between the Quakers and their Native American neighbors in the colony were magnanimous in nature. At least for some, there was a perceived gap between the idealized utopic society Quakers preached about and the realities of the economic interactions they maintained with the indigenous populations that surrounded them.

Such complexities of motivation and outcome are perhaps best embodied in the Quaker artist Benjamin West's iconic painting *Penn's Treaty with the Indians* of 1772 (fig. 14). As the art historian Beth Fowkes Tobin explains, the painting has been used for generations as a literal history textbook "illustration" displaying the supposed Quaker benevolence toward the Native Americans they encountered upon arriving in the New World. In order to understand West's important image in terms of its representation of Quaker ideals, Native Americans, mercantile values, and religious evangelism, a consideration of the lives of William Penn, the painting's ostensible subject, and West, the artist, is in order.

William Penn (1644–1718) was a Quaker follower of George Fox in England who decided to establish a utopic Quaker society in the New World. Coming from an affluent seafaring family headed by a prominent father with a strain of adventurism, Penn was in a sense an ideal candidate to establish a new colony in North America. Early in life he was influenced by Quaker missionaries and eventually converted to Quakerism in his early twenties. His father, Sir William Penn, was a highly respected naval officer whose service for the Commonwealth government of Oliver Cromwell garnered him recognition throughout the nation, and the family was given a land grant in Ireland as a result. Apparently a deft politician, the senior Penn managed to forge an alliance with Charles II during the Restoration of the monarchy only a few years later. Despite his father's royalist leanings, following a meeting with a Quaker missionary during his teens, the younger Penn began to gravitate toward Quakerism.

Eventually Penn met Fox and the two became friends. Penn's close personal association with the Quaker leader, in addition to his defiant public pronouncements of his faith, eventually led to deteriorating relations with both his own family and the Crown. Penn's missionary activities also hurt his reputation. Eventually he and a group of wealthy Quaker friends collectively purchased land in the colonies, what would roughly correspond in modern times to the southern part of New Jersey. Surprisingly, and apparently in an effort to solve multiple problems, King Charles II gave Penn a massive land grant to the west of his purchase in an effort to repay a debt owed to the Penn family and also to encourage Penn and his cohorts to leave England. This piece of land would eventually become Pennsylvania.[6]

Upon moving to the colony, in 1682 Penn would draft a charter for his land that embodied both democratic governmental ideals as well as Quaker spiritual values. Additionally the charter and other founding documents of Pennsylvania addressed relations with the indigenous tribes that had already been living in the area, most notably the Lenapes. With his charter, Penn also set up a deliberately redundant colonial government for Pennsylvania, consisting of a governor, a deputy governor, a Provincial Council, and a General Assembly, all of which were dependent on one another for the making of law, and all of which had limited terms. He apparently wished to take great care in the legislative activities of the government so as to avoid the corruptions he discerned in the monarchical parliamentary system of Great Britain.

Penn took up several themes of interest—mercantilism, morality, justice, and education—within the text of the charter. He desired to establish special committees of the Provincial Council to address each of these issues:

> A Committee of Justice and Safety to secure the peace of the Province and punish the Mall Administration of those who Subvert Justice to the prejudice of the publick and private Interest. A Committee of Trade and Treasury who shall Regulate all Trade and Commerce according to Law [and] encourage manufacture and Country-growth and defray the public Charge of the Province. And a Committee of Manners Educacon and Arts that all Wicked and Scandalous Living may be prevented and that Youth may be Successively trained up in Virtue and useful Knowledge and Arts.[7]

Penn here focuses on what one might expect in a legal charter of a new territory: public safety, commerce, and the like. Most important, though, and perhaps somewhat surprising, is his mention of "useful Knowledge and Arts" in the same category as "Manners Educacon." Apparently Penn deemed the arts important and useful enough to include, as he believed it had a potentially positive impact on public morals, perhaps thinking that knowledge of various crafts would give citizens occupations and thus lessen the possibility of "Wicked and Scandalous Living." This is significant, as we shall see. The visual arts in particular were seen by some Quakers as potentially uplifting in their application, provided images were used in particular ways. These are issues that both West and Hicks would later face in working as Quaker artists and in depicting Quaker ideals in their work.

In drafting the charter, Penn was also sensitive to Quaker relations with the continent's indigenous inhabitants. Indeed the subject was never far from his mind, as evidenced in both official and unofficial documents. In addition to his new charter, Penn authored several other documents in which he makes specific reference to his new indigenous neighbors in Pennsylvania. For instance, in a letter written prior to his departure from London to the chiefs of the Lenapes, Penn begins his hopeful correspondence with a bid to evangelize them:

> My Friends, there is a great God & Power that hath made the World & all things therein, to whom you & I and all people owe their Being & Well-being; and to whom you & I must give an account for all that we do in the world. This great God hath written his Law in our hearts, by which we are taught & commanded to love and help & to do good to one another. . . . This great God hath been pleased to make me concerned in your part of the world.[8]

Penn usually assumes a Christian universalism in his writings, as seen here; it is something he believed could overcome the real animosities between settlers and Natives. Thus his guiding assumption here is that his God is the God of the Lenapes as well and that his coming to the New World is the result of an act of divine providence, as opposed to one of economic and political exigency. The absurdity of this assertion seems lost on him, as the audience he was addressing did not necessarily share his faith, nor did they necessarily have any familiarity with it. Despite this, Penn insists that the "great God" binds the chiefs to him in "owing" their existence to Christ and for his imminent judgment that Penn assumes all people will face. We see such an unproblematic assumption of a commonality of beliefs and values in West's painting decades later; it served as a trope that glossed over the very problematic historical realities that sprang up in the course of Quaker and Native relations.

In addition to his political writings, which give us an inkling into his views on the arts and crafts, Penn is also well known for what is perhaps his principal theological work, *Primitive Christianity*. In this text Penn defines his ideal for a reformed and rejuvenated Christian practice, which he and his followers would strive to accomplish in Pennsylvania. Importantly for Fox and also Penn and other Quakers is the concept of the Inner Light, alluded to earlier. Penn begins *Primitive Christianity* with a brief but concise explanation of the term: "the light of Christ in man, as the manifestation of God's love for man's happiness."[9] This is important for Quaker belief and also for Hicks's art, as it sustains and extends Fox's earlier formulation of the "inner" and "outer" lives of the Christian. For Fox, Penn, and later Hicks, the cultivation of this inner spiritual realm via meditation and prayer (as opposed to ritual, practice, and scholasticism) was the key to attaining faith and salvation in Christ. This is because it represented for them the gift of love from Christ, which they believed was a potentiality in every human being. The Inner Light was also an imperative, as it was seen as the only route to salvation. In this we hear an echo of Martin Luther's *sola fide* doctrine.

The cultivation of this Inner Light was accomplished through a "primitive" practice of Christianity. According to Penn, one had to regain the *original* intent and practice of the early, pre-Roman Christian church as supposedly practiced by Jesus and his early followers. By regaining this more simplified and less ostentatious practice, one could avoid the corruptions of worldly temptations, which Penn called "high pretences and . . . deep irreligion" that plagued the more established churches of Europe, specifically Anglicanism and Catholicism.[10] Penn emphasizes this quality when he outlines the fundamental principle of Quakerism:

> That which the people called Quakerism lay down, as a funda-
> mental in religion, in this, That God through Christ, hath placed
> his Spirit in every man, to inform him of his duty, and to enable
> him to do it; and that those who live up to this, are the people

of God, and those that live in disobedience to it, are not God's people, whatever name they may bear or profession they may make of religion. This is their *ancient, first, and standing testimony*. With this they began, and this they bore, and do bear to the world.[11]

Penn's concern with Quakerism was always the maintenance of the "ancient" principles of Christ, which both predated and in a sense delegitimized the "showy" brand of Christianity proffered by the Vatican and the Crown. Also important in this quote is his insistence on the universality of the Inner Light, presumably applicable even to the "heathen" Natives of the New World. Thus in his letter to the Lenape chiefs, he "reminds" them of this principle, that they too are suffused with the Inner Light and as such bear certain duties and obligations to Christ. This assertion, while unsettling, was nonetheless framed in the discourse of fellowship and was an assumption universally shared by evangelicals of all denominations and at all times throughout the nation's history.

While Penn's ambition was to deal fairly with the Natives, following his death in 1718 relations between the Quakers and the various tribes in the region worsened substantially. Ironically one person who stands out in the course of this history of declining relations is Penn's son Thomas (1702–75). Thomas, who by then was embattled within the Quaker community due to his perceived misdealings with local indigenous tribes, wished for West to produce an image of retrospective unity among Quakers, and between Quakers and their indigenous neighbors in Pennsylvania. Thus while West's image postdates Penn's treaty by decades, it was nevertheless intended to idealize that event in the eyes of the present-day audiences of his own era.

Beyond the Penn family's own fluctuating relations with the area's indigenous tribes, the larger geopolitical situation in the mid-Atlantic colonies during the eighteenth century warrant mention in considering the context of West's work and the need for a symbolic reconciliation. The complicated and harsh political realities of these decades would greatly dampen the high ideals set forth in Penn's writings as well as in the charter. Ironically one of the main contributing factors to the political chaos in Pennsylvania before, during, and after the French and Indian War (1755–63) was the perceived pacifism attributed to the Quaker leadership by their political opponents in Pennsylvania.

The Quakers were eager to allow a diverse array of newcomers to settle inland Pennsylvania, and this inclusionary process only increased following the elder Penn's death. The colony saw immense population growth along with ethnic, linguistic, and religious diversification. While the Quaker-led Assembly in Philadelphia welcomed all comers, it did little to firmly establish or maintain social order, especially on the colony's western fringes. Rather it opted for an anti-authoritarian approach that assumed the settlers would become self-governing and peaceable via the discernment of their own Inner Light. This hands-off approach led to complex infighting between various groups, especially the indigenous tribes, the Scots Irish Presbyterian settlers, and German- and Dutch-speaking settlers (i.e., the "Pennsylvania Dutch"). The Quaker leadership was often targeted for blame. The new settlers, and even some within the Philadelphia elite, blamed the Assembly for failing to provide arms or clear legal guidelines in defense of the new settlements, which allegedly had been raided by Native tribes in the area. Charges of Quaker duplicity with Native American tribes quickly circulated, and intra-European resentments and tensions rose, eventually boiling over in the form of an armed march on Philadelphia in early 1764. A civil war was averted only by the diplomatic skills of Benjamin Franklin.[12]

As for the Natives themselves, a number of tribes known as the Wabanaki Confederacy sided with the French during the war, and after the war British forces responded harshly, leveling sanctions against those tribes, which included the Lenapes, whom Penn had attempted to court with his treaty decades earlier. Some Native leaders, most notably the Odawa chief Pontiac, launched counterattacks against European settlements in the region as reprisal for this treatment. This conflict is known as Pontiac's

War and took place primarily in the areas west of the colony. Despite this geographic remove, Pontiac's War fueled settler fears of indigenous deprivations in all parts of the colony. This in turn led to the rise of frontier vigilante groups in western Pennsylvania that were encouraged by anti-Quaker printed propaganda citing Quaker "pacifism" as the main reason for unruly Natives, both before and during the war. While such propaganda glossed over the political complexities of Pontiac's War, it was nonetheless effective in sparking action.[13]

One group in particular, coming from the frontier settlement of Paxtang, attacked a town that was home to members of the Conestoga tribe and killed twenty-one people, burning the entire village, despite the fact that the Conestogas were not part of the Wabanaki Confederacy. The attackers became known as the "Paxton boys" and were alternately praised and reviled in the press of the day, depending on the publisher's political stance. The upshot was that the Quaker community found itself quickly losing political credibility and eventually control of the colony established by Penn less than a century earlier.[14]

It is in this context that West's painting is best viewed in terms of what it can tell us about Quakers' ideals and their relationship to Native Americans. It is well known that Thomas Penn commissioned West to execute the painting in 1771 and that West, by then already living in London, worked on it in 1771 and 1772. The painting was purchased from Penn family heirs in 1851 by Joseph Harrison, who delivered it to Philadelphia for exhibition and then bequeathed it upon his death to the Pennsylvania Academy of Fine Arts, where it resides.[15]

While the details of the commission are well known, it will be helpful to consider West's execution of the work in the context of Thomas Penn's personal agendas and West's own career as well as the larger historical context in which Penn commissioned the piece. Like Penn and Hicks, West (1738–1820) was raised as a Quaker in Pennsylvania. Thomas Penn may have had a number of reasons for choosing West for the commission. First, West was already a rapidly rising star in the London art world. He had established himself as a history painter, a genre that at the time was considered "elevated" in intellectual terms in relation to other genres, such as still life. West's originality lay in his ability to seamlessly combine a grand style of large-scale history painting with contemporary events imbued with emotion. This combination of elements had previously been considered incompatible by leading academics, including West's friend and fellow painter Joshua Reynolds, who during this era served as first president of the Royal Academy of Arts in London.[16] In this sense West's work may be seen as quite daring for the time, and certainly would have made him stand out in relation to other prospective hirelings.

Second, in addition to his credentials as an academic history painter, West had Quaker origins and thus Thomas Penn may have been comfortable giving this sensitive commission to a fellow traveler in the faith. Third, West's reputation in London rested in large part on his larger-than-life persona, which he and his biographer John Galt capitalized on in writing a successful account of West's life. Throughout his career West was able to appeal to European patrons by citing his "exotic" status as a colonial specimen, claiming it gave him firsthand knowledge of Native Americans and their culture. As such, he would have been the perfect candidate to depict Penn with the Lenapes. West and Galt emphasized such exoticism in the biography, which, although much criticized by scholars, was popular at the time.[17]

In chronicling his life, West famously claimed that he first learned how to paint through his association with Native Americans who lived near his home in the rural suburbs of Philadelphia. He asserted that they taught him how to mix colors using natural pigments from the earth, and then how to apply these pigments to the face. As Ann Uhry Abrams has noted, many scholars have doubted the legitimacy of these claims. Regardless of the veracity of this now-iconic story of West's early life, it is known that as a young man he learned how to draw and paint by copying engravings belonging to family friends. His talent was recognized early on, and West soon gained the friendship and support of prominent citizens of Philadelphia, most notably Benjamin Franklin, whose portrait West would go on to paint. This support translated into financial backing, and in 1759 West was able to travel to Europe to refine his artistic skills in Italy.

According to Galt, West's early association with Native Americans, coupled with his identity as a "primitive" from the English colonies, garnered him attention in Rome, as his supposed intimate knowledge of indigenous American culture made him something of an object of curiosity to those he met in the city. West would later travel to London, where he settled permanently and went on to great success as a founder of the Royal Academy in 1768 and, following his friend Reynolds, eventually became president of the institution. West's letters from his long period in England indicate that he was well ensconced in the highest circles of London society, and eventually he was patronized by King George III.[18] Thus at the time of the commission from Thomas Penn, West's career was reaching a high point, as he was renowned on both sides of the Atlantic.

When we examine the composition of *Penn's Treaty*, we see some staples that West used time and again as an academically trained painter grounded in a classical tradition of history painting. The portly figure to the center left of the image, in the rather drab brown suit, represents William Penn. The ostensible purpose of the painting was to commemorate Penn's famous treaty with the Lenape Indians upon his arrival in Pennsylvania. West has said of his aim with this painting, "The great object I had in forming that composition was to express savages brought into harmony and peace by justice and benevolence, by not withholding from them what was their reight and giving them what they were in want of, as well as a wish to give by that art a conquest made over native people without sward or Dagder."[19]

West here praises Penn's ability to produce harmony with the Lenapes through persuasion rather than force. Like most Quakers, he perceived Penn as a man of higher morality due in large part

Quakerism, Skulls, and Sanctity

to this treaty. It was this nobility that West attempted to display. As Tobin has noted, in this quote West shows awareness of Penn's legendary offer to pay the Lenapes for land that he had already been granted by the king, indicating to his Quaker followers Penn's humility and generosity. In West's view, he also gained the Lenapes' favor by "giving them what they were in want of," in this case the textiles we see in the painting. The manufactured commodities of empire here take center stage as the item that, in the context of the image, produces docility in the Natives and thus communion between the two groups. As we shall see, displaying the Native in the act of internalizing mainstream mercantile values would become a cornerstone of the transformational imagery of the Gilded Age Indian boarding schools a century later. In another letter describing his perception of Penn's treaty, West would go even further than simply praising Penn and evoke the Christian faith as endowing the treaty with a divine significance: he thanks the letter's recipient for a gift he received that apparently was made from the wood of "the tree under whose spreading branches Wm. Penn held his Treaty with the Indian chiefs when he fulfilled the first duty of Christianity by rendering to others what they wished to be rendered to them—and thus conquering the savage without a weapon to denote any other conquest but that which justice delivered."[20]

As this second quote indicates, West and others characterized Penn's treaty as a form of "conquest," seeming to contradict the more common perception of the treaty as an act of divinely inspired benevolence. West shows amazement at Penn's ability to bring the "savage" to heal "without a weapon," as if this nonviolent exchange violated an expectation he might have had. In the context of Anglo-Indian relations throughout American history, Penn's nonviolent negotiation with the Lenapes does indeed stand out when one considers the openly genocidal aims of other settlers and explorers. That said, it is also important to consider the concept of colonial didacticism discussed in the introduction. The cultural historian Ella Shohat, in discussing images of colonization, explains that colonial didacticism generally consists of an "enlightened" colonizer, in this case Penn, bestowing "correct" values upon a less civilized Native, in this case the Lenape delegation. Even nonviolent interactions, exchanges, treaties, and so forth contained an element of indirect coercion, as a hierarchical relationship between the groups is assumed beforehand and yet goes unspoken. The peace is maintained so long as the Native simply accepts the bestowal of new knowledge and values from the colonizer.[21] This "knowledge" could be something simple or could be something more complex, such as the conveyance of a new religious cosmology. In all cases, colonial didacticism is a paternalistic discourse bent on reconstructing the Native in the image of the colonizer.

In this particular case we see the Lenapes engaging in a commercial exchange: Penn offers them a variety of commodities in return for a portion of their ancestral lands. And West displays their willing complicity in their own disinvestment. Tobin explains that their facial expressions and gestures indicate their acceptance of Penn's gifts and their overawed mental state upon seeing the dazzling objects. In fact one figure, to the right of the main group, has already covered his body in a green textile and carries another over his shoulder as he walks in the direction of the dark forest.[22] This may be taken as a sign of his newly acquired greed, as he apparently has more than he needs. Also, his compositional association with the forest is a common trope in American painting throughout the colonial era and into the nineteenth century.

The compositional alignment of Native figures with untamed forested areas in a picture is generally taken to connote their "primitive" qualities. For example, one may see this decades later in Asher B. Durand's famous painting *Progress* of 1853, the very title of which makes this equation explicit in a way that West's image does not. Like many American artists, Durand juxtaposes the civilized settlement, alight with modern technologies, with the untamed wilderness. On both sides he places figures: the settled part of the canvas is populated with Anglo-American figures, and the wilderness side is populated with Native Americans. While

Quakerism, Skulls, and Sanctity

both artists avoid displays of overt conflict, they nevertheless, in individual ways, reify the dualistic structure of civilization and savagery.

Also significant for the meaning of West's painting, the clothing worn by Penn and his cohorts does not date to the 1680s, when the treaty is believed to have been executed. Rather these are the fashions of West's own time, nearly a century later. Such clothing, which reads here as plain or unpretentious, was not how Quakers would have dressed in Penn's own time and indicates the retrospectively modernizing intent of West's composition. As the canvas was commissioned by Penn's son in 1771, such an anachronistic element seemingly contradicts any desire on Thomas's part for a historically unproblematic and accurate depiction of his father's treaty with the Lenapes. This disjunction therefore raises a fundamental question regarding the meaning of the image.

Tobin and Abrams both suggest that the image was intended to serve Thomas as a sort of visual resolution for the subsequently problematic relations between the Quakers and the surrounding tribes, especially following William Penn's death in 1718. Specifically Tobin argues that by dressing the elder Penn in eighteenth-century clothes, West and Thomas Penn wished to forge a visual and conceptual linkage between the two generations of the Penn family. Such a close association was desirable, as Thomas's relations with the Lenapes and other tribes was uneasy at times, and his treatment of them was not only contradictory to his father's stated moral ideals but also brought him into conflict with some of his fellow Quakers. Therefore West seems to be attempting a retroactive adjustment in order to smooth over difficult historical complexities.[23]

Indeed, when the historical record is consulted, relations between the groups, and even between internal Quaker factions, were problematized by a number of incidents that took place in the wake of William Penn's death. The two most well-known of these incidents were the Walking Purchase of 1737 and the controversial land sales conducted at the Albany Congress in

1754. Thomas Penn was a driving political force in both of these episodes, and his involvement caused him to lose considerable face among both Quakers and Natives, necessitating his commissioning of the painting by West. With respect to the Walking Purchase, Thomas claimed to have had a copy of a deed authored by his father that allowed the Quakers to lay claim to any lands west of the Delaware River that a man could walk to within a day and a half. Both the existence of this deed as well as Thomas's method of acquiring these lands opened him to criticism from multiple sides.

In order to extricate his family from a crushing debt, Thomas wished to purchase the Lenape lands north and west of Philadelphia for a cheap price, and then sell them on speculation at a much higher price. William Penn had established a deed in 1682 with Lenape sachems that firmly established lands that he had purchased at that time. This deed survives today in the collection of the Historical Society of Pennsylvania, and the parameters of the ceded territory are firm. In that deed William outlined the land he would purchase from the Indians and enumerated the goods he would give in return, which were substantial. He acquired a reputation for mostly just dealings with the Lenapes due to the fact that he offered to purchase this land, which was already part of the grant he had been given by the Crown.[24]

Interestingly his desire to purchase land already granted to him by the king seems to indicate a sliver of doubt regarding his true ownership. The grant specified that Penn could have dominion over unoccupied lands; apparently the Crown overlooked the fact that Pennsylvania at this time was occupied, which could nullify the grant. This oversight may of course have been intentional, as the Crown did not necessarily view the Lenapes as legitimate occupants. Regardless of intent, however, it seems that Penn sensed the contradiction and thus wished to compensate the Lenapes for the land.[25]

In his own dealings with the Lenapes, Thomas claimed that there was another, later deed, of 1686, that was negotiated between his father and the Lenapes, which allowed him to revisit the terms of

Quakerism, Skulls, and Sanctity

the 1682 deed and to expand upon the amount of land controlled by the Penn family. Historians widely doubt the legitimacy of this later deed, which was unsigned and, some believe, forged by Thomas and his agents at a later date. Nevertheless, arguing on the supposed legitimacy of this later deed, Thomas claimed it stated that he could purchase land "as far as a man could walk in a day and a half" beyond the boundaries of the 1682 agreement. With this document in hand, Thomas was able to leverage Nutimus, the chief negotiator for the Indians. He then hired three well-known athletes to run as far as they could, beginning from the starting line of the older agreement, and ending after a day and a half of exertion. The runner who made it the farthest from the starting line, and thus covered the most land, was offered a prize. With this tactic Thomas was able to acquire an enormous chunk of land, which he began selling on speculation before the purchase was even ratified.[26]

Proof of Thomas's method of acquisition exists today in the archives of Haverford College, where a group of letters and invoices indicate that he indeed paid a group of agents to conduct the purchase in this manner. He was required to pay agents for their trouble in executing the arduous "walk," and also had to pay a separate group to clear a path for the runners beforehand, so as to enable them to cover as much ground as possible. Additionally these documents suggest that he began planning the purchase as early as 1735, two years before the "walk" was actually executed in August 1737, as inquiries regarding the pricing of parcels of the new land predate the invoices for the services of his agents.[27]

In the context of this bizarre and unfortunate history, Thomas commissioned the painting from West. The historical anachronisms and inconsistencies mentioned earlier were therefore important in resolving contradictions. The "sobriety" of the fashions worn by the Quakers is in stark contrast to the chromatic explosion one sees in the clothing worn by the Lenapes on the right side of the painting. Tobin has interpreted this chromatic choice on West's part to a need to aesthetically polarize the two groups. The

Quakers are shown as a sober people with an aversion to excessive display; the Lenapes favor colors that suggest vanity. As mentioned earlier, their facial expressions also contribute to the aesthetic and conceptual polarization of the two groups. The Quakers appear calm and collected, and Penn's grand gesture suggests generosity and magnanimity. In contrast the Lenape representatives have animated and varying facial expressions, apparently in reaction to the appearance of the gifts being given to them. In other words, they are foolishly taken in by the spectacle of the commodities being offered and seem to be losing their bearings. The loss of self-control and cultural identity in the face of mercantile temptations was indeed a concern expressed by some Native leaders, such as Papoonon.[28]

Another important anachronism in the painting is the inclusion of people who were not present at the actual treaty. In a letter written a few years later to his brother William, West frankly tells him of the historical inaccuracies involved in his creative process:

> I could not neglect so favorable an opertunity as this . . . to send you the print of Wm. Penn's treaty with the Indians when he founded the Province of Pennsylvania. I have taken the liberty to introduce the likeness of our Father, and our brother of Reading, into the picture of the group of Friends [Quakers] that accompany Wm. Penn, that in the likeness of our Brother that stands imediatly behind Penn, resting on his cane. I need not point out the figure of our Father.[29]

Interesting in this letter, which is one of the very few original sources identifying those in the painting, West does not give a rationale for these inclusions. Whatever his motivations, apparently the visual association of his own family with the treaty mattered to West, as the artist indicates his father's presence by highlighting his face more brightly than those of the other Quakers. While all of the other figures in the composition have their gazes drawn by events unfolding in the rhetorical space of the picture, his father's role as de facto narrator is indicated by his mental detachment—he

Quakerism, Skulls, and Sanctity

appears in three-quarters view to be glancing out at the viewer. He is involved in the scene and yet his absence from it is tacitly acknowledged by his metanarrative engagement of our gaze. Such historical inaccuracies were hardly publicized at the time, however, as Thomas Penn badly needed West to execute an image of Quaker togetherness to repair his family's reputation after the Walking Purchase. Some colonial officials, including Benjamin Franklin and Sir William Johnson, even openly questioned the legality of Thomas's transactions.[30]

In considering the moral and religious overtones of the painting, especially as applied to the depiction of a perceived subaltern population, it is helpful at this point to draw parallels between this work and a later one by West that have conceptual and compositional similarities. *Christ Healing the Sick in the Temple* of 1817 (fig. 15) bears striking resemblances to the earlier, better-known work and offers us further insight into West's perception of subaltern populations, as well as the theological structure the two images share, despite their ostensibly different subject matter. West executed this painting on commission from the Board of Managers of the Pennsylvania Hospital in Philadelphia. Although the board had made overtures to West as early as 1800, the first version of the painting was not executed until 1811, and then was exhibited in London. The painting elicited such a positive response at the time that the directors of the newly established National Gallery in London offered to pay West a substantial sum for it. West agreed to the sale, then set upon doing a second version of the painting for the hospital, completed several years later. The image would prove important for the board: it metaphorically framed their work at the hospital in christological terms and was a significant source of revenue after they starting charging a fee to view it.[31]

The two paintings have different manifest content. One shows a biblical scene from the life of Christ as described in the Book of Matthew, while the other purports to give us a depiction that may be taken as both an allegory of mercantile ascent and a document of a key moment in the life of William Penn and the history of Quakerism. Even a cursory look at the two reveals that West drew parallels between the figures of Christ and Penn and, perhaps more unexpected, between the Lenapes and the mentally and physically ill.

Compositionally the two paintings clearly highlight the figures of Christ and Penn, as both are placed slightly to the center left in virtually the same location. Both assume very similar if not exactly identical poses, in each case intended to draw attention to the generosity of their acts. With respect to their poses, it is helpful to consider the wider context of such compositional devices in American painting around this time. The Philadelphia painter Charles Willson Peale famously gives us a central dominant male protagonist similarly posed in his painting *The Artist in His Museum*, a self-portrait of 1826. Peale, like Penn, was an impresario and entrepreneur; he opened a for-profit museum in Philadelphia that featured both works of fine art and specimens of natural history. Peale's purpose in opening his museum, beyond being simply entrepreneurial, was to educate the public through the displays contained within. Many of the objects in the museum, most famously the mastodon skeleton seen in the painting, were from Peale's personal collection. Peale and others at this time, fascinated by the "natural history" of America, were avid bone collectors. We see this interest in the collection and writings of Peale's fellow Philadelphian Samuel Morton, whose work in craniology will be discussed later in this chapter. The bones of ancient animals or peoples were often intended to establish a viable history for the continent, intended to ward off charges of American ahistoricism. The establishment of an ancient prehistory of the continent, through the excavation of either human or animal remains, was likewise a concern of Thomas Jefferson, who of course is more well-known for his diplomatic and political career. However, like Peale and others during the Enlightenment, Jefferson was an amateur archaeologist whose investigations were motivated by an overriding desire to discover the origins and evolution of all things in nature, with an aim toward their encyclopedic categorization.[32]

In his self-portrait Peale shows himself as the Enlightenment gentleman par excellence. He is the open-armed revealer of secrets, potentially life-altering for his audiences. Like the posed figures of Penn and Christ, we have the enlightened man generously bestowing not only gifts (commodities, knowledge, etc.) but also a new reality to the viewer. In this sense, the figures *within* these three images are a sort of cue or metaphor for how the actual viewer *outside* the painting is supposed to respond. The painted context may be contemporary, historical, or biblical, but the message remains the same: give thanks unto him who dispenses.[33]

A further linkage between West and Peale, aside from their mutual origins in the milieu of Enlightenment-era Philadelphia, was West's interest in collecting ethnographic objects. As mentioned, it is widely known that one reason for West's seemingly miraculous success both in Italy and in England was his "exotic" qualities in the eyes of the European elites who patronized him. As an American "primitive," he (supposedly) had access to places, people, and experiences that most "civilized" upper-class Europeans who had never ventured to the New World lacked. West emphasized this in his life narrative and apparently used it to his advantage, as seen in the famous *Borghese Gladiator* episode described in the biography by Galt. When asked by the Roman gentry his opinion of the famous statue, West replied that it was similar in conception to the physique of Native Americans. According to Galt, this answer apparently struck a chord with his audience, who valued West's alternative perception of the statue. Again, while the accuracy of this and other episodes in Galt's book may be questioned, the point here is the self-conceptualization propagated by West during his lifetime.[34]

West states in correspondence that he was able to paint ethnographically accurate depictions of Native Americans in *Penn's Treaty* and his French and Indian War painting *The Death of General Wolfe* because he had acquired a large array of ethnographic items while still in the colonies. As he put it in a letter to a friend, "By possessing the real dresses of the Indians I was able to give that truth in representing their costumes which is so evident in the picture of the Treaty."[35] West, like Peale, had an intellectual and artistic reputation that rested largely on their ability to acquire "exotic" trophies of the continent's "primitive" past, something that was perceived as giving them special insights into certain types of subject matter in their work.

West goes further in the two paintings under review, as both Penn and Christ are surrounded by a semicircular array of figures, in a fashion reminiscent of Raphael's *School of Athens*. The two central figures make outward-flowing gestures, bridging the gap between the various elements within each painting, and also between the viewer and the historical event depicted. In the case of Penn, he links the Quakers and the Lenapes on either side, and in the case of Christ, his gesture links foreground and background as well as left and right, each of which is inhabited by different constituencies. The open arms of the dynamic and slightly off-center Jesus cause the viewer to survey the wide array of social and psychological types: his followers, the physically disabled, the mentally ill, and the Jewish elders behind him.

In terms of West's compositional and aesthetic equation of the Native Americans and the mentally ill, it is helpful to briefly consider perceptions of both in early America, as well as the institutional contexts of those perceptions. Equating heathen indigenous persons with the mentally ill or spiritually possessed was by no means new at the time West was painting. It will be recalled that Cotton Mather, when writing about demonic possession during the witch hysteria that gripped the Massachusetts Bay Colony in the 1690s, equated the "pagan" Indians in the colony to those unfortunate Puritans who had fallen under Satan's spell. It is therefore worth briefly revisiting his text on the subject.

As discussed in chapter 1, Mather wrote in his tract *Memorable Providences, Relating to Witchcraft and Possession*, "There are Devils and Witches. . . . New-Engl. has had Examples of their Existence and Operation; and that *not only the Wigwams of Indians, where the pagan Powaws often raise their masters, in the shapes of Bears and Snakes and Fires, but the House of Christians*" (emphasis added). Such an equation allowed Mather and others to easily group together perceived nonconformists as threats to the colony's existence. All such persons were in need of spiritual conversion, and so the General Court doubled its effort to rectify the "lapse" in Christian morality.[36]

Mather would explicate his views on insanity even more extensively in his text *The Angel of Bethesda*, a little-known work in which the theologian attempts to play physician for the reader. Mather opines that both physical and mental illnesses are punishment for man's sinfulness, beginning with the Fall in the Garden of Eden as narrated in the Book of Genesis. He declares that the reader ought to be grateful to God for his grasp of reason, the lack of which is a divine punishment conferred upon the insane in recompense for their exceptional sinfulness. He then recommends daily prayer as a treatment for madness, conflating insanity with atheism. In Mather's logic both body and soul are God's creations; thus, if the soul drifts from God's will, the body will inevitably exhibit symptoms of that spiritual malaise.[37]

While Mather and other Puritans viewed insanity as a result of spiritual possession, by West's time definitions of insanity in America had evolved significantly and had come more in line with mainstream Enlightenment thought on the question. And perhaps surprisingly, this more "systematic" view of mental illness melded well with the discourse of "charitable" care given to the insane by Quakers in America. The insane were seen through a more scientific lens and were assumed to be in need of clinical surveillance and intervention. Such surveillance was needed, as the loss of reason became the new "heresy" of the Enlightenment, and so individuals affected by such a loss needed to be quarantined to protect the general public. This soon led to the establishment of scientific categorizations of insanity and to the founding of hospitals, clinics, and asylums that tended to the insane. The organization of a systematically "scientific" gaze in relation to insanity and demonic possession is likewise evidenced by the publication of the first medical treatise published in the United States to address the subject, Benjamin Rush's *Medical Inquiries and Observations upon the Diseases of the Mind*, in 1812.[38] Although not a Quaker himself, Rush was an evangelical Christian, having been educated in that vein during his youth.

Rush was also a leading physician in Philadelphia in the wake of the Revolution and was a staff member at the Pennsylvania Hospital for decades. In his treatise Rush discusses insanity and couches his recommended treatment in biblical verse, as West does in his painting. Rush divides his text into numerous chapters, each addressing a specific type of mental malady, categorized in an encyclopedic manner becoming of the Enlightenment. In one chapter, "Derangement in the Moral Faculties," Rush associates mental imbalance with what he refers to as a lack in the patient's "sense of deity." As proof of the possibility this state could arise in modern patients, he references biblical scripture multiple times, as if to reinforce the scientific legitimacy of his claim through this means. For example, he lists as primary causes of moral derangement the use of "ardent spirits" and "famine," or alcoholism and a lack of food. He links this latter cause to a verse found in the Deuteronomy 28:56–57, which warns readers to beware the moral degeneration that can occur during times of material difficulty, such as a famine. Like many of his generation in America, Rush would associate mental illness with moral decrepitude, violence, and poverty and legitimize these claims by reference to both Enlightenment-style categorization and an appeal to biblical verse. It was the combination of these problems, especially among the "lower orders" in Philadelphia, that would cause civic leaders, including Benjamin Franklin, to petition the Crown for the establishment of an asylum in which to contain the insane. As a result the Pennsylvania Hospital was founded in 1751.[39]

Recall that Foucault links Quakerism to the eighteenth-century rise of asylums in the English-speaking world. He asserts that

Quakers were driven by belief and political need to engage the mentally ill to a degree uncommon even among religious organizations. They courted private funding in setting up asylums in England and America, as this enabled them to, in a sense, "possess" insanity, to show their goodwill to the larger community. and to avert charges that *they* themselves suffered from mental delusions, a charge brought against Fox and his original followers in England in the seventeenth century. Foucault argues that it is therefore no surprise to read Edenic linguistic descriptions of Quaker asylums published during this era, as the Society had a vested interest in sanctifying their charitable work and making it seem like a mechanism of worldly salvation.[40]

Despite the pretense of "charitable" treatment, conditions at the hospital were inhumane, as many patients were confined to damp, cold cells with bars, and those deemed potentially violent were chained by the hands and feet.[41] However, because it was important for the hospital to be perceived as a humane institution, West was hired to produce a painting that was biblical and yet allegorical in its reference to the work of the institution: *Christ Healing the Sick in the Temple*. Thus in West's rendition, we have the conceptual merging of Quaker theological ideals and modern scientific rationalization, as seen in the graphic contrast between the graceful figure of Christ and the degraded figures of the ill that surround him, especially the insane boy to the right middle ground of the picture. The ill here are identified by their facial and bodily contortions, even requiring physical restraint from those around him.

As for West, a few decades later he did not perceive Native Americans as being in league with Satan in the literal, paranoid sense that Mather and other Puritans did during the witch trials. Nevertheless he saw them as morally deficient and in need of salvation at the hands of Penn. West believed that Penn had accomplished this goal through his act of commodity exchange, which he attempted to sanctify in his painting. His conception of the Lenapes as a subaltern group in need of Penn's generosity of spirit has been mentioned by scholars such as Tobin, who notes that their illuminated facial expressions upon seeing the commodities before them are tacitly set as a comparison against the self-controlled expressions on the faces of the Quakers. Interestingly, the Lenapes' reaction to the bestowal of mercantile values is both potential for their salvation and a confirmation of their avarice, commonly thought to afflict the insane as well.

We see a parallel in the perception of subaltern groups in correspondence regarding his commission to execute *Christ Healing the Sick in the Temple*. Appealing to West to accept the commission, Josiah Hewer, the president of the Board of Managers, writes of the hospital, "Its object is the relief of the *Maniacs and sick poor* in Pennsylvania; many thousands of these, of every nation and country, who have maintained an intercourse with Philadelphia, have enjoyed its benefits in common with the resident poor of our country. Conducted as the Hospital is, on a principle of *extensive benevolence*, it has attracted the attention of many charitable and well-disposed people, at home and abroad" (emphasis added).[42]

In an effort to induce West also to donate the painting to the hospital, Hewer emphasizes the broad-based charitable giving on which the hospital presumably depended in its efforts to aid the "Maniacs and sick poor." Important here is Hewer's conflation of the "sick" and the "poor." Poverty at this time was commonly seen as a mental and/or moral failing on the part of the impoverished; it is a viewpoint considered progressive when compared to the older view of sociological creationism to which many Puritans subscribed. It is also significant that the hospital treated both the mentally ill as well as the conventional ill, a distinction that West emphasized in the finished painting in the variety of figures shown. Indeed West was moved by the request from such a "benevolent" institution and agreed to complete the painting on a charitable basis, albeit after he was able to sell an identical copy to the National Gallery of London. He replied to Hewer, "The gratification it has long afforded me, in hearing of the celebrity of those laws, by which that Hospital is governed; the

Quakerism, Skulls, and Sanctity

relief it affords to the sick poor and the benign aid it gives to the afflicted in general has placed it among the first Institutions. . . . I therefore accept the offer."[43]

Important for West and his fellow Quakers involved in the transaction is the charitable nature of the institution and its dedication to the aiding of the "sick poor." Such principles were similar to the elevated values embodied in Penn's treaty and were rarely if ever spoken of as forms of modern institutional imprisonment and surveillance. In fact West would go on to write about the painting's subject matter and how he felt that it was a theme appropriate for the hospital: "The subject I have chosen is analogous to the Institution: It is the Redeemer of Mankind extending his aid to the afflicted of all ranks and conditions. The Passage in from Matthew, chapter 21, verse 14 & 15: 'And the blind and the lame came to him in the Temple, and he healed them. And when the chief Priests and the Scribes saw the wonderful things that he did, and the children crying in the temple "Hosanna to the Son of David!" they were displeased.'"[44]

In his enthusiasm for the painting, West saw its narrative as paralleling the moral mission of the hospital itself, and, as he states, the subject becomes an analogue to that mission. Whatever the realities of life in the hospital, a discourse of "morality" and "relief" was commonly deployed in reference to these newly organized institutions of surveillance and incarceration and was important to their perceived viability, especially in religious or other charitable contexts.[45]

This was important in more general cultural terms as the treatment of insanity evolved over the course of the eighteenth century, from family care to the less personal public care offered by clinics. As this transition from private to public, from the personal to the impersonal, was potentially disruptive to the community, we have a necessary parallel to the discourse of institutionalism in a common refrain in Quaker culture: the doing of Christ's work on earth. For West and the hospital managers, an image could apparently embody these more charitable ideals, as it was a literal illustration of a biblical verse and an allegorical representation of the work of the hospital and of Quaker ideals more broadly. However, this "doing of works" in this world was a source of controversy within Quakerism, as we shall see. Many Quakers objected to the actual engagement in works as well as the propagandizing of these works via mechanisms of publicity, such as bold public pronouncements and the fabricating of certain types of images. Perhaps in being geographically separated from Pennsylvania and inhabiting the cosmopolitan cultural milieu of the London art world, West felt immune to such considerations and was able to execute the painting without qualm.

That the two paintings were perceived as similar in their themes and intents was made explicit by Samuel Coates, a friend of West's and the secretary to the Board of Managers. Coates himself was a physician who regularly interacted with and treated insane patients at the hospital.[46] In a letter to West, Coates discussed the two paintings, as he wished to express to West the managers' "full approbation of the subject thou hast chosen." He says of *Penn's Treaty*, "The first Indian Treaty with Penn, was of thy own delineating," as if in simply making an image of the event West had somehow authored its historical significance.[47] Such a belief in an essential linkage between imagery and the ontological reality of persons or events in history recurs throughout the correspondence that addresses these two paintings, and indeed was often taken as a measure of the intellectual quality of a history painting. Coates and others conferred on West the abilities of a divinely inspired genius, exemplified in his god-like ability to "delineate" an event that took place decades before his birth. This was a nod to the success of the memorializing function intended by West and his patron Thomas Penn, as *Penn's Treaty* was clearly seen as establishing an iconic sense of communion among Quakers.

Coates would go even further in his praise of *Christ Healing the Sick*. The painting was soon installed in a gallery adjacent to the hospital and was available for public viewing. In the visitor's guidebook, Coates, like Galt, places West among the greats of

Western painting, including Raphael, Poussin, and Daniele Da Volterra. He then writes that upon entering the exhibition gallery at the hospital, "we cast our eyes upon Mr. West's Picture—suddenly, as if by magic, all these chef-d'oeuvres of the art [history] ebb and crowd back in the tide of our memory, but soon flow and vanish away."[48] Both paintings were seen as works of inspired genius and as working in the service of Quaker ideals.

In Quakerism, recapturing the "primitive" aspect of Christian faith was of paramount importance. Both George Fox and William Penn sought an "authentic" version of Christian faith and practice, which they perceived as existing prior to the "corruption" of the church by the papacy in Rome in the Middle Ages. And in West's aesthetically linking Christ and Penn, as well as the historical milieus in which each executed his "miraculous" works, he implies that Penn, in his benign dealings with the Lenapes, has, at least momentarily, recaptured the spirit of Christ, free of the corruptions endemic to larger Anglo-Indian relations.

With all of this in mind, we can look at the two images side by side. In *Penn's Treaty*, West places the Quakers to the left of Penn and the Lenapes to the right. The situation in *Christ Healing the Sick in the Temple* is slightly more complex. Here he places the Jewish elders and Christ's followers in the background and to the center and left. In contrast, the ill are placed either in the foreground or to the right, curling around to the right background. Such a pictorial trope allows West to make further allusions. Not only do Christ and Penn compositionally echo one another, but the various figures surrounding them likewise echo one another. The Quakers take on the role of Christ's (Penn's) followers, and the "savage" Lenapes assume the role of the ill and disabled. In both cases, each oppositional group is conveniently demarcated, and the subaltern group is portrayed as in need of assistance from the divinely inspired central figure and his followers.

The architectural background of each image supports such a reading. According to West's friend Coates, the brightly illuminated room behind the red curtain to the left of Christ's head represents the Holy of Holies, a sacred inner sanctuary inside of the ancient Temple of Jerusalem believed to contain the Ark of the Covenant. Traditionally both Jews and Christians believe that at one time the Ten Commandments given by God to Moses were contained within the Ark. As such, the Holy of Holies was a spiritually rarefied area within the Temple, and only the High Priest of the Temple was permitted inside, and only once a year, during the Jewish holiday of Yom Kippur. Coates describes West's inclusion of this symbol:

> We must not forget to mention here the boldness of the Artist in placing the bright circle of glory, which surrounds the head of Christ, close to the spot which exhibits the seven lights of the mysterious luminary in the *Sanctum Sanctorum* of the Temple. A common artist would have been afraid lest the accidental background might have outglowed the brightness of the light which emanates from the beloved Son of Him who said, "Let there be light." Conscious of this power, the Artist places the one nearly upon the other, and, by this most orthodox contrast, exemplifies the rising dawn of the Messiah's glory upon the slow-retiring twilight of the fulfilled types of the Mosaic law.[49]

Coates's equation of Christ's act of healing with the prescriptions of Mosaic law attempts to establish a spiritual lineage between Jesus and the biblical patriarch. Likewise West compositionally likens Christ's act of healing with Penn's act of mercantile exchange. In a similar vein, behind Penn's head we see another classical-themed structure, albeit in secular guise: a newly constructed brick house (also an anachronism used by West) frames Penn's head. The archway of the house stands immediately to the right and behind Penn, and above it the initials "W.P." and the year "1683" are inscribed. The structure serves multiple functions: it historically contextualizes the image and identifies Penn, and it serves as a marker of the "progress" being made by the Quakers within the savage confines of Pennsylvania, even at this early date. The structure may clearly (and favorably) be compared to the "primitive" housing of the Lenapes at right. But in terms of the comparison here, it is a background structure that likewise contextualizes the profundity of Penn's act, much as the Holy of Holies sets a biblical contextualization for Christ's act. Penn's "temple," his gift to the New World, is the progress wrought by the Quakers in the wilderness. As Christ emerges from the ideal space of the Holy of Holies into the rough-and-tumble of his historically present world, so Penn emerges from the structure of civilization into the wilds of the New World in an effort to "heal" the Lenapes through the peaceful conference of commercial values.

As West's depiction of Penn's ideal behavior toward the Lenape shows, well before the eras of aggressive frontier expansion and classical pseudoscience in the nineteenth century, Native Americans served as a conceptual nexus for artists, illustrators, and others who were increasingly concerned about the rapidly growing nation's racial tensions and perceived spiritual malaise, commonly noted in the writings of the country's most well-known ministers and missionaries.[50] West's fellow Quaker Edward Hicks (1780–1849) often lamented such conditions in his sermons and letters as well as in his autobiography. For example, in a letter to his friend Samuel Hart, Hicks writes the following regarding some of his fellow Quakers: "[I was] at one time so offended at the inconstant conduct of some of my fellow members that was high in profession but low in practice that I was almost ready to do as some weak disciples had done . . . go back and walk no more with him [Christ] but was admonished by the wise saying of Peter 'Lord to whom shall we go that hast the word of everlasting life.'"[51]

Hicks regularly saw contradictions between Quaker doctrine and the actual practices of many of his brethren. As seen in the example of the prophet Papoonon, some Native American leaders were quick to discern what they saw as the "greed" of Quaker merchants, and Hicks at times seems to concur with this evaluation in his private correspondence. This is in stark contrast to the idealized utopic vision of society and nature he offers us in his *Peaceable*

Kingdom series. In an effort to resolve these contradictions, Hicks relied on biblical verse, which would also play a key role in the intended meaning of his paintings.

To understand Hicks's *Peaceable Kingdom* series and its references to Native American subjects, we must understand the brand of Quakerism practiced by him and his family, and also the historical genesis of the events he depicts in this series. To do this, it will be necessary to consider briefly Hicks's perception of William Penn and his sons, as well as Hicks's reception and use of the retroactive historical and aesthetic idealization of Penn by West in *Penn's Treaty with the Indians.*

Hicks was born to Anglican parents in Pennsylvania during the Revolution; because his mother died when he was young and his father incessantly traveled for business, he was effectively orphaned. In addition to these misfortunes, his father's Loyalist political leanings during the war led to his professional ruin afterward. The young Hicks was thus left in the care of David Twining, a friend of the family. Hicks's religious education began during his childhood on the Twining farm, where the family was Quaker. Following Twining's death, Hicks was forced to strike out on his own, and wound up being an apprentice at a coachmaker's shop.[52] Thus Hicks and his family saw the extremes of affluence and position, poverty and ruin, fluctuations that would give him a lifelong fear of financial desperation. This narrative of a "fall from grace" would recur in evangelical Christian discourse. It is an early life trajectory that the Mormon founder Joseph Smith would also experience and that became the driving force behind his own embrace of spiritualism a generation later.

Hicks's experiences at the coach shop were mixed. Both he and subsequent scholars have concluded that this was a key moment in his life. By his own telling, while an apprentice he experienced a moral decline due to his questionable social associations, often turning to music and drink for solace. At the same time it was this perceived moral decline that led him to renounce loose living and commit more fully to his Quaker faith. Concurrently the skills he acquired as a coach painter allowed him to launch a career in the visual arts.[53]

Hicks's newly acquired spiritual fervor and painting skill led to simultaneous careers as a Quaker preacher and a visual artist. Ironically it was these twin callings that led him and his family down a road of near-constant financial uncertainty, plaguing him well into middle age. Around this time Hicks met a fellow Quaker named John Comly, who would prove to be a valuable lifelong friend. Comly encouraged Hicks in his ambitions as a preacher, but first discouraged his activities as a painter, seeing them as a materialistic distraction from his more important work of saving souls. Judging from surviving documents, Comly felt strongly that Hicks's passion for painting was the source of his troubles in life, and he went so far as to attempt to intervene financially on Hicks's behalf. In a letter he wrote to Hicks's cousins Isaac and Samuel, Comly implored the two for assistance in releasing Hicks from the "mire of paint": "But what would it be for Isaac & Samuel Hicks to loan their cousin Edward such a sum, without interest as wants relieve him, set him at liberty to run on his Master's errands, unshackled; help him out of his deep mire of paint, and set his feet, thro the blessing of Heaven on firm ground."[54]

In making his argument for a substantial no-interest loan on Hicks's behalf, Comly sets Hicks's current financial duress as a polar opposite force to his "Master's errands," a reference to his sacred obligation to Christ to spread the word of the Inner Light. It was *also* Hicks's attachment to preaching that held him and his family in chronic financial straits, however, as Quaker preachers of this era were commonly unpaid volunteers.[55]

While Hicks endured the logistical difficulties and social indignities associated with chronic financial dependence, and while his closest friends and family members often bemoaned his "mire of paint," one must also consider the specific nature of Hicks's beliefs in order to understand his attachment to the seemingly unprofitable occupations of painting and preaching. Hicks's religious views were intense and strident, and like other

Quakers he perceived the lesson of the Bible to be present and operative in his everyday life, often drawing allusions between the two in his letters, his sermons, his memoir, and his images.

Also important in the discussion of the historical evolution of evangelical imagery and texts is the changing reality of the institutional contexts of the production, distribution, and consumption of evangelical imagery. One reason for the prevalence of the appearance of Native Americans in the work of Hicks, which no prior American artist had depicted to such a degree, was the rise of newer technologies of reproduction that became more commonplace in the wake of the Revolution and the economic expansion of the new nation. More opportunities existed for the dissemination and thus appropriation of such imagery, as serialized publications became more accessible. Also, affluent philanthropic venues such as the Pennsylvania Hospital proliferated in the latter eighteenth century, expanding demand for evangelically inspired imagery.

With these changing contexts in mind we may consider Hicks's use of imagery as well as the specifics of his Quaker faith, and how these two factors were combined by the artist in his *Peaceable Kingdom* series. Hicks was the nephew of the famous Quaker preacher Elias Hicks, who was controversial and well-known in Quaker society in America in the early nineteenth century. Elias led a faction of Quakers—who subsequently became known as the "Hicksites"—down a spiritual path that he felt led to the cultivation of the Inner Light, the ultimate goal of his brand of Quaker worship and practice. The Hicksites preferred inner meditation over traditional Christian dogma and doctrine—especially that of the Catholic and Anglican churches—and also displayed an aversion to public religious ritual. In his *Memoirs*, Hicks writes of his enthusiasm for Elias and his brand of Quakerism, even comparing his cousin to the original twelve apostles of Jesus, as well as early Christian luminaries such as Tertullian and Origen.[56]

Elias's teachings were often in contrast to the beliefs of the orthodox Quaker faction, perceived by him and his followers to be too urbane and materialistic, as they tended to focus on the external practice of works of faith in the world. Elias, whom Edward refers to in his memoirs as a "butt of Orthodox persecution," instead focused his preaching on the inward cultivation of the soul, which could be shared with others only following intensive periods of meditation and prayer in which the worshipper had reached a proper sense of the "inwardness" of paradise, as opposed to its external, materialistic manifestation. Edward's and Elias's distaste for the orthodox faction is also evident in Edward's *Memoirs*, where he quotes his cousin who derisively refers to them as "beasts of prey," "creatures that range in darkness," and "false brethren."[57] In the heat of such disagreements, both factions claimed to represent "true" Quakerism as advocated by Fox and Penn generations earlier. These doctrinal differences led to a schism within the movement in 1827. Edward sided with his uncle's faction during this period, and historians have sometimes seen the formal evolutions in his *Peaceable Kingdom* series as an aesthetic response to these divisions within Quakerism.[58]

Hicks is best known for his *Peaceable Kingdom* series, of which he made dozens of versions, often as gifts for Quaker friends. Details of the images vary in response to external events, but the overriding theme and composition remain similar throughout. In the background of early versions, Hicks gives us a reversed compositional formula based loosely on printed reproductions of West's *Penn's Treaty with the Indians* and renders a symbolic image of the Quaker vision for the New World. Hicks's perception that Penn's treaty was analogous to and the fulfillment of biblical prophecy is illustrated throughout the series, and he uses both text and image to forge a conceptual link between the two.

For example, one early version, executed on commission for Hicks's friend Joseph Parrish (fig. 16), is a visual analogue to a verse from the book of the prophet Isaiah 11:6, a trope also intended to communicate Hicks's adherence to his uncle's version of Quakerism, which emphasized the pursuance of a spiritual Inner Light. This Inner Light of Christ was to be cultivated by the Quaker practitioner at the expense of material gain and shared with others in the service of mutual salvation. Thus in the Parrish version of 1823–25, Hicks establishes the staple compositional formula for the entire series by marshalling all familiar elements.

On the frame surrounding the central image is a version of the famous text from Isaiah: "The wolf also shall dwell with the lamb & the leopard shall lie down with the kid & the young lion & the fatling together & a little child shall lead them." In the foreground of the painting itself a small androgynous child holds a tree branch in its right hand and embraces a lion with its left arm.[59] The branch in this and other early versions of the series has been interpreted as an embodiment of Hicks's ideals for a utopic society in the New World, more specifically as a grape branch. As such, it represents both the royal lineage of Jesus going back to King David of the Old Testament and also Christ's sacrifice on the cross, or a variation on the wine-blood metaphor of the Eucharist.[60]

Art historian Alice Ford argues that the child is wearing "First Day" clothing, a fashion associated at the time with the attendance of Quaker services.[61] Thus the central figure is a sort of modernization of the ethic spelled out in Isaiah's miraculous prophecy, as the Quaker child has the power to unite seemingly adversarial species in defiance of natural laws; the predatory lion, for example, is made docile by the child's embrace and does not attack the other animals. Quaker viewers, such as Hicks's patron Parrish, would have seen such scenes as inspirational and miraculous.

In the background Hicks inserts the pictorial device of the natural bridge, which frames a reenactment of Penn's treaty. This trope was taken from a popular geography book of the time, the *New American Atlas* by Henry Schenk Tanner of 1823. The bridge was an important metaphor for Hicks, as it symbolized the bridging of differences between groups, both within and outside of Quakerism. The growing divide between Quaker factions drove Hicks to execute these paintings, which were symbolic attempts to proffer peace and unity.[62] The miraculous gathering in the

Quakerism, Skulls, and Sanctity

foreground is echoed by the equally miraculous gathering in the background, between Penn and the Lenapes. Both scenes visually correspond to the biblical prophecy painted on the frame. This prophecy served as a conceptual and doctrinal cornerstone for Quaker practice, as it highlighted the power of the Inner Light, a force, if properly cultivated, capable of bridging the gap between what might otherwise be perceived as "natural" enemies.

It is well-known that Hicks derived this composition and other versions of the theme from preexisting formulas painted by a variety of artists, then synthetically combined these elements into the finished products of his series. Hicks actually derived West's scene of Penn's treaty from the frontispiece of a popular biography of Penn titled *A Brief Memoir of the Life of William Penn, Compiled for the Use of Young Persons*. The book was written by Priscilla Wakefield and contained woodcut illustrations based on West's original composition, but reversed.[63]

Hicks had seen an engraved copy of the child done by an English engraver named Charles Heath (fig. 17). In Heath's version too an angelic child holds a branch of peace and embraces a ferocious lion. Both children are surrounded by varying animal species and are in an Edenic setting, with peace reigning. Heath's engraving is from an original drawing by Richard Westall, a member of the British Royal Academy. It is thought that Hicks saw it in a popular 1815 edition of the Bible first published in London by White, Cochrane and Company and later circulated in the United States.[64]

To sum up, Hicks foregrounds a Christ-like child in an Edenic landscape accompanied by a cadre of exotic animal species. The species coexist in harmony, in miraculous defiance of their ordinary relations. This is coupled with a classicized and very liberal interpretation of Penn's treaty with the Lenape Indians in the background, for Quakers believed that William Penn's prophetic treaty with the Lenapes in 1683 laid the groundwork for their Peaceable Kingdom in America and fulfilled Isaiah's prophesy. Hicks alludes to this in his *Memoirs*, in which he draws conceptual parallels between the visionary Penn and Jesus.[65] All of these factors were taken into account by the artist in his conceptualization of the Quaker utopia.

Unfortunately Hicks's prophetic vision of New World harmony was by the 1820s unfulfilled. In the wake of Penn's death, a series of intervening territorial and doctrinal disputes between Quakers and various Native American groups, as well as between competing Quaker factions, prevented its full realization.[66] Despite Hicks's desire to symbolically unify Quaker factions, Quakers and Native Americans, and multiple generations of Quaker leaders past and present, even he wrote of his distaste for the ideology of some of his "false brethren" in Quakerism. He accused them of hiring "formidable auxiliaries" in the form of lawyers and "hireling" priests in an effort to "prosecute and persecute" those of the Hicksite persuasion and to silence their unorthodox Quaker views through lawsuits and public humiliation.[67]

Hicks's fantastic vision, while grounded in biblical verse, may also be seen in the context of contemporary science in his native Philadelphia and beyond. While such connections have not been entirely lost on previous historians, their full ramifications in terms of linkages between Quaker theology and various pseudosciences have yet to be uncovered. In his *Memoirs*, Hicks writes of his interest in popular scientific theories of the time and attempts to link these theories to his own Hicksite version of Quakerism. Carolyn Weekley has noted that Hicks subscribed to the ancient medical theory of humorism, which over the course of the nineteenth century descended from being a generally accepted medical theory to being widely discredited due to advances in medical research and chemistry.[68]

Hicks's interest in humorism is significant for this discussion, as he used it as an intellectual device to explain his own nature, the Quaker schism, and the culture and behaviors of the Native Americans whom he depicted so many times in the *Peaceable Kingdom* series. This medical theory has roots in ancient Greek medicine and was popular among physicians and the lay public for millennia, up to the nineteenth century in Europe. The theory was first applied

Quakerism, Skulls, and Sanctity

systematically to the study of human health by the ancient Greek physician Hippocrates in his text *On the Nature of Man*, where he explains humorism as the coexistence of four fundamental fluids in the human body. He called these fluids blood, phlegm, yellow bile, and black bile. The key to human health was a balance and proper mixing of the four fluids ("humors"). An imbalance in the proportion of the fluids led to pain and disease. The later Greek physician Galen then associated the humors with various human temperaments: choleric, phlegmatic, sanguine, and melancholic. Each temperament was assumed to bring with it certain behaviors and attitudes, and it was believed that every individual had a specific combination of the four temperaments, based on the proportional presence of the four humors. For example, if one was choleric it was thought that one had an excess of yellow bile, which in turn led to an aggressive, domineering personality. The theories of Hippocrates and Galen reigned in Western medicine until they were overturned by medical research in the mid-nineteenth century. Hicks lived during an era when this theory—later viewed as pseudoscientific—still maintained some credibility.[69]

In his *Memoirs*, Hicks often frames his own experiences and perceptions of social realities in reference to humorism and seamlessly blends this consideration with biblical verse and Quaker teachings. For instance, when discussing his religious transformation to Quakerism at the tail end of a downward spiral in his life, he describes the onset of alarming physical and mental changes which he saw as both providential and pseudoscientific: "About midnight I was awakened with the same alarming symptoms I was attacked with the year before . . . when I was only saved from death by a miracle. . . . My friend the Doctor gave me body relief, but my mind was too solemnly impressed to be cured by anything but a heavenly physician. *From this time on my appearance was changed somewhat from a sanguine to a melancholy cast*" (emphasis added).[70]

He links this medical assessment of his altered state to his emerging interest in Quakerism, crediting his increased attendance at Quaker meetings to his transformation: "I found myself within reach of [a] Friends' meeting at Middletown [Pennsylvania], and went to it, and though I had often been there, I do not recollect that I had been at that meeting since my serious turn. Be that as it may, I think that I had a precious meeting, for I continued to walk five miles to that meeting every First Day."[71]

Importantly, Hicks here expresses an assumption shared by many pseudosciences of his time: that one's internal state, or "temperament" in humorist terms, has a direct correlation with one's external bearing or appearance. Thus Hicks tells the reader that he not only felt differently but that he had a new "cast" as a result. He links his transformation in character and appearance to an emerging spiritual revelation within himself; perhaps he sensed the assertion of his own Inner Light.

While Hicks describes his own key moment in life in both spiritualist and pseudoscientific terms, in other sections of his *Memoirs* he perceives others around him in similar terms, feeling that his idealist theories of spirit and body are universally applicable to all persons and all situations. Thus he describes the nature of humanity as compared to lower animals, all of which in his view were created by God and all of which were endowed with various faculties. While humans are differentiated from lower animals by the faculties of reason and free will, humans themselves are differentiated in terms of their various temperaments: "The animal body of man was the finishing work of all animated nature, and consequently the highest order of terrestrial creation; being compounded of the four principal elements—Earth, Air, Water and Fire. As either of these predominated in the animal economy, it gave rise to the constitutional character or complexion, called by the physician and philosopher—melancholy, sanguine, phlegmatic and choleric. Hence arises that astonishing variety in the appearances and actions of men and women, as creatures of this world."[72]

Hicks saw man as the product of divine creation, a terrestrial being in the "higher" likeness of God. Central to man's creation was the endowment of the human body with the four humors,

Quakerism, Skulls, and Sanctity

which differentiated humans from one another. Hicks would then take this theory and apply it to the problems within Quakerism. Not only did he see all humans as subject to the humors, but he attributed mostly negative humorous traits to those Quakers of the orthodox sect that disagreed with his views. It is this consideration that brings us back to his *Peaceable Kingdom* paintings.

As part of his interest in the humors, Hicks attributed traits to other persons but also saw metaphoric links between people and animal species in terms of temperament. It was these links that he used when he symbolically mapped the theological woes of the Quaker schism in his paintings. As such, four of the common species Hicks repeated in the series were also associated by him with various temperaments, symbolic of the religious landscape in which he found himself. Hicks claimed that the wolf represented the melancholic type, the leopard represented the sanguine, the bear the phlegmatic, and the lion the choleric. The animals he chose for the series were thus based in Isaiah's prophecy and yet were also associated symbolically with pseudoscientific ideas.[73]

With all of this in mind, it is no surprise that in many versions of the *Peaceable Kingdom*, including the Parrish version shown here, Hicks shows the divine child embracing the choleric lion. The choleric temperament was one of aggression; thus we have the miraculous sight of the child making the choleric king of the beasts docile. In a like fashion the wolf was associated with the melancholic nature, which Hicks saw as quiet and yet deceptive. The wolf's tendency toward stealth and isolation covered a greedy disposition, and it was this animal that he commonly associated with those in the orthodox sect of Quakerism, given what he saw as their pious proclamations and yet materialistic way of life. In the series, the wolf is made docile as well, often shown lying peacefully next to a kid, per Isaiah's prophecy.[74]

The entire series, with its docile adversarial animal species, divine children, and assortment of peacemaking Quaker exemplars, may be taken as a general statement on Hicks's part expressing a desire for spiritual unification of all Quakers. The question remains, however, as to where Hicks received his artistic inspiration for the zoological metaphors he uses in the paintings. While their conception is biblical, his visual sources were modern, and while his general compositions were derived from West, Westall, Heath, and the Wakefield book, Hicks also likely derived ideas for the depiction of animals from the work of the American illustrator Alexander Anderson (1775–1870) and the French biologist Georges Cuvier (1769–1832). In Anderson we have an illustrator who was well known in America in the nineteenth century for his biblical illustrations. He not only illustrated several editions of the Bible published by a variety of firms in New York, Philadelphia, and Boston, but he also did engravings to illustrate publications put out by the American Tract Society, an evangelical organization dedicated to Christian pedagogy.[75]

Hicks may have copied the poses for some of the lions in the series from Anderson's illustration of a Bible edition widely circulated in the United States at the time.[76] This represents another instance of Hicks's reliance on a popular, mass-produced visual medium, contradicting the common perception of his work as being strictly primitive in nature. Anderson would illustrate a number of biblical scenes and when depicting lions of course includes the hero Daniel. In this popular narrative from the Old Testament—one that fascinated American evangelicals throughout the nineteenth century—the condemned Hebrew prophet Daniel is cast into a den of lions by the Persian king Darius of Mede, only to be found the following morning miraculously untouched by the beasts. In the *Peaceable Kingdom* series, Hicks's child likewise tames the carnivorous beast in defiance of the laws of nature. Daniel was able to tame the lions and thus save himself through faith, which is mirrored in Hicks's child.

At this point it is also helpful to understand common perceptions of Native Americans in the country at the time. Even Hicks, who by the standards of the day was fairly progressive in his view of them, at one point in his *Memoirs* refers to Native Americans as having a "murderous" nature, albeit in response to the injustices done to them.[77] It is tempting to conclude that the twin scenes in many of the images of his series may be read in reference to both Isaiah's prophecy and the story of Daniel. As Daniel tamed the wild beasts, so the Quaker child tames the menagerie. One might say further that in defying the general norms of Anglo-Indian relations in the colonial era, Penn sought to "tame" the "wild" Indians by which he and his compatriots are surrounded in both West's and Hicks's paintings of his treaty.

Anderson is commonly considered by historians to be an innovator in woodcutting technique in America and a central figure in the rise of mass print culture in the early nineteenth century. He was the son of a Scottish immigrant who owned a print shop, and thus he learned the trade early in life.[78] In addition to his religious commissions, like Hicks, Anderson often depicted a wide variety of animal species, some shown with anthropomorphized features. And like Hicks, Anderson also ventured into depictions of the human form, often showing different social classes and racial groups, including slaves harvesting sugar cane. Regardless of his specific subject matter, though, Anderson displays a representational concept similar to that of his contemporary Hicks. Both portray a harmonious natural order mirrored in their depictions of human figures. All animals and persons have a peaceful and secure place in nature and in the social structure, and any conflict is generally averted. However, this representation is clearly at odds with the rapidly changing political and social realities of the growing young country, as incursions into the frontier and race-based slavery in the southern states significantly increased social and political tensions even within the Anglo-American population.[79]

While Hicks's affinity for Anderson is to be expected given their similar cultural grounding and outlook, his reliance on Cuvier is somewhat surprising. Cuvier was a renowned French scientist, one of the towering figures of the late Enlightenment in Europe. He is remembered for a number of significant theoretical innovations, including his theory of geological catastrophism and his complex encyclopedic system of species. Alice Ford has suggested that Hicks received his inspiration for the tiger cubs in the series from engravings that illustrated the English-language publication of Cuvier's *Le Règne Animal*, translated as *The Animal Kingdom*. If Ford's contention is correct, it links Hicks aesthetically and intellectually to one of the leading geologists and zoologists of the era. Cuvier's views on the evolution of the planet were importantly at odds with the later gradualist adaptation theory of Darwin. Cuvier favored a catastrophist view of geological change, arguing that a series of catastrophic natural events such as floods had periodically and suddenly occurred, thereby causing a change in the physical makeup of the planet and its organic population. Strangely, Cuvier's views actually relate to those of Hicks and other radical Christians of the Second Great Awakening, who commonly perceived Noah's flood as an event that led to the subsequent genesis of modern humans and animal species. In fact Hicks painted the biblical flood in one of his own works.[80] Such a conceptual overlap supports the strong affiliation between cutting-edge scientific thought and evangelical Christian thought during the early nineteenth century.

An even more provocative and overt link between Quaker spiritualism and popular racial science is present in the collaboration between Hicks's fellow Quaker Samuel Morton and the lithographers John Collins and Thomas Sinclair. While Hicks's nod to popular science remains subtle and covert in his work, the discourse of Morton and his followers in the field of craniology makes explicit the assumed logical similarities between a very speculative science and its counterpart in the evangelical communities of America. Morton's intellectual and social connections to Quakerism require a bit of consideration, as the rigorous education he received at Quaker schools has been credited by his biographers as one of the central contributing factors to his subsequent interest in medicine. In addition to this, Morton's stepfather was a well-known mineralogist in Philadelphia, and thus the boy's dual interests in spiritualism and science took root at an early age.[81]

Morton was the son of an Irish immigrant to Philadelphia and an American Quaker mother. His father, who was an Anglican, died when Morton was an infant, and his mother raised the child in her own family's faith. Morton began attending Quaker schools and meetings in early childhood and maintained a consistent religious affiliation with the Society until his twenties, when he reverted to Anglicanism. Despite this, Quakerism was to play a significant part in his intellectual development. While Morton's generally strong educational background was the result of his Quaker schooling, his specific professional interest in medicine was piqued upon meeting one of his mother's physicians, Joseph Parrish. At this point it is critical to recall that Parrish was a devout Quaker himself, and was one of Hicks's more avid patrons, owning one of the *Peaceable Kingdom* paintings. Parrish took the young Morton under his wing, instructing him privately in his office. From these initial classes Morton eventually branched out and began taking classes at the University of Pennsylvania, from which he received his medical degree in 1820.[82] It is in his early religious training and internship with Parrish that we can best see the heavy influence of Quaker thought in Morton's subsequent life.

Following his graduation from the University of Pennsylvania, Morton studied in Scotland at the University of Edinburgh under Robert Jameson, who would also teach Darwin slightly later. It was likely in Edinburgh that Morton came under the influence of the Scottish phrenological movement, then led by George Combe (1788–1850). The two would meet years later, in 1838, when Combe, who by then was a transatlantic leader in the propagation of the new pseudoscience, was on a lecture tour in Philadelphia.[83]

Phrenology was a pre-Freudian science of the mind that originated in Germany during the Enlightenment; its principles were progressively articulated by a series of entrepreneurial practitioners, most notably Johann Gaspar Spurzheim (1775–1832) and Franz Joseph Gall (1758–1828). It was from Spurzheim that the Scottish Combe and Morton would learn of phrenology, and the publication of his wildly popular book *The Constitution of Man*, which was a veritable handbook on the uses and practices of the pseudoscience, cemented his reputation on both sides of the Atlantic. Basically phrenology (from the Greek *phren* and *logy*, "mind discourse") sought to explain empirically that which in traditional metaphysical terms could not be apprehended by the senses: the internal soul or character of a person. It was a materialist science that claimed to offer insight into the inner workings of the minds of humans, claiming that these workings could be discerned in the outer shape and proportion of the skull. Although a discredited pseudoscience by modern standards, phrenology was at the time on the cutting edge of science and shocked people by claiming to offer insight into the mind via a route other than conventional metaphysics. It found a ready audience during the Enlightenment in both Europe and North America.[84]

Morton was enamored by Combe's brand of phrenology, as it combined metaphysics and empirical analysis. Combe claimed that although the phrenological traits of a person were clearly visible in the shape of that person's skull, these attributes ultimately derived from God and thus constituted a sort of "natural law" to which we were all beholden. And yet despite these divine origins of the phrenological faculties, Combe—following his teacher Spurzheim—famously claimed that one could effectively alter one's phrenological characteristics by "exercising" particular phrenological organs in the brain. If one wanted greater intelligence, for example, one simply needed to exercise the part of the brain (the phrenological organ) that corresponded with the faculty of intelligence. Combe sought an overall balance of phrenological organs, which may be viewed as an extension of humorism, with its fixation on the compositional balance of bodily humors. Combe's appeal lay in his ability to flatter his middle-class audiences by casting phrenology as a democratic science capable of being practiced by all thoughtful persons.[85]

Combe and Morton would go on to collaborate on Morton's famous pseudoscientific tome *Crania Americana; or, A Comparative View of the Skulls of Various Aboriginal Nations of North and South America*. Combe's intellectual endorsement of Morton's work was an important factor in its subsequent perceived legitimacy. The book was a text of craniometry, the science of collecting, cataloguing, and categorizing skulls based on a series of exacting measurements using a variety of scientific instruments, such as the "facial goniometer." The book's overriding agenda was to empirically establish a number of "facts" regarding the nature of race worldwide. In order to understand this, we must examine Morton's own intellectual grounding and his perceptions of race, including his perceptions of Native Americans and African Americans.

Morton was a disciple of the German naturalist Johann Friedrich Blumenbach (1752–1840), who is known today as the naturalist who innovated the field of comparative anatomy, something that would serve as a forerunner to Morton's own work. Blumenbach evaluated the skulls of various "races" of humans, aiming to ascertain the relative degree of "civilization" in each of his designated races. In the appendix to his book on the topic, *On the Natural Variety of Mankind*, Blumenbach specifies five racial categories, begging a comparison on the reader's part. In some cases he even illustrates various skull types side by side (fig. 18). Blumenbach's scheme, however, was not strictly descriptive in intent. He meant to draw evaluative comparisons between his races: Caucasian, American, Ethiopian, Malay, and Mongolian. Blumenbach believed that all of humanity descended from Adam and Eve in the Garden of Eden, thus attempting to lend biblical authority to his writings in addition to their obvious empirical appeal. He attributed physiological differences such as skull shape, skin color, hair texture, bodily proportion, and so forth to environmental factors. He viewed the Caucasian race as the most civilized and beautiful, but rejected the notion that the races were differing species. He believed all humans were of the same species and had the same creationist origins, and differences in culture and appearance were due to what he termed "degenerations" brought about by environmental factors.[86]

As Blumenbach states in relation to the Caucasian race during his discussion of the five races, "Color white, cheeks rosy . . . in general that kind of appearance which, according to our definition of symmetry we consider most handsomest and becoming." This quote is suggestive for a number of reasons. First, Blumenbach, like many other scientists and artists during the Enlightenment, assigns specific chromatic metaphors when differentiating the five races: Caucasians are "white," Ethiopians are "black," Americans are "copper," Mongolians are "yellow," and the Malay are "tawny." These are common categorizations and chromatic metaphors still used in popular speech in the United States in the twenty-first century, in discursive contexts ranging from institutional to colloquial.

Further, Blumenbach echoes myriad aesthetic assumptions regarding beauty that may most effectively be linked to then-current German academic discourse as embodied in the writings of the art historian Johann Joachim Winckelmann, whose popular definition of aesthetic beauty relied on his perceptions of classical Greek statuary, filtered through Roman copies and the works of the High Renaissance. Winckelmann saw beauty as a potential ideal, attained by the artist with the combination of ideal parts into a synthetic whole. In his description of the Caucasian, Blumenbach similarly points to Caucasian anatomy as being the ideal of the five races, containing the "most handsomest and becoming" attributes according to the law of "symmetry," another value of classical Greek art and architecture. All else falls short due to the vagaries of climate and other races' inability to properly adopt to those climates.[87]

In fact Blumenbach seems to imply by the "rosy cheeks" of the Caucasian race that it was the closest to their common ancestors Adam and Eve and thus the most blessed of the human races, as their skin tone allowed them to blush, as Adam and Eve did when banished from the Garden. The importance of rosy cheeks as a sign of God's favor is reiterated later in the Old Testament in the Book of Jeremiah. There God tells the prophet Jeremiah that those without the capacity to blush are those who have no shame, and therefore "they shall fall among those who fall," a reference to their impending damnation. From Blumenbach's reading, then, it is only a small step to the notion that the darker-skinned races are farther from salvation.[88]

Morton complimented Blumenbach's efforts in the text, at one point referring to his mentor's system of categorization as "imperfect, yet it is, perhaps, the most complete that has hitherto been attempted."[89] While he agreed with his mentor's five-race system, Morton would significantly alter Blumenbach's monogenist view by introducing his own version of racial categorization, called polygenism, whereby the five races were different species created at different times by God. Morton and Combe argue in the book that the Caucasian race had attained the highest level of civilization and that the American and Ethiopian races were lagging far behind, not due to climatic factors as Blumenbach maintained but due to static, unchanging racial characteristics that were the results of God's creation. These static characteristics, they claimed, were visible in the skulls of persons of the "inferior" races that Morton collected.[90]

As further proof of his polygenist claims, Morton turned to art criticism, pointing to Egyptian hieroglyphs and pictographs, many of which were just being rediscovered during that era, in the wake of the Napoleonic invasion of Egypt. He reasoned that pictures of the human head done in ancient Egypt closely resembled the proportions of the skulls he possessed in his collection, therefore, the racial characteristics were unchanged from thousands of years earlier. This was significant for, as Morton and others believed, the world had been created by God only shortly before that time, and so racial characteristics were apparently *intended* by God to remain static for eternity.[91] While such argumentation may sound shocking to the modern reader, it is important to recall that at this time such thinking was deemed scientifically valid by some, and Morton's skull collecting practice was designed to prove the legitimacy of polygenism.

Morton's intellectual investment in his skull collection, together with his measurements, overlooked the complicated economic and political realities of Philadelphia during the antebellum era.

Morton and Combe apparently chose to overlook the fact that the "lowest" race in their hierarchy in fact had a large thriving middle-class culture in the city, which was a hotbed of abolitionism at the time. Morton attained his "Ethiopian" skulls from the local poor in Philadelphia, whose remains were cast off or sold by the local almshouses and hospitals, such as the Pennsylvania Hospital. Morton regularly performed dissections on the cadavers of the poor and collected their body parts for his own purposes. Such a practice contradicts the publicly stated aims of such "charitable" religious institutions.[92]

Morton would measure the proportions and facial angles of each skull, then calculate their interior volume. He took these measurements to be a sign of the relative cranial capacity of each specimen, which he assumed could serve as a gauge for evaluating the intelligence of the specimens. He aggregated his data based on Blumenbach's racial system and assigned average measurements to grouped specimens from each race. It was based on these calculations that his polygenist claims were legitimized.[93]

The historian Ann Fabian recently uncovered a plethora of sources from which Morton collected his skulls. Fabian tells us that Morton and his agents in the field collected skulls from around the world and targeted cemeteries, slave plantations, battlefields, catacombs, and prisons, all of which contained a ready supply of human remains and were overseen by personnel willing to sell them.[94] Morton himself confirms his reliance on disciplinary institutions such as the prison in a letter to Combe regarding the skull of a convict he had recently acquired. He describes the man, named "Peirce" in the letter, as a violent criminal, a cannibal who fed on human flesh. Morton was fascinated by Peirce's story and was at times attracted to skulls of the criminally insane, as he felt they could offer insight into the behaviors of such persons.[95]

We see in his personal correspondence that at one point Morton worked with the painter George Catlin in collecting specimens. Catlin had famously traveled to the Upper Missouri River Valley in the 1830s and 1840s in search of indigenous portrait subjects.

In a letter to Morton, Combe writes, "Mr. Catlin did not send me the skulls, but I presume you have got them, as I told him that you would call for them."[96] This is a surprising connection, as Catlin was well known then and now for his desire to preserve the memory of what he perceived to be the "vanishing" Native on the nation's dwindling frontier: "I have flown to their rescue—not of their lives or of their race (for they are 'doomed' and must perish), but to the rescue of their looks and their modes, at which the acquisitive world may hurl their poison . . . and trample them down and crush them to death; yet, phoenix-like, they may rise from the 'stain of the painter's palette,' and live again upon canvas."[97]

The notion of Natives as a "vanishing race" was popular among Anglo-American artists and intellectuals throughout the nineteenth century. Some perceived the Native as a noble and yet tragic figure whose "authentic" or "primitive" culture was inevitably going to be destroyed by the advancement of white civilization on the American frontier. Catlin viewed his "Indian Gallery" as an artistic attempt to preserve the doomed Native for future generations, heroically bestowing an aesthetic afterlife on the unfortunate race.

Characteristically Morton's collaborator Catlin simultaneously valorized the Indian and ceded the race to inevitable doom at the hands of civilization. This viewpoint is best summarized in his famous before-and-after image of the Assiniboine leader Wi-jun-jon, whom he painted before and after a diplomatic trip to Washington (fig. 19). This representational formula, which would become a staple of Indian boarding school visual discourse during the Gilded Age, effectively conveyed the sense of inevitability in Catlin's perceptions of the Native. Apparently part of Catlin's mission, as Combe notes in his letter, was collecting skulls for Morton, perhaps an unwitting gesture in the degradation of the public perception of Native Americans. Morton would categorize all indigenous Americans as not only one singular race, but a race that was craniologically inferior to the Caucasian race. To this end, Morton offers an illustrated comparison between a Swiss skull (fig. 20) and the indigenous skulls illustrated in his book. This skull, which may have been that of a convict, Morton nevertheless deemed a specimen indicating a higher attainment of civilization, as discernable in the steeper facial angle. Morton and Combe believed *all* Caucasian skulls indicated such superiority, regardless of the background of the individual. In this way, Morton kept race at the center of his polygenist discourse.[98]

At this point, it will be helpful to briefly consider the work and lives of Morton's two main artistic collaborators in the making of the *Crania Americana*. John Collins (1814–1902) and Thomas Sinclair (1805–81) were both Philadelphia-area Quakers who were hired by Morton to do the elaborate illustrations for his tome. Collins came from a family of Quaker artists. His grandfather had been a painter in the court of George III in England; after immigrating to America, he opened a print shop that printed Bibles and currency. He later opened another print shop with John's father. After attending Haverford College, Collins moved to Philadelphia and opened a lithographic firm, where he specialized in doing reproductions for artists and scientists. He was a cousin of Morton's wife, and this likely precipitated his commission for the *Crania Americana* illustrations. He worked with Sinclair at his business, eventually selling the firm to Sinclair after failing to turn a profit for many years. Collins eventually gave up printmaking and, like Hicks, worked as a Quaker preacher.[99]

In his work Sinclair traversed the typological distinctions and exhibited great technical prowess. He fluctuated between spiritual and scientific illustration, depending on the nature of his commission. The lithograph shown in figure 21 was executed around 1845 and indicates a knowledge of evangelical Christian ideas and culture in the United States during the Second Great Awakening. Sinclair shows us nine men gathered ritualistically around an altar with an open Bible. The title *Christian Union* refers to the unification of the denominations brought about by the apparent arrival of the new millennium, symbolized by the miraculous appearance of the Holy Spirit in the form of a dove hovering above the altar. The men react in joy and amazement,

Quakerism, Skulls, and Sanctity

some even embracing their theological nemeses. Like Hicks, who was still active around this time, Sinclair references Isaiah's prophecy with the symbol of the lion and the lamb lying together peaceably. In the background are an African slave and a Native American, both of whom are likewise stunned by the appearance of the Holy Spirit. The Native, like those in West's painting, drops his weapons upon seeing the dove. Sinclair is giving us another vision of race in American visual culture from this era. The Indian is transformed from pseudoscientific subject to evangelized subject, miraculously dropping the implements of his savagery. In this commission Sinclair seems to be forwarding the seemingly contradictory notion that evangelization *could* actually change the savage, at least to some degree.

The reproduced lithographs in the pages of Morton's *Crania Americana* were a cornerstone of his argument for polygenism. Their perceived scientific legitimacy was contingent upon a string of representational relationships that Morton openly discusses, apparently in an attempt to convince the reader of their viability and accuracy. For instance, in reference to the book's frontispiece (fig. 22), Morton acknowledges that the image is several steps removed from the subject himself. It is a reproduced portrait of Big Elk, a leading chief of the Omaha tribe. Morton explains that the image was taken from life by the famous portraitist John Neagle, also of Philadelphia. Neagle's image was copied as a drawing by a Philadelphia artist, M. S. Weaver, and Weaver's drawing was then copied in lithographic format by Sinclair. Recognizing that such an extended chain of representations might be seen as problematic, Morton is careful to praise each artist in turn, declaring the "beauty and accuracy" of this series of depictions of the chief.[100]

Morton's argument represented a significant departure from the more mainstream thinking of Blumenbach and others, who attempted to bridge the biblical-scientific divide with monogenism. While Morton also wished to bridge that divide, his comparatively static view of racial attributes posited a multicreationist logic and would also serve as an intellectualized justification for the existence of slavery in America. Anyone believing that the North-South divide on the questions of race and slavery was absolute in the antebellum era need only consider the social and intellectual links between Morton and his most enthusiastic followers, Josiah Nott (1804–73), George Gliddon (1809–57), and the Swiss American professor Louis Agassiz (1807–73).

While he viewed both Native Americans and African Americans as craniologically inferior to the Caucasian race, Morton's views on slavery were ambivalent. In diary entries he kept during a sea voyage to Barbados in 1834, he discusses slavery on the island. In theory he advocated a gradualist approach to its abolition, but he nevertheless perceived the slaves around him as "carefree" when compared to free persons. He also expresses concern about slavery's abolition on the island, citing the security of the slave-owning class as well as possible economic drawbacks, such as the freed slaves refusing to work. He wrote that the island's black population "have in my eyes a very repulsive appearance. They have the genuine African face, are . . . stupid in their manner, and singularly uncouth in their deportment," a comment which emphasizes not only his ambivalence toward abolition but his clear contempt for persons of the "Ethiopian" race.[101] Morton's perception of the physiognomy of the slaves, with their "genuine African face," is linked in his thinking to their alleged character; thus he also describes them alternately as "uncouth," "stupid," and "carefree."

Morton sought to rationalize and contextualize what he perceived as both qualitative and quantitative distinctions between his encyclopedic racial categories by referencing ancient archaeology and biblical narrative. He was by no means alone in this intellectual project, as it represented in both Europe and North America an attempt to accommodate traditional Christian creationist narratives with an increasingly daunting wave of modern scientific skepticism. While some, like Blumenbach, opposed slavery on moral grounds, it is important to remember that both nineteenth-century Indian policy in the United States as well as the perpetuation of the slave economy were supported by these categorizations of race. Thus while Blumenbach and Morton may have been ambivalent on the topic, this was not true of their most avid American followers, Nott and Gliddon, who collaboratively sought to *justify* slavery's existence by reference to the theories and skewed theologies of their intellectual mentors, thereby facilitating devastating consequences for their suspect racial theories.

An astounding example of this need for justification is manifested in Nott and Gliddon's pseudoscientific text *Types of Mankind* (1854), which, like Morton's *Crania*, is a tour de force in its manipulation of text and image. Indeed, in a letter Nott sent to Morton, we see his admiration for Morton as well as his intellectual struggle to rectify his Christian beliefs with his scientific knowledge:

> I have read the "Crania" with great pleasure & instruction & feel assured that it will add not a little to your reputation. Your conclusion that the races, as far as facts can trace them are <u>distinct</u>, I think is the only one which reason can arrive at. . . . You have gone far enough according to my notions to blow [?] up all chronologies, although it may not be very <u>politic</u> to say so in these days of Christian intolerance. The Bible, if of divine origin, was clearly not intended to conclude, in its code of beautiful morals, the whole range of natural science, for it shows no knowledge beyond the human knowledge of the day & its great ends did not require any other. Even the Septuagint account is far too short to take in the events of Egypt, to say nothing of geological formations which are now placed before the "beginning" of Moses.[102]

Nott here displays his skepticism of other Christians, who in his view disavow modern science in an effort to legitimize the biblical narratives to which they were beholden. However, the issue at play here is not that Nott was an unbeliever. He too was beholden to his Christian beliefs; however, his ambition was to make them relevant in modern times by accommodating them with newer scientific ideas. Nott also saw opportunity in this endeavor to justify the most controversial of all topics: slavery.

Nott clearly states his intellectual ambitions on the title page of *Types of Mankind*, whose verbose subtitle is *Ethnological Researches, Based Upon the Ancient Monuments, Paintings, Sculptures, and Crania of Races, and upon their Natural, Geographical, Philological, and Biblical History*. Nott was attempting a totalizing and definitive statement on the origins, categorization, and comparative status of the races, the categorization of which was to be based on the work of his mentor Morton in *Crania*. It is not surprising, then, that the book was dedicated to Morton's memory. Morton had died three years prior to the book's publication, in 1851, and Nott placed a reproduction of a bust portrait of him as the frontispiece.

While Nott does periodically exhibit skepticism regarding creationist narratives, the book's overriding agenda is nevertheless the establishment of separate, stable racial categories with the aim of rationalizing slavery in America. Such hierarchies provided the same logic during this era to those wishing to forcibly solve the Indian question via extermination, concentration, or assimilation. In his preface to the text, Nott's colleague Gliddon makes explicit reference to the patriotic character of the book, citing the "cis-Atlantic" quality of the scholarship (presumably in tacit comparison to that being conducted in Europe) as well as his view of the book's production as "eminently characteristic of American republicanism" due to the book's exclusively private funding.[103] In these senses, Nott and Gliddon's text goes beyond Morton's in the explicitness of its political aims.

Nott and Gliddon invited the Harvard professor and naturalist Louis Agassiz to contribute the main theoretical essay of the book. Aggasiz, following the lead of his colleagues, attempted to establish autonomous origins for the various human races by likening each racial category to the climatic region of the earth from which they derived and claimed that these origins paralleled the presence of animal species specific to those regions. By so doing, Agassiz hoped to establish via a "natural history" of man and animal that the races were distinct in terms of both origin and subsequent development. As he put it, "Here, again, it cannot escape the attention of the careful observer, that the European zoological realm is circumscribed within exactly the same limits as the so-called white race of man, including, as it does, the inhabitants of southwestern Asia, and of north Africa, with the lower parts of the valley of the Nile. We exclude, of course, modern migrations and historical changes of habitation from this assertion. Our statements are understood to be referring only to the aboriginal or ante-historical distribution of man."[104]

By establishing these "essential differences" through an appeal to the "natural" distribution of animal species and human races, Agassiz implied that the different races, like the various animal species, had inherently different characteristics due to climatic adaptations, which lent them different "natural" roles in society. And as Morton and others asserted, this meant, first, that God had created the races and distributed them to these various regions, and, second, that these God-given differences, confirmed by the climates of the world in which they were first dispersed, lent each group certain comparative traits. Morton's friend and fellow craniologist James Aitken Meigs summed it up by asserting that the static conditions of race led the white race to the greatest share of power and wealth and placed the Ethiopian in perpetual servitude and slavery.[105] Agassiz agreed with Meigs, summing up his findings on racial attributes as "instinctively directed by the All-Wise and Omnipotent, to fulfill the great harmonies established in Nature."[106] For Morton, Nott, Gliddon, Aggasiz, Meigs, and other American naturalists, this was the ultimate outcome of their painstakingly empiricized theories: the merging of theology and science in the service of enslavement.

From Aggasiz's conclusion in the essay, the rest of the book becomes a largely pro forma fulfillment of his theoretical pre-scription. In the main section of the text, Nott uses illustrations of various sorts, from sketches of ancient hieroglyphs and tomb paintings to reproductions of skulls such as those Morton had in his own collection. Interestingly, Nott acknowledges that while figure 23 is a synthetic illustration taken from multiple ancient

Egyptian archaeological sources, and then transcribed by various artists, it is nevertheless a scientifically accurate depiction of four ancient races as seen by the Egyptians, upholding the thesis of the book, as these races still existed in the nineteenth century in the same fashion as depicted by the Egyptians. He explains that the "American" race is missing here because it was unknown to the Egyptians at the time.[107] With "scientific" illustrations such as these, coupled with Aggasiz's authorial voice opening the book, Nott was able to confidently assert in reference to the flood narrative in Genesis, "The language of Scripture touching the point now before us is so unequivocal, and so often repeated, as to leave no doubt of the author's meaning. It teaches clearly that the Deluge was *universal*, that every living creature on the face of the earth at the time was destroyed, and that *seeds* of all the organized beings of after times were saved in Noah's Ark."[108]

It is unclear if Hicks was personally acquainted with Morton, Collins, Sinclair, or any of Morton's other collaborators. What does emerge, though, is an alternative history of race and representation within the strongly Quaker milieu of antebellum Philadelphia. Many of these people clearly shared religious beliefs and intellectual interests, lived in the same city, and had overlapping social relations. Beyond their shared relations with Joseph Parrish, both Morton and Hicks published books with Merrihew & Thompson, a Philadelphia publishing house. Hicks's spiritual memoirs were published by them in 1851, and in the same year they also published the third edition of Morton's lesser known *Catalog of Skulls of Man and the Inferior Animals*. Additionally the two shared certain intellectual influences, as Hicks's interest in zoology led him to consult Cuvier, also one of Morton's mentors, whose encyclopedic system he repeatedly cited in the *Crania*.

What clearly emerges from all of the topics discussed in this chapter is a Quaker discourse on race and salvation. The encounter of the racial and spiritual Other in the form of the Lenapes served as the founding myth of Quakerism in America and also as a historical and aesthetic rallying point for the attempted reuni-

Quakerism, Skulls, and Sanctity

fication of the Quakers by Hicks and others in the wake of the schism. Conversely, evolving ideas about and representations of race as seen in Morton's work would ironically serve not as a sign of mercantile cooperation and spiritual unification but as a sign of the heightened authoritarian view of race popularized during the era of mass enslavement in America.

With this in mind, I hope to forward in this and other chapters of this book newer histories of Christian evangelical movements in America and their deployment of visual imagery in support of their projects of hierarchization and Americanization. In the next chapter, we will see an interesting conceptual parallel to Morton's pseudoscientific racial hierarchies in the teachings of the Mormon founder Joseph Smith. Like Morton and other antebellum thinkers, Smith perceived Anglo-Americans as superior to other racial groups, and he sought a legitimization of this assumption in his theological teachings. In both cases we see the merging of theology, entrepreneurialism, and scientific racism in the establishment of newer bodies of knowledge.

1. John Choate, *Wounded Yellow Robe, Henry Standing Bear, Timber Yellow Robe; upon Their Arrival in Carlisle*, n.d. Albumen mounted on card. Courtesy of the Carlisle Indian School Digital Resource Center, http://carlisleindian.dickinson.edu.

2. John Choate, *Wounded Yellow Robe, Henry Standing Bear, Timber Yellow Robe; 6 Months after Entrance to School*, n.d. Albumen mounted on card. Courtesy of the Carlisle Indian School Digital Resource Center, http://carlisleindian.dickinson.edu.

3. Freake-Gibbs painter, *John Freake*, 1671–74. Oil on canvas. Worcester Art Museum, Worcester, Massachusetts/ Bridgeman Images.

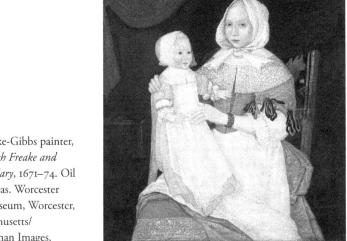

4. Freake-Gibbs painter, *Elizabeth Freake and Baby Mary*, 1671–74. Oil on canvas. Worcester Art Museum, Worcester, Massachusetts/ Bridgeman Images.

5. Thomas Smith, *Self-Portrait*, c. 1680. Oil on canvas. Worcester Art Museum, Worcester, Massachusetts/ Bridgeman Images.

6. Artist unknown, Seal of the Massachusetts Bay Company Charter, 1629. Engraving. Private Collection, Peter Newark American Pictures/ Bridgeman Images.

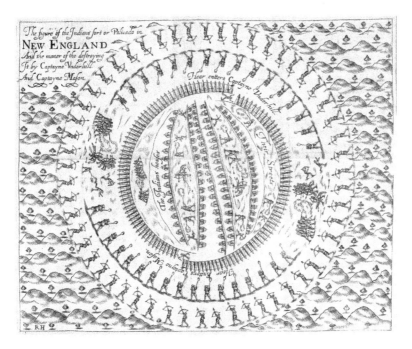

7. Possibly Richard Hearne, untitled, c. 1638. Engraving. Illustration from John Underhill, *Newes from America*, 1638. Courtesy of New York Public Library.

8. Paul Revere, untitled (Hellmouth). Engraving. Illustration from Jacob Green, *Vision of Hell*, 1773. Courtesy of New York Public Library.

9. Anonymous. Engraving.
Illustration from *Bickerstaff's
Boston almanack*, 1767. Courtesy
of New York Public Library.

10. John Chester Buttre, *Elliot, the
First Missionary among the Indians*,
c. 1880. Engraving. Courtesy of
New York Public Library.

11. David Oswald, 2018. Ink on paper. After C. C. A. Christensen, *Joseph Smith Preaching to the Indians*, c. 1879

12. Frère Luc, *France Bringing the Faith to the Indians of New France*, c. 1675. Oil on canvas. Pôle culturel du Monastère des Ursulines.

13. John Verelst, *Portrait of Hendrick*, 1710. Oil on canvas. Library and Archives Canada, acc. no. 1977-35-4. Acquired with a special grant from the Canadian Government in 1977.

14. Benjamin West, *Penn's Treaty with the Indians*, 1771–72. Oil on canvas. Pennsylvania Academy of the Fine Arts, Philadelphia. Gift of Mrs. Sarah Harrison (The Joseph Harrison Jr. Collection).

15. Benjamin West, *Christ Healing the Sick in the Temple*, 1817. Oil on canvas. Courtesy of Pennsylvania Hospital Historic Collections, Philadelphia.

16. Edward Hicks, *The Peaceable Kingdom of the Branch*, c. 1823–25. Oil on fireboard. Yale University Art Gallery.

17. Charles Heath (after Richard Westall), *The Peaceable Kingdom of the Branch*, 1815. Engraving. American Bible Society.

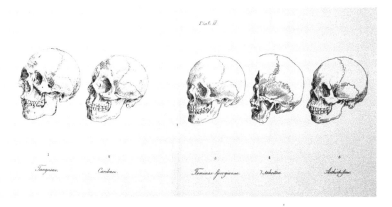

18. Johann Blumenbach, illustration of the five races, 1795. From *De Generis Humani Varietate Nativa*. Courtesy of New York Public Library.

19. George Catlin, *Wi-jun-jon, Pigeon's Egg Head Going to and Returning from Washington*, 1837–39. Oil on canvas. Smithsonian American Art Museum. Gift of Mrs. Joseph Harrison Jr.

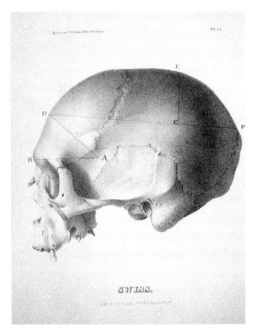

20. John Collins, untitled (Swiss skull), 1839. Lithographic reproduction. Illustration from Morton, *Crania Americana*. Courtesy of New York Public Library.

21. Thomas Sinclair, *Christian Union*, 1845. Lithograph. Library of Congress.

ONGPATONGA.

[BIG ELK.]

CHIEF OF THE OMAWHAWS.

Drawn for Morton's Crania Americana by M.S.Weaver.

Lith. of T. Sinclair, No 79 S. Three St. Phil?

From the original painting by J. Neagle.

See page 292

22. Thomas Sinclair, from drawing by M. S. Weaver, from original painting by John Neagle, *Ongpatonga (Chief Big Elk)*, 1839. Lithographic reproduction. Illustration from Morton, *Crania Americana*. Courtesy of New York Public Library.

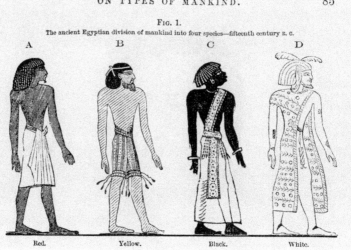

FIG. 1.
The ancient Egyptian division of mankind into four species—fifteenth century B. C.

A   B   C   D

Red.   Yellow.   Black.   White.

23. Artist unknown, comparative racial illustration. Woodcut.
From Nott, *Types of Mankind*, 1854. Harvard University Libraries.

24. David Oswald,
2018. Ink on paper.
After Del Parson,
The First Vision, 1988.

25. David Oswald, 2018. Ink on paper. After C. C. A. Christensen, *The Hill Cumorah*, c. 1870s.

26. David Oswald, 2018. Ink on paper. After Arnold Friberg, *Lehi and His People Arrive in the Promised Land*, 1950.

27. David Oswald, 2018. Ink on paper. After Arnold
Friberg, *The Prayer at Valley Forge*, 1976.

28. David Oswald, 2018.
Ink on paper. After
Arnold Friberg, *Samuel the
Lamanite Prophesies*, 1950.

29. David Oswald, 2018. Ink on paper. After Arnold Friberg, *Two Thousand Stripling Warriors*, 1950.

30. David Oswald, 2018. Ink on paper. After Arnold Friberg, *Nephi and Laman*, 1950.

31 David Oswald, 2018. Ink on paper. After John
Scott, *Jesus Christ Visits the Americas*, c. 1960s.

32. David Oswald, 2018.
Ink on paper. After
Heinrich Hofmann,
Christ at 33, 1894.

33. Orson S. Fowler, *Indian Chief/Black Hawk*, 1869. Engraving. Illustration from Fowler, *The Practical Phrenologist*. Courtesy of New York Public Library.

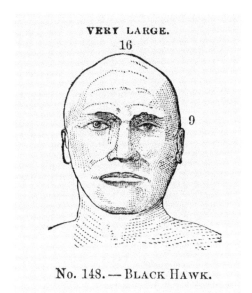

VERY LARGE.
16

9

No. 148. — BLACK HAWK.

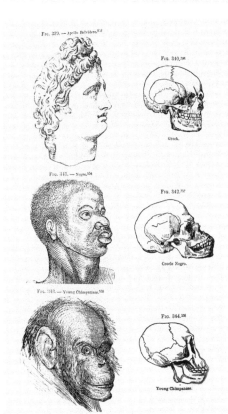

34. Josiah Nott. Illustration from *Types of Mankind*. Courtesy of New York Public Library.

35. John N. Choate, *Tom Torlino, a Navajo, as He Arrived and Three Years After*, 1882. Albumen. Courtesy of the Cumberland County Historical Society, Carlisle, Pennsylvania.

36. John N. Choate, *Tom Torlino, a Navajo, as He Arrived and Three Years After*, 1885. Albumen. Courtesy of the Cumberland County Historical Society, Carlisle, Pennsylvania.

37. Frances Benjamin Johnston, *Debating Class, Carlisle Indian School*, 1901. Albumen print. Frances Benjamin Johnston Collection, Library of Congress.

38. Frances Benjamin Johnston, *Kindergarden Children Washing and Ironing*, 1899. Albumen print. Frances Benjamin Johnston Collection, Library of Congress.

39. Anonymous, *Captain Pratt and Indian Prisoners in the Courtyard at Ft. Marion*, c. 1875. Albumen. National Park Service, Castillo de San Marcos National Monument, St. Augustine, Florida. Courtesy of New York Public Library.

40. Frances Benjamin Johnston, *Negro, Eagle, Indian*, 1899. Cyanotype print. Courtesy of Hampton University Archives.

Southern Workman.

DEVOTED TO THE INDUSTRIAL CLASSES OF THE SOUTH.

VOL. VIII.   HAMPTON, VA., JANUARY, 1879.   NO. I.

ON THE THRESHOLD.

41. E.W., *On the Threshold*, 1879. Reproduced engraving. From *Southern Workman* magazine. Courtesy of Hampton University Archives.

42. Frances Benjamin Johnston, *Stairway to Treasurer's Residence: Students at Work*, 1899. Albumen. Frances Benjamin Johnston Collection, Library of Congress.

43. Frances Benjamin Johnston, *Old Time Cabin*, 1899. Albumen print. Frances Benjamin Johnston Collection, Library of Congress.

44. Frances Benjamin Johnston, *A Graduate's House*, 1899. Albumen print. Frances Benjamin Johnston Collection, Library of Congress.

45. Joseph Palmer, modeler, from life mask by Clark Mills, *Zotom (Kiowa)*, c. 1877. Plaster. Life-size. Smithsonian National Museum of Natural History.

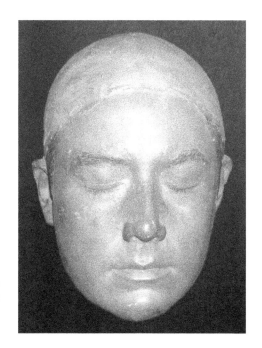

46. Anonymous, cover of 1895
catalogue of the Carlisle School.
Printed illustration. Courtesy
of the Cumberland County
Historical Society, Carlisle,
Pennsylvania.

3

Mormonism, Light and Dark

Mormonism, more than any other messianic Christian movement that took root during the Second Great Awakening, has proven to be the most well-organized and -financed from an institutional perspective. So it is unsurprising that the textual and visual accompaniments of Mormon doctrine are likewise the most involved in terms of nuance, complexity, and internal narrative cohesion. When examining the visual culture of Mormonism, formally known as the Church of Jesus Christ of Latter-day Saints (LDS), it is important to take several factors into consideration. In addition to its complex relationship with Native Americans and other non-European groups, it must be considered in relation to the context of the Second Great Awakening, which was a time of fragmentation and diversification within the nation's Christian population. Such diversification allowed for newer and more inventive spiritual and aesthetic narratives, something we see in abundance in Mormon culture.

This chapter considers the doctrine of Mormonism through close analysis of the LDS's foundational texts, especially the *Book of Mormon*, and elaborates the theological and mythicohistorical narrative believed by Mormons to be the word of God as translated and transcribed by the movement's founder, Joseph Smith (1805–44). Modern editions of the *Book of Mormon* contain a number of striking illustrations thought by Mormons to represent accurate historical, documentary depictions of various moments described in the text. I analyze these images in depth, with special attention to the manner in which race is explained in Mormon doctrine. In a parallel vein, I examine the larger context of race relations in America during the Second Great Awakening in order to place Smith's writings in a larger context of meaning beyond simply his own very reflexive references within the *Book of Mormon*. Finally, I take into account actual interactions between Mormon settlers and Native Americans in Utah as a counterpoint to the idealized depictions of race relations in the *Book of Mormon*.

The rise of Mormonism, and its appeal to so many erstwhile Christians in the United States and Western Europe, is intimately linked to the role of western movement as conceived as both spiritual and political escape from tyranny. In this sense the Mormon migration from the original mecca of Nauvoo, Illinois, to the extremely unlikely and inhospitable frontier confines of what was then the Utah Territory may be seen as a veritable latter-day echo of the Puritan escape westward across the Atlantic from the tyranny of imperial Anglicanism roughly two centuries earlier. And beyond this, the provocative narratives contained within the *Book of Mormon* attempt to establish a quite literal, direct lineage between Mormonism's nineteenth-century westward pilgrimage and that of ancient biblical Israelite tribes millennia earlier. As Smith wrote in what Mormon scholars refer to as the Wentworth letter, "We believe in the literal gathering of Israel and in the restoration of the Ten Tribes; that Zion (the New Jerusalem) will be built upon the American continent; that Christ will reign personally upon the earth; and, that the earth will be renewed and receive its paradisiacal glory."[1]

Smith, like other radical Christians during and before this era in American history, was concerned with the fulfillment of what he saw as divine prophecy on the American continent. This in itself was nothing new in the Second Great Awakening. However, in the case of Mormonism Smith constructed a quite literal narrative of Anglo-Israelite historical and theological continuity, which is something that sets Mormonism apart from earlier radical

Christian groups like the Puritans, who viewed such allusions primarily as literary trope and metaphor. In fact the very literalness of this contention, of an actual physical connection between the Tribes of Israel and the inhabitants of the New World, has been sought out by generations of Mormon archaeologists, who have looked for ruins of early Israelite settlements in what today we would call southern Mexico and Central America. Indeed some Mormon archaeologists, including Milton R. Hunter, claim to have unearthed such evidence, arguing that the iconography on certain pre-Columbian ruins make reference to the ancient presence of the light-skinned "Nephite" families as well as Christ in Mesoamerica in ancient times.[2]

And as Mormons believe that their earlier ancestors in the New World spawned not only lighter skinned Anglo-Americans but also darker skinned Native Americans, intimate interactions between the groups are believed to have occurred regularly for thousands of years in the Americas. Evangelical activities involving the two groups have likewise been a constant, as the lighter skinned "Nephites" have sought to save their darker skinned "Lamanite" brethren. This complex relationship and its theological justification are discussed in greater depth later in this chapter. For now, it is sufficient to note that Smith claimed that his knowledge of Native Americans, their spiritual "plight," and the necessity of their conversion was given to him during a divine vision by Moroni, an angel and ancient prophet in the Mormon tradition. In the Wentworth letter, Smith continues his autobiographical narrative by linking this awareness to the purpose of his mission on earth: "I was informed [by Moroni] that I was chosen to be an instrument in the hands of God to bring about some of his purposes in this glorious dispensation. I was also informed concerning the aboriginal inhabitants of the country, and shown who they were, and from whence they came; a brief sketch of their origin, progress, civilization, laws, governments, of their righteousness and iniquity, and the blessings of God being *finally withdrawn* from them as a people was made known unto me" (emphasis added).[3]

Smith, like many evangelical reformers of the Second Great Awakening, believed he had been divinely chosen to ensure the salvation of unbelieving populations. The "final withdrawal" of blessings from the Native Americans would become a cornerstone of his evangelism.

Historians commonly date the Second Great Awakening to the first half of the nineteenth century, with an apogee taking place from the 1820s through the 1840s.[4] It was during these years that a host of new, radical forms of evangelical Christianity spread rapidly westward across the continent. In addition to Mormonism, the Millerite movement of William Miller was prominent and would later evolve into Seventh-Day Adventism. Significantly both of these movements revolved around charismatic, dominant early leaders, each of whom shared not only messianic spiritual belief systems but a pointed entrepreneurial sense that allowed them to attract devotees from other Christian sects, and even to induce these devotees to follow them into the wilds of unfamiliar and at times dangerous territory. A competitive, mercantile-like ethos imbued all such theological movements during the Awakening, as each seemed to fulfill exigencies apparently unfulfilled by more mainstream, established Christian denominations and were thereby able to convert new adherents on a large scale.

The competition for adherents and the need to be perceived as doctrinally "correct" could spill over into politics and even outright civil warfare. In this context, Smith and his Mormon movement apparently struck a chord with many, both for better and worse. Not only were Mormons deemed doctrinally irregular by more mainstream Christian groups, but their life practices were such as to encourage deep suspicion and contempt. These perceptions translated eventually into civil strife directed against Smith, his brother, and his adherents more broadly. The historian W. Paul Reeve has even argued that Mormonism's early practice of polygamy—later banned by the Church—was so disturbing to other Christians that Mormons were, for a long time, perceived as congenitally deficient due to their supposedly "immoral" reproductive habits. Reeve argues that Mormons occupied an awkward cultural and political space, as they were deemed neither "white" nor "nonwhite" well into the early twentieth century, due in large part to these practices.[5]

Beyond this perception of the Mormon as doctrinal and congenital Other, on a personal level Smith himself felt constantly under duress if not outright threat, judging from entries in his personal journal. In one entry he wrote:

> My family was kept in a continual state of alarm, not knowing, when I went from home, that I should ever return again; or what would befall me from day to day. But notwithstanding these manifestations of enmity, I hoped that the citizens would eventually cease from their abusive and murderous purposes, and would reflect with sorrow upon their conduct in endeavoring to destroy me whose only crime was in worshipping the God of heaven, and keeping his commandments; and that they would soon desist from harassing a people who were as good citizens as the majority of this vast republic.[6]

Many questions are raised when one considers the status of Mormonism in America during the Second Great Awakening. Primary among them is the "subversive" doctrine of Mormonism, and thus the status and identity of the *Book of Mormon* itself. Further, as many of the most well-known Mormon images are reproduced in the book's modern editions, they are a convenient starting point for understanding the meaning and significance of these images for Mormon adherents. Also, the relationship between Mormon imagery and the words contained within Mormon texts is crucial to understanding the culture of this evangelical movement.

The historian Candy Gunther Brown offers a helpful analysis of the status of what she terms "the Word" in evangelical religious movements and effectively places Mormonism within this analysis. She argues that in evangelical culture, scriptural words contain a mystical connotation beyond simple linguistic connotation and denotation; thus her use of a capital "W" in evangelical contexts.

She states that evangelicals share a belief that the Word existed before time because it is the Word of God spoken or written by various prophets. As such, the world was in effect *created* by the Word—the spoken will of God—as it exists in a temporal rather than a transcendent realm. As Gunther Brown puts it, "The Word existed before the world's creation and spoke the world into being."[7]

Gunther Brown traces the history of Christian evangelical activity and the unique role of Mormonism in that history. The term "evangelical" is derived from the Greek *euaggellion*, which translates as "good news." It was first used by Protestant followers of Martin Luther during the Reformation in the sixteenth century to describe their own church in Germany. By proclaiming themselves thus, early Protestants could subvert the ecclesiastical hierarchy of the Catholic Church, which sought to insert itself between the Word and the lay public. This claim was originally intended to liberate lay Christians from what was seen as the tyrannical control of Rome, thereby in effect personalizing and sanctifying the practice of faith.[8]

In America in the nineteenth century evangelicals still largely believed in the transcendent quality of the Word. While the Mormons shared this belief, they went a step further and in so doing broke with mainstream Protestant tradition. Mormons maintain that the writings of Joseph Smith are a prophetic iteration of the Word and are therefore canonical to a degree on par with the Bible itself. Thus Smith and his followers refer to themselves as "latter-day saints," an appellation intended to convey the transcendent viability of his writings and the great faith of those who adhere to them. In this sense, the Word is a *living* thing embodied in the faith and works of Mormon practitioners to this day.[9]

According to the introduction of the 2007 printed edition of the *Book of Mormon*, the book was first printed in 1830 as an "English translation" by Smith. He was able to translate the book's text "by the gift and power of God" from its original form in an ancient language he refers to as "reformed Egyptian."[10] The introduction to the book goes on to describe the text's significance:

The Book of Mormon is a volume of holy scripture comparable to the Bible. It is a record of God's dealings with the ancient inhabitants of the Americas and contains, as does the Bible, the fullness of everlasting gospel. . . . The book was written by many ancient prophets by the spirit of prophecy and revelation. Their words, written on gold plates, were quoted and abridged by the prophet-historian named Mormon. The record gives an account of two great civilizations. One came from Jerusalem in 600 B.C., and afterward separated into two nations, known as the Nephites and the Lamanites. The other came much earlier when the Lord confounded the tongues at the Tower of Babel. This group is known as the Jaredites. After thousands of years, all were destroyed except the Lamanites, and they are the principal ancestors of the American Indians.[11]

This passage raises several key concepts pertinent to the Mormon cosmology and the subsequent treatment and representation of Native Americans. The first line informs the reader that the *Book of Mormon* is to be taken as seriously as the Bible, as it too is the word of God. This word, the excerpt explains, was written originally by several ancient prophets through divine revelation and inspiration, again a cornerstone idea held by Christians. Several centuries later Mormons believe that these original prophecies and revelations were abridged by a divinely inspired historian named Mormon, from whom the modern text and church get their name. The introduction of the *Book of Mormon* explains their modern translation and transcription:

After Mormon completed his writings, he delivered the account to his son Moroni, who added a few words of his own and hid up the plates in the hill Cumorah. On September 21, 1823, the same Moroni, then a glorified, resurrected being, appeared to the Prophet Joseph Smith and instructed him relative to the ancient record and its destined translation into the English language. . . . In due course the plates were delivered to Joseph Smith, who translated them by the gift and power of God. The record is now published in many languages as a new and additional witness that Jesus Christ is the Son of the living God and that all who will come unto him and obey the laws and ordinances of his gospel may be saved.[12]

Important in these introductory passages are a number of items. In addition to being perceived as divinely inspired prophecy, the *Book of Mormon* is also seen as a "record." Thus the book is *both* the word of God and an accurate, objective recording of historical events. This linkage or correspondence between the divine and earthly realms is one aspect that gives the book's narratives such a compelling quality; it is an association common to most messianic American religious movements dating to early colonial times. This basic dualistic structure of thought, linking the material realm and the metaphysical realm, was likewise a hallmark of much Puritan writing, as seen, for example, in Winthrop's "city upon a hill" metaphor in his sermon "A Model of Christian Charity." For Winthrop, this divine city—a metaphor presented in the fifth chapter of the Book of Matthew—was to be approximated in the utopic towns of New England. Their streets would be paved in gold due to the piety and industry of their faithful inhabitants, a sign to the world of the "chosen" status of the Puritans.[13] In both traditions, we see various prophetic figures attempt to elevate the empirical to the status of the divine through literary fiat. In the case of Mormonism, it is likewise important to remember not only what links it to Puritanism but also what sets it apart: Smith's belief in the *literal* voyage of ancient Israelites to the Zion of the Americas. Historical accuracy therefore takes on the utmost importance in Mormon culture.

To create a record of historical events, the LDS has, throughout much of its history, sought visual analogues to accompany the Word put forth by Smith in the *Book of Mormon*. The role of images has indeed been important—and controversial—within Mormon culture. The controversy echoes still in modern discussions of aesthetics in Mormon culture, indicating a perceived epistemological and aesthetic continuity between the original text and later illustrations of that text. For example, one Mormon leader, Boyd Packer, addressed at length the role of aesthetics in relation to Mormon doctrine in a speech he delivered in 1976 titled "The Arts and the Spirit of the Lord." Packer expresses disappointment with artists who have worked within or for the Church in depicting sacred scenes. He acknowledges that while many of these artists have been talented, "few have captured the spirit of the gospel of Jesus Christ and the restoration of it in music, in art, in literature."[14]

Packer attributes this shortcoming to what he sees as the "temperamental" nature of artists. He urges all creative people to remember that their gifts are God-given and as such ought to be used responsibly, in a manner that "invite[s] the Spirit of the Lord." Much visual art and music has failed to appropriately depict doctrine because, according to Packer, "you don't teach sacred, serious subjects with carless, scribbled illustrations."[15] Nonetheless Packer praises certain Mormon artists, notably the Danish painter C. C. A. Christensen (1831–1912), whose work (fig. 11) I discuss as an example of ideal artistic production in the context of Mormon culture. Packer's perception of Christensen's Mormon-themed paintings is significant and worth quoting at length:

> Some years ago I was chairman of a committee of seminary men responsible to produce a filmstrip on Church history. One of the group, Trevor Christensen, remembered that down in Sanpete County was a large canvas roll of paintings. They had been painted by one of his progenitors, C. C. A. Christensen, who traveled through the settlements giving a lecture on Church history as each painting was unrolled and displayed by lamplight. The roll of paintings had been stored away for generations. We sent a truck for them, and I shall not forget the day we unrolled it. . . . Brother Christensen was not masterful in his painting, but our heritage was there. Some said it was not great art, but what it lacked in technique was more than compensated in feeling. His work

has been shown more widely and published more broadly and received more attention than that of a thousand and one others who missed that point. . . . I do not think Brother Christensen was a great painter, some would say not even a good one. I think his paintings are masterful. Why? Because the simple, reverent feeling he had for his spiritual heritage is captured in them. I do not think it strange that the world would honor a man who could not paint very well.[16]

In his characterization of Christensen's work, it is clear that Packer's criteria for judging visual art pertains to how the artist serves the Church by subordinating his or her "temperament" to the "appropriate" depiction of the "Spirit of the Lord." For Packer, Christensen was not a technically superior artist, but an artist who imbued his depiction of Mormon history with true feeling. Christensen is also praised for his missionary work, as he used his paintings to illustrate his teachings.

As we shall see, the Mormon self-perception as persecuted Other parallels Smith's theological writings and narratives throughout the *Book of Mormon*. The book revolves around a long-standing spiritual—and supposedly historical—war between two ethnic groups, the sanctified Nephites and the unholy Lamanites. The metaphor of tribal identification, based among other things on skin tone, has always been central to the Mormon identity. Concurrently the movement's unorthodox doctrine, while having a stunning internal sense of coherence and narrative logic, has come under fierce attack from without. In part a reaction to this criticism, the Church has historically employed artists to execute academic-style images that are intended to serve as reinforcing empirical "proof" of the historical legitimacy of the events described in the *Book of Mormon* and in Smith's extended autobiography, as conveyed in *The Pearl of Great Price*, one of the other canonical texts in Mormon theology. Image making in Mormonism goes beyond the creation of a sense of "communion" within the LDS, as Morgan and Promey would have it. I will discuss in depth the aesthetic strategies used by the various artists employed by LDS and Mormon definitions of race and their subsequent characterization of and interactions with the continent's indigenous population.

Smith, being the founder of Mormonism, was perhaps the most entrepreneurial of all the prophetic figures of the Second Great Awakening. According to the *Teachings of the Presidents of the Church*, a series of authoritative texts by the Church's leadership, Smith was born in Vermont in 1805 to parents who were, at the time, financially well off. However, financial reversals soon forced the family to move. The presence of Smith's family in America has been dated to the 1600s by Mormon genealogists.[17] If true, this makes it likely that his early American ancestors, who presumably lived in New England, were Puritans. As alluded to earlier, when reading Mormon texts and considering the theological concepts proffered by Smith in the *Book of Mormon*, one senses strong parallels between Puritan and Mormon thought, making Puritanism a likely intellectual source for Smith's teachings.

In the wake of the family's financial reversals, during which Smith's father lost a farm due to crop failure, they relocated to western New York State when Smith was still a child. It was there, in the "burned over district" of the Second Great Awakening, that Smith's career as an evangelist would begin. The family settled in the small town of Palmyra, though despite the town's size, Smith recalled that there were seven Christian denominations competing for converts. Smith relays that none of these denominations appealed to him, for, young though he was, he perceived doctrinal inconsistencies in each. He writes, "In the midst of this war of words and tumult of opinions, I often said to myself: What is to be done? Who of all these parties are right; or, are they all wrong together? If any one of them be right, which is it, and how shall I know it?"[18] Additionally during this period, Smith claimed that his family was indigent and thus he received only a cursory education, spending most days working on a farm with his father.[19] This combination of logistical and economic desperation with newfangled evangelical thought is common among Americans both during the Second Great Awakening and at other times. One sees this in the teachings of the Puritans, who steadfastly—and wishfully—envisioned their wilderness land grant as a divine city with golden streets.

So, compounding Smith's intellectual confusion at this point in his life were his concerns regarding his family's low social and socioeconomic status, which apparently left an indelible impression on the young Smith, as he mentions it repeatedly as a formative factor in his early identity. Not only was he confused and even mystified by the seemingly contradictory teachings of the Presbyterians, Methodists, and Baptists in the community, but one gets the sense from his narrative that such concerns were never far from his mind, and no doubt impacted his desire for *deliverance* from his declassed state. For Smith, this deliverance would be both spiritual and material, as becomes evident in subsequent Mormon doctrine, where references to riches and largesse become a sort of double metaphor, bridging the divide between theology and materialism.

Smith's disillusionment with the denominations in the area led him to independent Bible study. He claims that in 1820, following a reading of a verse in the Book of James, he walked to a grove of trees near his home and began praying. At this point, he states, he received his first vision, which consisted of a pillar of light and two figures levitating above him. Smith writes that the figures were male, and one said to him, "This is my beloved son! Hear him!" (fig. 24). He thus interpreted the vision as representing God the Father and Jesus Christ. In LDS, this event is generally believed to be the start of his evangelical ministry. Of this vision Smith writes, "It no sooner appeared than I found myself *delivered* from the enemy that held me bound."[20] This sense of deliverance would become the cornerstone of the narrative Smith constructs in the *Book of Mormon*. Indeed one may say that the perceived need for such a deliverance not only drove the proliferation of denominations during the Second Great Awakening more broadly but was also a conceptual foundation in Puritan thought, Quaker thought, and even the Social Gospel of the Gilded Age.

The depiction of Smith's "first vision" in figure 24 was executed by the Mormon painter Del Parson (b. 1948) in 1988. In a
formula that is virtually canonical to Mormon art dating to the
mid-nineteenth century, we see the earthly individual, in this
case Smith, juxtaposed with the otherworldly figures of God and
Christ or an angel or prophet. Such images are modern in their
emphasis on the possibility of divine revelation occurring in the
most banal, unexpected contexts. Yet they also have a distinctly
ancient, timeless quality, metaphorically echoing the miraculous
visions and occurrences contained in biblical verses.

Also significant in this image are stylistic tropes common in
the history of Mormon art. The metaphor of lightness, in both
chromatic and spatial terms, is characteristic of Mormon aesthetics
and also Christian aesthetics more broadly, dating back to medieval
painting. The figures here, and in Smith's textual account, are
defined by their forms of lightness: the white and gold aura that
surrounds them and composes the space they inhabit within
the image, which distinguishes them from the foreground space
inhabited by the figure of Smith. Their clothing conforms to this
chromatic program and alludes to a biblical era, also in contrast
to Smith's modern attire. All of these tropes visually negate the
temporal and spectral distances inherent in such a conception.
Together with the very academic style used by the artist, the
scene accomplishes a sense of believability important to Mormon
art. In other words, it establishes theological tradition, relating
again to the sense of communion described by Morgan and
Promey. This is of course no coincidence, as Parson was trained
as an artist at Brigham Young University, where he received
both a BA and an MFA. He began receiving commissions from
LDS in the early 1980s, and his work was done in consultation
with Church requirements, as it was widely used to illustrate
Church publications.[21] In figure 24 we have an image that is
intended, at least for LDS adherents, to break down contextual
and chronological barriers between the late twentieth century,
the Second Great Awakening, and biblical times.

What sets Mormon visual culture apart is not only its systematic and oddly coherent internal logic but the degree to which Smith and his followers, including Brigham Young, linked the use of imagery to the foundational texts of the LDS, as seen in figure 24. This insistent linkage between text and image, seemingly in defiance of historical logic, has maintained near universal credibility among LDS followers to this day. Thus throughout the Church's nearly two-hundred-year history, one sees waves of imagery being appropriated by Mormon theologians and scholars in an effort to continually renew Smith's original message for subsequent generations of followers and converts.

It is therefore common to see paintings such as those by the late nineteenth-century painters Carl Bloch (1834–90) and Heinrich Hofmann (1824–1911), neither of whom had any known association with LDS or knowledge of Mormon theology, deployed by the Church in the illustration of various biblical narratives. These biblical narratives were construed as being intimately interwoven with the "latter-day" narratives spun by Smith in the *Book of Mormon*, which Mormons commonly see as a complement to and extension of these themes and narratives in a New World context.

We also see the work of numerous twentieth-century Mormon artists—most notably that of the painters Arnold Friberg (1913–2010) and John Scott (1907–87)—used as illustrations for the text's stories, thereby establishing a cultural and conceptual continuity between the mid-nineteenth-century text and twentieth-century visual culture. All of these appropriations and conceptual associations serve to establish the internal coherence of Mormon doctrine. Indeed when reading Mormon literature and viewing the images used as illustrations of that literature, it is easy to forget the very real cultural and historical ruptures that exist between them. In the work of Christensen, Parson, Bloch, Hofmann, Friberg, and Scott, it is not difficult to discern the clear art historical precedents and models used by each artist. Such precedents were no doubt desired by their Mormon patrons, as the sense of aesthetic and historical familiarity adds to the credibility of the *Book of Mormon*'s stories. Because of this, when Mormon leaders and publishers select artworks to accompany their teachings, theological concerns are not the only consideration. Credible aesthetic tropes are sought after as well.

In the wake of his first vision, Smith claims to have had a discussion with Jesus, in which Smith asked him which denomination was the most righteous. Jesus replies that none are righteous, and so Smith began a period of intensive public questioning of doctrine, which led him to be derided by leaders of the local denominations. In response to this, Smith engaged in further prayer and eventually had more visions, which, together with his first vision, are considered the foundational events of the "restoration" of the early Christian church that Mormons seek to effect.[22]

After being derided by local sectarian leaders, Smith launches into a compelling section of his story, in which he sets himself up as a visionary, prophetic, Christ-like figure persecuted by the uncomprehending officials of his community. This is not surprising given the nature of Smith's theological beliefs. The philosopher and historian Simon Critchley contends that in Mormonism, the Trinitarian idea of God becoming man has a parallel in the notion of man becoming God. Each individual practitioner of Mormonism is a potential "saint" in a very immediate sense.[23] Smith's telling of the story in fact not only relates to his sense of being persecuted by the ruling class of his community, but even reminds one of the misfortunes of Jesus as described in the Gospels, where the Savior had to contend with the incessant questioning and harassment of the Pharisees. Smith writes:

> I continued to pursue my common vocations in life until the twenty-first of September, one thousand eight hundred and twenty-three, all the time suffering severe persecution at the hands of all classes of men, both religious and irreligious, because I continued to affirm that I had seen a vision. . . . Having been forbidden to join any of the religious sects of the day, and being of very tender years, and persecuted by those who ought to have been my friends

and to have treated me kindly, and if they supposed me to be deluded to have endeavored in a proper and affectionate manner to have reclaimed me—I was left to all kinds of temptations. . . . In consequence of these things, I often felt condemned for my weakness and imperfections.[24]

The next vision occurred in 1823 and consisted of Smith being visited by the spirit, in angelic form, of the ancient prophet and historian Moroni. As mentioned previously, the *Book of Mormon* credits Moroni with the abridging and editing of the prophetic writings of several earlier prophets, including those of his father, Mormon, whose written commentary is contained within the book itself and after whom the book is named. During this vision, which Smith claimed happened in his bedroom one night, Moroni charged him with being God's modern prophet. He informed Smith that the first step in his role as prophet would be unearthing two golden plates on which he had inscribed all the earlier prophetic writings. Moroni had buried the plates—conveniently—on a hillside outside of the town of Manchester, New York, where Smith and his family were currently residing.[25]

After prophesying about the coming apocalypse and the subsequent dawning of a new millennium, quoting various biblical verses, Moroni then instructed Smith that he should not retrieve the plates for a period of four years and then should not show them to anyone who was not authorized to see them. Smith was instructed to go to the hill each subsequent year on the same date as his initial vision until Moroni allowed him to take the plates out of the spot in which they were buried. In 1827 Smith writes that he was finally allowed to remove the plates by Moroni, who was present for each annual pilgrimage.[26]

C. C. A. Christensen's series of paintings addressing the life of Joseph Smith is called the "Mormon Panorama," considered crucial documents regarding the Church's early history. The revelation of the golden plates by the angel Moroni is depicted in figure 25. Like many subsequent artists employed by LDS, Christensen was professionally trained. He studied at the Royal Academy of Art in Copenhagen in the 1840s and 1850s, where he converted to Mormonism. He subsequently painted only for the Church and translated the *Book of Mormon* into Danish. He was also employed as a missionary and traveled throughout Scandinavia in the second half of the nineteenth century in the service of Mormon evangelism. He eventually emigrated to the United States in 1857 and settled in Utah to live among his spiritual brethren; there he became a historian of Mormonism, specifically of his own evangelical activities in Scandinavia.[27]

In figure 25, *The Hill Cumorah*, Christensen has painted the critical meeting of Smith and Moroni on the hillside in 1827. This image, which may be seen as the founding revelation of the Mormon movement, corresponds to the event described in the *Book of Mormon* as well as in Smith's *Pearl of Great Price*. Christensen, as he characteristically does, paints the scene in a manner clearly influenced by the romantic movement of the early nineteenth century, which was quite popular in northern European countries. Smith kneels in awe before Moroni, who is depicted in Christological fashion, defined by his glowing brightness, which dramatically illuminates the densely forested nighttime landscape. Smith looks up at the angel with hands extended in anticipation of being given the plates that would soon become the *Book of Mormon*. The drama of the scene is reinforced visually by the sharp diagonal on which it takes place, a diagonal axis to which Smith is visually beholden by his position and which Moroni easily hovers just above. The relative relationship of each figure to the surrounding landscape indicates their respective status as inhabiting the earthly (Smith) and heavenly (Moroni) realms. This is a formula repeated by Mormon artists throughout Church history; a similar composition was used by Parson for his depiction of Smith's first vision, also set in a wooded area.

Importantly, Christensen makes use of bright white and yellow tones in describing the divine body of Moroni, and this is in heavy contrast to the earthy tones of the background and Smith's clothing. This aesthetic treatment would become a staple in Mormon imagery and visually indicates some of the core aspects of the Mormon faith as well as reasons for Mormon missionary work. Pertinent to this is the sentence at the end of the paragraph cited earlier from the *Book of Mormon*'s introduction: "After thousands of years, all were destroyed except the Lamanites, and they are the principal ancestors of the American Indians." Here we start to see the convergence of aesthetic metaphor and scriptural doctrine as pertaining to race within Mormonism. Another central aspect of Mormon teaching is the belief that an ongoing cosmic battle for moral supremacy is taking place between the Nephites and the Lamanites, two Israelite tribes thought by Mormons to be the early ancestors of modern humans. This idea, and the ramifications it has had for race relations in the history of Mormonism, requires closer examination.

In very broad terms, the aesthetic metaphor that equates salvation with skin lightening was not uncommon in the country over the course of the nineteenth century, and in fact sees a parallel in the beliefs of various Christian denominations across time. While this is perhaps most startling in the Mormon doctrine that spiritual transformation could result in lightened skin, the references to whiteness as signifying spiritual purity and elevation are not unique to Mormonism and may be partly the cultural inheritance of medieval Christian iconography. As I discussed in my first book, this visual trope is not unique to Mormonism, but is something integral to Christian visual culture historically and is crystallized by the art historian Albert Boime. Boime discusses the ideological coding of such uses of color in art, as chromatic metaphors are often confused with ideological categorizations of race. Thus black and red have obvious connotations for race, especially in American art history. But when looking at the broader history of Christian art, color usage has at times been taken as a valid metaphor not only for race but also for the spiritual duality of Good versus Evil.[28]

This time-honored chromatic metaphor occurs repeatedly in the *Book of Mormon*, in both visual and textual form. While

Christensen's painting of Smith's vision alludes indirectly to this idea, we see it spelled out even more explicitly in textual form in the text itself. In the introduction, Smith states the following in reference to the visitation he received from Moroni in his room in 1823: "I betook myself to prayer and supplication to Almighty God. . . . While I was thus in the act of calling upon God, I discovered a light appearing in my room, which continued to increase until the room was lighter than noonday, when immediately a personage appeared at my bedside, standing in the air, for his feet did not touch the floor. He had on a loose robe of most exquisite whiteness."[29]

Here we see a reference to whiteness as a sign of spiritual enlightenment and transcendence. As discussed in chapter 1, this equation of whiteness with salvation was hardly new in the time of Smith and can be readily seen in the writings and visual imagery of Puritanism centuries earlier. Interestingly Smith's testimonial regarding this mystical experience closely parallels the treatment of Moroni in Christensen's painting. Perhaps taking a cue from his spiritual mentor Smith, Christensen depicts Moroni as hovering above the earth, wearing a loose robe, and glowing in exquisitely bright yellow and white tones. What makes this more than a passing metaphoric reference is Smith's larger narrative throughout the *Book of Mormon*.

After Smith retrieved the golden plates, he and his family temporarily moved to Pennsylvania to escape the increasing hostility of members of the local denominations in Palmyra, who reputedly attempted to steal his plates on multiple occasions. The LDS characterizes Smith's translation of the plates as his first act in "establishing God's kingdom on Earth." Once in Pennsylvania he needed to divine (interpret) the plates, as the script they contained was in "reformed Egyptian," according to the *Book of Mormon*. Smith explains that the box buried on the hill that contained the plates also contained other items, specifically what he calls "Urim" and "Thummim." These were two smooth stones attached to a breastplate that, when worn properly, allowed him to divine the text on the plates and thus translate it into English. The names he gave the stones are actually derivative of ancient Hebrew terms used to describe the vestments worn by ancient priests and were thought to have conferred the power of divine mediation on the individual who wore them. Smith then dictated the contents of the plates to his friend Oliver Cowdery, who transcribed the text. Following four months of translation, the transcription was brought by Smith, Cowdery, and another friend to the publisher E. B. Grandin in Palmyra and was printed in early 1830.[30]

In Smith's story we see an overarching narrative driven by a need for divination and, in a sense, the discovery of gold. For Utah was perceived as the final stopping point in the search for a new Zion, and its settlement echoed the Mormon narrative of westward movement of the Hebrew patriarch Lehi and his family, from Jerusalem to the "bountiful" Americas. This journey, conceptualized as both spiritual and physical, is the central narrative in the *Book of Mormon*. The West as bounty was a concept broadly shared during this era by competing religious denominations as well as secularists, as evidenced in the national obsession with gold that drove many settlers to the West in the 1840s and 1850s.

This association between divination, treasure, and spiritual transformation has not been lost on art historians who examine the art of this period. One, Charles Colbert, observes that spiritualism was a central practice in the life of Hiram Powers, the leading American sculptor of the antebellum era. In fact Powers, like Smith, claimed to have otherworldly visions while in his bedroom at night, and once claimed that his sculpture *The Greek Slave* was conceived during such a vision. In this sense, "spiritualism" refers to the act of communicating with or divining signs from other realms through acts or objects of mediation, something central to the practice of both men.[31]

From this perspective, Smith's use of divining tools in his translation of the plates has a close parallel. Colbert argues that some of Powers's work executed during this period reflects his own interest in divination, specifically his interest in the divination of gold.

Colbert draws a connection between Powers's use of symbolism in his sculpture *California* and the popularized use of a divining rod, a superstition adopted by some at the time in the rush to get rich quick. The use of a stick or other implement for purposes of divining the subterranean location of gold was widespread, and Smith's collaborator in the translation of the plates, Cowdery, was a practitioner of such techniques. In his sculpture *California*, Powers displays his affinity for the practice of dowsing by placing a divining rod in the left hand of an allegorical female figure. The rod points toward the valuable-looking gemstones depicted at the base of the figure, indicating the validity of divination in the discovery of treasure. While Smith was not a visual artist and may not have known of Powers's work, he clearly was a creative individual and prolific writer who, like Powers, fabricated work out of a desire to divine both spiritual and material treasure. As such, one may see Smith as a fellow traveler to the artistically inspired spiritualists of the era.[32]

Given that Smith claimed to have successfully translated the plates into English from "reformed Egyptian," it is possible to analyze the narratives contained within the *Book of Mormon*, together with the imagery used by the Church to illustrate those narratives. While these narratives are complex in detail and broad in scope, for the purposes of this discussion they may be summarized as follows.

Smith's story centers on a cosmic and historical struggle between two sets of descendants of an ancient Israelite family believed to have fled to the Americas during the fall of Jerusalem to Babylon in the sixth century BCE: the light-skinned descendants of the beneficent prophet Nephi and the dark-skinned descendants of his evil brother, Laman, who had plotted to murder Nephi and doubted the grace of God. Nephi and Laman were two sons of the Hebrew prophet and elder Lehi. He was a faithful man, who, after receiving a vision from God foretelling the imminent fall of Jerusalem due to the iniquity of its inhabitants, wisely gathered his family and fled the doomed city. Through this first part of the

Book of Mormon, which, like the Bible before it, is subdivided into smaller books, chapters, and verses, Smith brilliantly interweaves biblical references with what are very American fantasies and aspirations of deliverance. At one point in the First Book of Nephi, Smith describes Lehi's departure thus: "And it came to pass that he departed into the wilderness. And he left his house, and the land of his inheritance, and his gold, and his silver, and his precious things, and took nothing with him, save it were his family, his provisions and tents, and departed into the wilderness."[33]

In this evocative passage Smith offers time-honored American themes that he would repeat throughout the *Book of Mormon* and that appear throughout the history of American spiritual writing in general. The visionary Lehi, through the grace of God, leaves behind his corrupted ancestral land with the hope of salvation in a better place. This trope of departure into the wilderness is accompanied by Lehi's heightened practical and moral capability, as he willingly leaves behind his material possessions: inheritance, gold, silver, and so forth. This opening narrative played out in Smith's own life, as he and his family were repeatedly forced to move due to the hostility and persecution of competing religious denominations. He and his followers eventually made their way to the town of Nauvoo, Illinois, then on the edge of the American frontier. The "journey out" was also central to the histories of the Puritans and Quakers. Smith, being a highly literate Christian, was no doubt familiar with biblical narratives of this sort (as the Exodus of the Jews, for instance) and also with the early history of America. As mentioned earlier, it has been said by the LDS that his early ancestors lived in New England during the Puritan era.[34]

Eventually Lehi and his family make their way to the Irreantum, presumably a large body of water, although its exact location is not known. Upon arriving at the coast, Nephi is instructed by God to construct a large ship (reminiscent of Noah's Ark), which they use to traverse the sea and make their way to the waiting utopia. Smith writes that God attempts to quell Nephi's fear regarding the daunting journey by using the metaphor of lightness: "I will also

Mormonism, Light and Dark

be your light in the wilderness; and I will prepare the way before you."[35] In a later passage Smith explains the indestructability of the ship, as it was in effect a Godly vessel: "Now I, Nephi, did not work the timbers after the manner which was learned by men, neither did I build the ship after the manner of men; but I did build it after the manner which the Lord had shown unto me; wherefore it was not after the manner of men."[36]

Following the divinely inspired construction of the ship, Lehi and his people set off on their journey. Smith depicts the journey as harrowing, as Nephi's brothers and relatives begin to lose faith in the journey and rebel. Eventually Nephi regains control of the ship through his faith and with divine intervention guides the ship through a violent storm to its destination in the promised land:

> And it came to pass that after we had sailed for the space of many days we did arrive at the promised land; and we went forth upon the land, and did pitch our tents; and we did call it the promised land. . . . We did begin to till the earth to plant seeds, which we had brought from the land of Jerusalem. And it came to pass that they did grow exceedingly. . . . There were beasts in the forest of every kind . . . which were for the use of men.[37]

The arrival scene likewise has a visual counterpart in the book (fig. 26). It was executed under commission to the Church by Friberg, who himself was a practicing Mormon. In 1950 he was hired by the Church to produce several large-scale epic religious scenes, some of which would later be used as official illustrations of various narratives from the *Book of Mormon*. Like that of other Mormon artists before him, Friberg's painting style betrays a heavy grounding in academicism and the art of the Renaissance. As in many of the illustrations Friberg executed for the book, he attempts to give the scene a spontaneous, snapshot-like appearance through the foreshortening of the boat and placing the viewer just over the edge of the craft at a vantage point that allows us to see both the reaction of the travelers and the coast of the promised land in the distance. The aging Lehi and his wife lean over the edge with expressions of great relief; in fact Lehi seems to be offering a prayer of thanks to God at the moment depicted.

Friberg, the son of immigrants, may well have related to the narrative of migration outlined on the book. As a young child, his parents converted to Mormonism after arriving in the United States. Friberg was academically trained at the Chicago Academy of Fine Arts and later would study under Norman Rockwell in New York at the Grand Central School of Art. Stylistic affinities with Rockwell are clearly evident in the great sense of academically inspired detail, the intensive lighting, the restrained color palette, and the depiction of theatrical emotion. Friberg joined the U.S. Army during World War II and depicted patriotic subjects for recruitment posters. This influence is evident in his later work, *The Prayer at Valley Forge* (fig. 27), in which George Washington is shown kneeling in prayer prior to that key battle of the Revolution. He would do his series for the *Book of Mormon* at the request of Adele Cannon Howells, a high-ranking member of the LDS and president of the Primary, a pedagogical subdivision of LDS dedicated to the education of Mormon children.[38]

During the journey into the wilderness of the Americas, not all was well with Lehi and his family. Smith relates that two of Lehi's sons, Laman and Lemuel, began speaking out against their father as they increasingly lost faith in his divinely sanctioned deliverance from Jerusalem. The two also resented their younger (and favored) brother Nephi, who repeatedly exhorts them to greater faith in response to their various misdeeds. As such, these characters come to represent the opposite of faith in the *Book of Mormon*. In fact their doubting would lead to civil strife within the family and later among their descendants in the New World. Because of this rupture, in practical terms Smith's agenda, and that of his Mormon successors, has been to seek out and save the damned descendants of Laman, the Lamanites, which they accept as a God-given obligation. A verse in the book instructs the reader on the appearance of a Lamanite and elaborates on the reason for this appearance, which is rooted in Laman's pride and doubt: "And he had caused the cursing to come upon them, yea, even a sore cursing, because of their iniquity. For behold, they had hardened their hearts against him, that they had become like unto a flint; wherefore as they were white and exceedingly fair, and delightsome, that they might not be enticing unto my people the Lord God did cause a skin of blackness to come upon them."[39]

When Lamanites are depicted in the book's illustrations, they most often appear in a belligerent, warlike posture in relation to the Nephites. An example is figure 28, a painting by Friberg illustrating the story of Samuel, a "converted" Lamanite prophet who boldly proclaimed his newfound faith to the Nephites from the top of a wall of Zarahemla, an ancient city Mormons believe to be the center of the ancient Nephite civilization in the Americas. At this point in the book's narrative, the previously favored and lighter skinned Nephites fall into iniquity in the eyes of God due to their materialistic habits. Samuel, a Lamanite who saw the light, as it where, is sent by God to exhort the Nephites to change, and many of them initially reject his warning. Friberg here shows us the dramatic scene from ground level, as the Nephites attempt to silence Samuel.[40]

It is important to note that in Mormonism, the Lamanites do have the potential to be saved, despite bearing the physiological mark of their ungodly ancestor. Smith intended the story of Samuel to give the reader the sense of a redeemed Lamanite, noting that physiology alone does not automatically predetermine grace. And yet Smith and his followers have continually sought out the Lamanites around the world in an effort to redeem them. That persons of darker skin are assumed to be in need of such salvation is established in the book's introduction, which tells us that the "Lamanites . . . are the principal ancestors of the American Indians."[41]

Indeed, the conversion of Lamanites remains a central concern for Mormon missionaries, and conversion narratives play a central role in Mormon literature. Despite the fact that the *Book of Mormon* recounts in detail the earlier salvation of some righteous

Lamanites,[42] modern Mormons have nonetheless continued to focus their missionary efforts on dark-skinned peoples of Polynesian and indigenous American descent, perceiving them as the descendants of the heretical Laman. As early as the beginning of the 1830s Smith dispatched missionaries to the western frontier. His friend Cowdery put it this way in a letter to fellow missionary Hyrum Smith, brother of Joseph:

> We left you last fall we arived at this place a few days since which is about 25 miles from the Shawney indians on the south side of the Kansas River at its mouth & delewares on the north I have had two interviews with the Chief of the delewares who is a very old & venerable looking man after laying before him & eighteen or twenty of the Council of that nation the truth he said that he and they were very glad for what I their Brother had told them and they had received it in their hearts etc—But how the matter will go with this tribe to me is uncirtain.[43]

The Nephites eventually saw their civilization destroyed at the behest of God due to their wicked practices; oddly the Lamanites were the only surviving group in the Americas following this catastrophe. This is how Smith explained the presence of Native Americans upon the arrival of European settlers in early modern times. From this perspective, the establishment of the Mormon Church and the conversion of darker skinned Others has become an attempt at the "restoration" of the great Nephite civilization that existed prior to the fall from grace. This restorative aspect of Smith's narrative seems most influenced by the Garden of Eden scenario in the Book of Genesis. Smith and his cadre are thus "neo-Nephites" who seek their own improvement and redemption through self-salvation and the salvation of racial Others, in this case race being originally interpreted as a spiritual signifier.

There are thus some Mormon images, such as figure 29, again executed by Friberg, where the saved or converted Lamanites are shown in what is intended to be a positive light in contrast to the unbelieving state of their ancestor Laman. Here the artist illustrates another point in the book's narrative, where a large army consisting of two thousand saved Lamanites are enlisted by the Nephite prophet and warrior Helaman to fight an enemy army of unrepentant Lamanites. In the compelling image Friberg positions us at eye level with the soldiers, who bear arms in a good cause. These are the correctly docile Lamanites, whose possession of weaponry poses no threat to Nephite civilization. Above them in the background Helaman is perched on a horse issuing commands. As with all Nephite heroes throughout the book's stories, Helaman resembles a sort of medieval Nordic warrior firmly in command of those underneath him. While Lamanites are occasionally depicted in images and in the text as redeemable, it is in their submission to Nephite rule that they truly fulfill the Mormon prophetic mandate.[44] The message in the text and in this image is clear when taken in context: the Lamanites (Mormonism's dark-skinned Other) become good when accepting the faith, and become heroic when agreeing to forge alliances with their spiritual and racial superiors in the destruction of any of their own kind who fail to adopt said faith.

The ideal of spiritual purity is also depicted in text and illustrations. Smith describes Nephi, Lehi's good son and the progenitor of the Nephites, in moral and physiological terms: "And it came to pass that I, Nephi, being exceedingly young, nevertheless being large in stature and also having great desires to know the mysteries of God, wherefore, I did cry unto the Lord; and behold he did visit me, and did soften my heart that I did believe all the words which had been spoken by my father; wherefore, I did not rebel against him like unto my brothers."[45]

In this description of Nephi, written in the first person in order to give a sense of authenticity to the text, Smith draws distinctions between Nephi and his wicked older brothers. Nephi's largeness of stature may be taken as both a moral and a physical description, and both qualities are shown in Friberg's depiction of Nephi interacting with his brothers (fig. 30). Despite the potential for a Lamanite to be saved, when they appear in images with

Nephites they are commonly shown in a subordinate position. Thus Nephi, depicted in a manner becoming a Teutonic warrior, rebukes his brothers for their lack of faith in God and obedience to their father, while simultaneously displaying his industry. He is shown in a Vulcanesque posture, fabricating the weapons and tools necessary for the survival of the new Zion, an indication of his skill and leadership. His brothers, in contrast, cower below his outstretched, authoritative left arm. One turns away in embarrassment, and the other two cover their faces as if unable to confront Nephi's righteousness head-on. Such didacticism is commonplace in Mormon art, which exists because of LDS patronage and is intended to instruct followers of the doctrine in the proper way of life, as embodied and acted out by these mythic characters.[46]

According to the narrative, despite their initially sanctified position in relation to the Lamanites, the Nephites eventually backslide into spiritual corruption and thus require a visitation from Jesus, which Smith claims took place in their settlement in the Americas. This miraculous visitation, believed to have happened following Jesus's death on the cross, is dramatically depicted by a number of artists employed by LDS. Perhaps the most iconic image of the resurrected Christ was executed by the illustrator John Scott, who worked on commission for the Church in the 1960s (fig. 31). Perhaps surprisingly, Scott made his name in the 1930s as a commercial freelance illustrator of popular pulp magazines, a widely consumed form of entertainment and visual stimulation in the country throughout the mid-twentieth century. They often contained outlandish or even lurid narrative subject matter, ranging from science fiction and crime dramas to romanticized characterizations of the Old West. The commission from LDS therefore represents something of an anomaly in Scott's career, unlike most other artists employed by the Church, who were often longtime members.[47]

In his rendering of Christ's return to the Americas, it is evident that Scott had at least a cursory knowledge of pre-Columbian architecture, as the buildings surrounding the scene contain a fair

Mormonism, Light and Dark

amount of detail. Bound in a bright white toga, Scott's version of Christ to some degree coincides with traditional Mormon depictions of divinity. The scene is nonetheless intended to be disturbing to Mormon viewers. The once-great Nephite civilization is in partial ruin, a visual indication of their descent into iniquity, as described in the *Book of Mormon*. Smith tells us that Christ needed to return to the Nephites in order to revitalize their flagging society and remind them of the grace of their ancestor Nephi, whom he addresses during the visit. Christ speaks to the Nephites and reminds them of their ongoing need for faith and baptism, citing these as the difference between salvation and damnation. Knowing the Nephites have fallen into doubt, Christ then invites them to touch his stigmata as proof of his presence. Scott shows us the moment just before they approach him. In Mormonism this visitation is also the fulfillment of a prophecy mentioned earlier in the book and is taken as divine proof that there was indeed an ancient Nephite civilization (which they call "Bountiful") in Mesoamerica.[48]

Scott attempts to capture for his patrons the much-desired sense of historical accuracy in architecture and in the terrain and foliage of Mesoamerica. He likewise adds a distinctly Mormon twist to the clothing of the Nephites, mostly an odd combination of biblical and pre-Columbian attire. And yet an unintended humorous aspect creeps in, in the figure of the woman with the small child kneeling in awe to the right of Christ. Her costume appears ahistorical, in keeping with middle-class American fashion from the 1960s.

The principle of purity is seen in figure 32, originally executed in 1894 by the German painter Heinrich Hofmann, and used as a frontispiece in modern editions of the *Book of Mormon*. Hofmann, a devout Lutheran, portrays a Teutonic Christ with high forehead, strong expression, and piercing eyes that would be distributed globally throughout the twentieth century and has served as an ideal standard in modern Christian imagery, well beyond the confines of Mormonism. The painting was initially reproduced by the publisher Franz Hanfstaengel in Munich in the late nineteenth century. By the mid-twentieth century the image was well-known throughout the Christian world. Clearly Friberg's depictions of various Nephite exemplars share a physiognomic heritage with the figure depicted by Hofmann. Beyond the immediate context of Christian visual art, however, and given the historical context in which Hofmann painted, his Teutonic Christ resonates with criminological "goodness," in keeping with then-common aesthetic hierarchies.[49]

The Teutonic features of Hofmann's Christ—later influential in Mormon visual culture—may be related to multiple visual influences. From an artistic perspective, Hofmann was no doubt familiar with Germanic art historical prototypes for depicting Christ and Christ-like figures. One such example dating from the Renaissance is Albrecht Durer's famous self-portrait of 1500, in which Durer assumes the role of divinely inspired genius and artist, to the point of taking on near-Christological features. Durer's image, given the historical context of Reformation-era northern Europe, may best be seen as a response to the enhanced social role of the newly emergent artist of the Renaissance: brilliant, creative, individualistic, and self-confident. Indeed the image's iconography is visible evidence for these invisible mental attributes: the piercing gaze, the spotlight illuminating the top of the head, as well as the worldly success of the artist as seen in his fashionable clothing. The image is secularized by the artist's signature, dating, and brief biography, all painted around the artist's imposing figure, a gesture largely unprecedented in European art up to this point. Ironically this secular treatment of the genius artist would become a popular prototype that would merge with the depiction of divine figures, when Renaissance artists became the new visionaries of Western culture, replacing the medieval cleric as the mediator of the beautiful and the mysterious. This transition from medieval metaphysics to a more secular, modern version of metaphysics was brought on in no small part by the mercantile revolution and rise of Protestantism.[50]

Mormonism, Light and Dark

Both Renaissance and academic stylistic influences are central to Hofmann's work. He studied at the famed Düsseldorf Academy in the 1840s, associating with a group of artists known as the Nazarenes, who specialized in classically inflected depictions of the life of Christ. Following his study of religious art in the German academy, he studied in Rome in the 1850s under the tutelage of the German painter Peter von Cornelius.[51] In both situations, Hofmann's training was grounded in idealization of the subject, but also in naturalism. The relationship between the ideal and the natural in visual art was central to Germanic theories throughout the Enlightenment and held sway into the early twentieth century.

Specifically the influential German art historian Johann Joachim Winckelmann (1717–68) wrote that artists should look to nature for inspiration, but in order to gain a "higher" aesthetic mastery they needed to "correct" the flaws in nature. This was done by synthetically combining bits and pieces from nature into a "higher" idealized whole through the imagination, producing a work that superseded nature itself. The prototype for Winckelmann's ideal was classical Greek sculpture.[52] Painters like Hofmann and others of his generation would have been taught under the lingering influence of Winckelmann's aesthetics, absorbing the expectations for what constituted beauty per Winckelmann's system. Specifically, in relation to Hofmann's education, the Düsseldorf Academy was founded by the painter Wilhelm Lambert Krahe in 1762. Krahe was a close associate of Winckelmann's, and the teaching at the Academy was heavily influenced by the latter's ideas on aesthetics through the nineteenth century. In addition to the general influence of the school, Hofmann also traveled extensively in Italy, where he studied under von Cornelius, who was a classically trained painter of religious subjects and had previously been the president of the Düsseldorf Academy.[53]

While Hofmann was undeniably grounded in classical depictions of the divine, he was also an artist living and working in the nineteenth century, and as such his vision was inevitably impacted by the visual conventions of his own era. Winckelmann's ideas blended with ideas from other fields of knowledge to form conventions regarding definitions of beauty as well as moral goodness, as in Boime's ideas regarding the metaphoric power of color. Beginning in the Enlightenment, thinkers across Europe, including in Germany, were busy constructing new systems of vision, in accordance with specifically modern technological and scientific advancements. Winckelmann's work in art history represents one such system. Concurrently, as European scientists invented more and more nuanced instruments intended to enhance the human senses and perception of the natural world, artists likewise depicted the natural world in a more systematized manner, according to the emergent conventions of an encyclopedic or naturalistic worldview.

As discussed in chapter 2, the German naturalist and anatomist Johann Blumenbach established one such perceptual system. He invented the pseudoscience of craniometry in the late eighteenth century, which would go on to influence how scientists, artists, and the general public would perceptually categorize humanity for centuries, up to our own time. Hofmann, being an exceptionally well-educated painter, traveled throughout Europe in pursuance of his studies, spending time in the Netherlands, France, and eventually Italy, where he clearly absorbed lessons from the Italian Renaissance. As an academic painter of his caliber, Hofmann would have likewise been exposed to anatomical studies under von Cornelius and his instructors at the Düsseldorf Academy. Thus one may firmly state that Hofmann absorbed not only aesthetic theory but a newly systematized way of empirically observing nature.

If we examine both systems of knowledge side by side, it becomes apparent that for Winckelmann and other aestheticians of the era, the standard for beauty and thus a sense of elevation in what one would call "high art" was the physiological form of classical Greek sculpture, at least as it was perceived by him and others during the Enlightenment, though filtered through Roman copies. Simultaneously, for naturalists like Blumenbach, a Nordic or Teutonic physiognomy became the standard for elevation in the newly racialized sciences of the time. It is fair to suggest that as Hofmann and many other academic artists working in Europe during the nineteenth century tended to Aryanize Christ as a measure of his moral superiority, there was an epistemic overlap with the thinking of the pseudoscientists.

A critical consideration in this context is the actual ethnic identity of Jesus. While it would seem, from a historical perspective, that he would have to have been of Semitic origin (as opposed to northern European), this issue was not universally resolved in the nineteenth century. Art historian Annette Stott has offered insight on this issue in her work on the Anglo-Israelite movement of the late nineteenth century. There were some at the time who claimed that the Anglo-American population of the United States were descendants of ten lost tribes who came from northern Israel in biblical times. These tribes contrasted the more well-known Twelve Tribes of southern Israel, who were taken to be ancestors of the modern Jewish people. The idea was that these lost northern tribes were actually of fair Caucasian ethnic stock and eventually migrated to other parts of the world. As we have seen, a variation of this idea is the central narrative in the *Book of Mormon*, which conceives of the Nephites as a light-skinned people who migrated across the ocean to the New World from Israel. Images of Jesus as a northern European would logically fit in with this scheme and would aesthetically and racially align him with Anglo-America. In addition Anglo-Israelism was a millenarian movement which posited that a Second Coming was imminent and that those of Anglo-Saxon lineage were best suited to be saved due to their alleged ethnospiritual affinities with the Savior. All such theories of Anglo-American exceptionalism, whether racial, political, or spiritual, reinforced the sense of ownership of the continent that would be the foundation of the doctrine of Manifest Destiny. Thus contemporary aesthetic theory, pseudoscientific thought, and popular spiritualism all impacted the perception and representation of Jesus as a northern European ethnic type.[54]

These hierarchies were not merely the purview of visual artists like Hofmann, but were even more popularly known through the emerging field of criminology. By the late nineteenth century certain aspects of pseudoscientific thought, credible a few decades earlier, began to wane in influence due to intervening events, such as the Civil War and Emancipation. Nevertheless criminologists in many countries, including France, the United Kingdom, Italy, and the United States, made use of more advanced techniques in photography and other representational technologies in the establishment of what were supposedly newer and even more systematized empirical bodies of proof that allowed the police and general public alike to spot a potential criminal on the street.

Theorists and practitioners such as Francis Galton in England, Alphonse Bertillon in France, Cesare Lombroso in Italy, and Thomas F. Burns in New York used photographic mug shots arranged deliberately so as to imply underlying physiological characteristics shared by all criminals. Lombroso in particular used synthetic visual arrays, which he believed illustrated various types of criminals, the category being indicated by the lettering on the sides of the image. He felt that congenital predispositions to crime could be discerned by the trained eye of the detective. Although these theories were not always explicitly tied to race, a complex web of environmental and congenital determinism generally underwrote their perceived credibility.

Despite regional and cultural differences between them, what united these criminologists was a firmly held belief—assumed to be borne out by archived empirical data—that criminals shared not only behavioral tendencies but physiological traits. As a result certain visual clichés became accepted as markedly criminal: dark skin, a prominent forehead, bushy eyebrows, a narrow skull crown, a thick nose, and so forth. In fact during his time as police super-intendent Bertillon went so far as to construct elaborate synoptic tables drawn from fragments of mug shots taken by the Paris Prefecture of Police. For his part, Burns constructed an elaborate photographic "Rogues Gallery" that would later be published in book form and distributed to members of the public. From this point it was only a small conceptual leap to the conclusion

Mormonism, Light and Dark

that physiological traits shared in common by particular ethnic groups indicated a greater possible congenital predisposition to criminality. Some went so far as to claim that criminals displayed in their physiology certain "atavistic" rudiments held over from more "primitive" tribal times or lower species of primate—thus Lombroso's infamous claim that darker skinned southern Italians were more criminally prone than lighter skinned northern Italians.[55]

The ideal, Aryanized version of Jesus is, by implication, the polar opposite of its darker double in nineteenth-century visual discourse in both Europe and the United States. Mormons believed that modern Native Americans had inherited the morally deficient traits of their ancestral Lamanite tribe, despite the efforts of some Lamanites to attain salvation. Beyond the confines of Mormon doctrine is the more well-known and widespread phrenological view of the indigenous American that was current through much of the nineteenth century, a view that had its roots in the pseudoscientific categories of Blumenbach and others during the Enlightenment.

According to this view, as popularized by Samuel Morton, George Combe, and later the entrepreneurial Fowler brothers of New York, Native American "destructiveness" was to be seen in the shape, size, and proportions of the skulls found in collections such as Morton's. Such a view was arrived at through the measurement and/or manual examination of a skull (or alternatively the head of a living person), as conducted by a phrenologist. The resulting pseudo-empirical findings were popularized in publications, such as those of the Fowlers, containing copious illustrations intended to prove the racial hierarchies (fig. 33).[56]

"Destructiveness" was a common phrenological attribute assigned to Native Americans, and it made sense to many Euro-American readers of the time, as the indigenous population was often blamed for a wide variety of atrocities that took place on the frontier during white settlement. Indians were generally perceived as constituting an obstruction to Anglo advancement and "progress," and as such their main attribute was seen as "destructiveness." Phrenological and craniological analysis merely lent a veneer of scientific legitimacy to what were political and racial hostilities caused by territorial disputes. It is in this context that the Mormon notion of the "destructive" Lamanites found a parallel. Despite Mormonism's very real doctrinal and political differences with more mainstream evangelical groups, and despite Smith's ostensibly abolitionist view of slavery, racial Others were nevertheless seen in a similar light by both Mormon theologians and pseudoscientific practitioners.[57]

While Native Americans, African Americans, and non-Anglo immigrants occupied the role of dark "double" on phrenological charts and in the criminological archive, the opposite association between the perceived "perfection" of the classical Greek aesthetic and the appearance of an Aryan physiognomy is not difficult to find in pseudoscientific illustrations. Here we may tie the antebellum polygenism to the millennial spiritualism of the Anglo-Israelist movement. The earlier discussion of Josiah Nott's and George Gliddon's *Types of Mankind* (fig. 34) may be viewed in this light. Nott and Gliddon associate Greco-Roman aesthetics with a perfected "Greek" skull. In their hierarchy, the "Negro," with his craniologically debased skull, is midway between the "Greek" and the "Chimpanzee." The proportions of the Greek skull resemble those of the modern Caucasian skulls collected by their friend Morton. Not surprisingly, the Greek skull at the top of their hierarchy representationally overlaps Winckelmann's ideal standard of beauty, the physiology of the classical Greek statue. This offers another instance in which skull shape, size, and proportion are associated with intellectual and moral capacities.

The aesthetic and epistemological slippage inherent in Nott and Gliddon's analysis apparently did not occur to them in the writing of their text. They assume a perfected proportion in their hypothetical Greek specimen, an assertion that overlooks the real ethnic differences between modern Greeks and the Germanic peoples of northern Europe. Also, they use a crude illustration of the head of the famous Apollo Belvedere sculpture, a statue that was actually not Greek but an imperial Roman copy of a lost Greek original. Despite all of these inconsistencies, in their zeal they simply assumed unproblematic aesthetic and ontological corollaries between ancient sculpture, modern ethnic types, and supposed internal capacities.

The vagaries of Anglo-American perceptions of Native Americans certainly contributed to conflict on the frontier, but the harsh material and logistical realities of the West played an overarching role in the violence that took place between settlers and the various Native tribes they encountered. It is therefore important to consider not only Mormon ideals and pseudoscientific preconceptions in relation to Native Americans, but the lived experience between the groups as each struggled to survive in what was a changeable climate and shifting alliances.

It is clear from surviving works that Mormon artists such as Christensen continued to attempt to positively frame Mormon-Native relations. In figure 11 Christensen gives us a formula that is by now familiar in the history of American visual culture. We see a sort of encounter image that avoids any reference to overt confrontation or violence, instead favoring what seems to be a constructive interaction between the brave and gifted representative of Anglo-American faith, aesthetics, or scientism. The painting was part of the "Mormon Panorama" series, the visual history of Mormonism from Smith's first vision in 1823 to the arrival of his followers in Utah in 1847, in the wake of his murder. These works were intended for educational purposes, as they were used to illuminate Mormon lectures, and also memorialized Smith as the heroic prophet and founder of the Church.

This formula of encounter may be dated to colonial times and was deployed by more famous artists throughout the nineteenth century in visualizing life on the frontier between settlers and Indians. It is somewhat reminiscent of George Catlin's famous image, in which he depicts himself engaged in a bit of aesthetic didacticism vis-à-vis the savages of the Mandan tribe of the upper Missouri River Valley. Like Catlin, who bestows new and revelatory artistic knowledge onto the "savage," Smith bestows revelatory spiritual knowledge onto the Natives, shown attentively listening. Even more so than Catlin, however, Christensen aesthetically polarizes the Mormons and the Natives. Smith's skin, and that of his followers sitting behind him, is depicted as extremely light, almost shining. In contrast, the Natives' skin is an unnatural high-pitched red tone, something an academically trained painter like Christensen would have recognized. It must therefore be concluded that this chromatic polarity was intentional on Christensen's part, perhaps a metaphor depicting the polarized spiritual identities of the two groups. This is hardly surprising when one considers the core beliefs regarding race commonly held in Mormonism. Christensen's painting successfully conveys the lineage of the "stained" Lamanites, here in modern guise, and the "pure" Nephites, here represented by Smith and his cohorts.[58]

It is also tempting to read the painting in psychoanalytic terms. Smith serves as a visual bridge between the denizens of civilization behind him and the denizens of the wilderness in front of him. On the one hand, this could be seen as a symbolic reference to the westward movement of Mormonism, which paralleled the larger westward movement of Anglo-America at the time. On the other hand, the wilderness often is assigned feminine attributes in contrast to the perceived order of civilization. Thus Smith's assertive and domineering gesture may also be seen as gendered, as he juts forward into the receptive semicircular formation Christensen uses to arrange the Native audience. From this perspective, it is the symbolic "penetration" of nature, wilderness, or infidelity by the forces of civilization and Christian faith.

The historian Ned Blackhawk offers a more complex reading of Mormon interaction with indigenous Americans upon their arrival in Utah. Smith led the Mormons from upstate New York to Ohio, and eventually to the town of Nauvoo, Illinois. While in Nauvoo, Smith became a powerful force both politically and militarily, as he formed a small private army known as the Nauvoo

Legion. In fact some newspapers of the day referred to Smith as General Joe Smith, albeit in many cases this was intended as a sardonic reference to his paramilitary status.[59]

Along with the press's often unflattering characterization of Smith and his "deluded" followers, the presence of this force in Nauvoo, together with Smith's aggressive conversion activities, his political aspirations, and his alleged practice of polygamy, eventually aroused the ire of the non-Mormon town leaders. Smith was increasingly taken seriously as a threat to public order in the town. When he directed his troops to destroy the presses of a local newspaper that had accused him of practicing polygamy, he and his brother Hyrum were imprisoned in a nearby town. A vigilante mob stormed the jail, eventually shooting the two. Following Smith's violent death, his status as a prophet and thus martyr within the Church was only enhanced.[60]

Smith's friend Brigham Young took up the mantel of leadership of a faction of the Church when controversy arose as to Smith's proper successor. Young led the largest faction to Utah, a migration that would precipitate their encounter with the local tribes in the territory. Blackhawk explains that following their migration, which took three years, the Mormons incorrectly believed that the Utah Territory, then still not fully incorporated in the United States, was a sort of virgin land, akin to the fabled promised land of Bountiful as described in the *Book of Mormon*. This was of course a common perception at the time on the part of Anglo-Americans coming from the East; the frontier even held biblical associations for many with the Garden of Eden. When the Mormons did encounter the native Ute and Paiute tribes, violence erupted, for they had expected the region to be cleared by God in order to facilitate the celestial "gathering" they had anticipated in what they saw as their new Zion.[61] Contemporary news accounts detail the violence; one article in the *Morning Courier* of Louisville, Kentucky, reported that during one battle Mormon soldiers killed forty "Utah Indians" and that these results had an "excellent effect" on the Indians, who had been "very quietly disposed" since then.[62]

Apparently the mainstream society's distaste for Mormonism was outstripped by its distaste for Native Americans.

Blackhawk argues that Young and his followers were in a precarious position in Utah. They were themselves a persecuted minority in relation to both more mainstream Christian groups and the federal government, who viewed them as undesirable and so actually encouraged their westward migration. Once in Utah they were faced with radical Otherness in the indigenous tribes and their religious practices. They thus behaved "tactically" in an effort to try to control the tribes without provoking a high-profile incident that might draw the attention of the federal government. They attempted to convert the Paiutes in order to gain them as allies against the more powerful Utes, although they viewed the Indians as unredeemable due to their perceived childlike quality.

Despite these tactics, violence did periodically break out, and the Mormons faced difficult economic conditions in dealing with the tribes. They were at once forced to sustain their Paiute allies and were simultaneously under duress from the threat of regular Ute raids of their farms and livestock. The Utes were forced to do this due to the fact that the Mormons, protected by the remnants of the Nauvoo Legion, forcibly settled the valleys once controlled by the tribes. As they were driven out of the fertile areas, the Utes had no regular access to food and thus raided Mormon home-steads. This cycle of violence continued through much of the early history of the Mormon presence in Utah.[63] Despite these logistical problems, media characterizations of Mormon settlement were not uniformly negative. Some outlets, such as the *Morning Post* of Pittsburgh, maintained a decidedly pro-Mormon bent, emphasizing the extraordinary quality of Mormon accomplishments such as missionary work and the establishment of new utopic settlements in unlikely locales. Sickness, death, and conflict are de-emphasized in such reports.[64]

From the Mormon perspective, conditions in Utah began to stabilize only during the Civil War. This was due to the influx of new federal troops into the territory, when the size of the army ballooned due to recruitment. However, this stability came at a cost, as conflicts arose between troops and various tribes, resulting in the deaths of hundreds.[65] This "clearing" of the territory would facilitate Mormon hegemony in the area, and subsequently a large colony developed and prospered. By the time Utah was granted admission to the Union in 1896, the Mormons had largely succeeded in fulfilling one of Smith's prophecies as laid out in the *Book of Mormon*. It was to be yet another "city on a hill" founded in an American wilderness, although like many other such utopic communities in the Americas, it was built on ideas of spiritual predestination and racial supremacism.

This linkage is discussed repeatedly in the *Book of Mormon*, as spiritual salvation and light skin are conflated. This conflation is furthered in Mormon visual culture, which relied heavily on rather stereotypical racial depictions of the Nephites and Lamanites, mirroring the ongoing categorization and regulation of race in the country throughout the nineteenth century, well after the abolition of slavery and the Civil War.

The negative perception of and interaction with Native Americans would continue and intensify following the Civil War, as the rapidly expanding and industrializing nation required swift reunification in order to facilitate its rise to the status of an emerging industrial world power. Such exigencies would lead to a reconfiguration and merging of evangelism and pseudoscientific thought vis-à-vis the Native during the Gilded Age, resulting in the Social Gospel.

4

The Social Gospel, Christ's Kingdom on Earth

While definitions of race played a central role in Mormon doctrine and practice, the relationship between race and evangelism would become even more widespread and systematized during the Gilded Age. In investigating this relationship, I will discuss two of the most prominent evangelically inspired institutions of that period: the Carlisle Indian Industrial School in Pennsylvania and the Hampton Institute in Virginia. Both were residential boarding schools, one located in the former Union, the other in the former Confederacy. These two very similar schools, coexisting and sharing a near-identical curriculum and philosophy, prove that the evangelical agenda was nationwide and transcended the North-South cultural divide historians often deem so important. As Morton's craniology appealed to both northern and southern racists prior to the war, the Social Gospel espoused by these institutions appealed to liberal-minded reformers across the Mason-Dixon line.

What strikes one as strange about the vast and systematic efforts at Indian evangelization and education during the Gilded Age—the era of the Social Gospel—is the seeming lack of historical awareness on the part of the progressive reformers who spearheaded these efforts. This becomes apparent only when one comparatively examines the surviving documentation from this period in relation to that of the earlier periods discussed in previous chapters. The fact that indigenous proselytizing and

Anglo-Indian interchange dated back to the early decades of Puritan settlement in Massachusetts Bay, under the auspices of the General Court, seemed lost on Richard Henry Pratt and Samuel Chapman Armstrong, the founders of these two most prominent evangelical boarding schools.

In discussing ideas of salvation, race, and representation during this era, it is important at the outset to note the unique contextual attributes to be found in American culture at this time, as these attributes differentiate the methods used by reformers from those used in previous eras. The first task, then, is to grapple with the characteristics of the Gilded Age, and then to define the agendas of and methods used by those who advocated what historians have called the "Social Gospel."

The Gilded Age was an era that, broadly speaking, stretched from the end of the Civil War and its aftermath in the 1860s and 1870s through the early years of the twentieth century. Generally it was a time of significant demographic, technological, and economic change in the United States. The period saw rapid industrialization and the creation of a new economy and jobs, which led to unprecedented quantities of both internal migration and foreign immigration. One result of these phenomena was the sudden and dramatic increase in the populations of American cities, especially those on the eastern seaboard and those in the interior that served as railroad hubs. As cities grew, their character and layout changed. Population density shot up, and with it increases in demand for infrastructure, which drove further building and other industrial activity. Beginning earlier in the century, as the railroads were built to transport goods, services, and people from the outlying rural areas to these cities, more land on the frontier was needed to accommodate the laying of track. This led to increased tension and outright conflict with indigenous tribes that inhabited these areas. In addition, the increased presence of railroads, especially during the productive boom after the Civil War, promoted travel and permanent settlement en masse in regions that had previously been sparsely populated.

As these changes unfolded, demographic groups that in earlier times would have lived apart from one another came increasingly into contact, often competing for resources in the emergent industrial society of mass production. As economic competition intensified so did economic inequality, with some Americans becoming fabulously wealthy "robber barons," while many others lived in dire poverty. The squalor and injustice that mark the era were common themes in literature and visual culture during this time, perhaps most vividly captured by the photojournalist Jacob Riis. Such disparities fostered desperation and resentment and led to an increase in crime in the country's growing cities. This, along with the newer immigration patterns, made American cities much more alienating and anonymous places than they previously had been.

Faced with these changing social conditions, political leaders and social reformers sought to create institutions and programs that would alleviate ethnic and class-based social tensions, or that would "cultivate" or "improve" the lower orders.[1] It is thus during the Gilded Age that institutions of social and cultural improvement appear for the first time: museums, parks, organized sport, and a quantitative uptick in public and private educational institutions. One also sees a qualitative change in the pedagogy of these institutions, based on the emerging belief that a systematic and standardized education for the masses of students would serve as an antidote to the ills of modernization, as cited by Riis and others.

Prior to the progressivism of the Gilded Age, formalized education in America had been the purview of an elite class of Anglo-American men. The proliferation of new colleges, urban public education systems, and boarding schools during this time thus represents a significant change in course in terms of public policy and social organization. Education, or more properly "civilization," was seen as important given the influx of Others from both within and outside of the country. It was a means by which one could assimilate and stabilize what was a potentially menacing and disruptive mass of newcomers by making them part of the larger social fabric.

During the Gilded Age, then, many social reformers preached the Social Gospel. The historian Sydney Ahlstrom has offered a helpful characterization of this new ideology, pointing out that American Christians living during the latter part of the nineteenth century found themselves confronted with an epistemological crisis brought about by two factors: the widespread acceptance of evolution, as explained in Darwin's *Descent of Man*, and what Ahlstrom terms "positivistic naturalism." Under the doctrine of positivistic naturalism, all truth was empirical in nature, and thus any idea vying for legitimacy in the public sphere needed to have a discernable applicability to contemporary social and political problems, and beyond this needed to be perceived as having a "scientific" basis.[2]

These challenges to conventional Christian theology forced denominational leaders to frame evangelical activities in pragmatic terms that could be applied to evolving social problems in American society. The challenge was to create the "kingdom of God" on earth, as the evangelist Walter Rauschenbusch summed it up. Thus, despite the secular economic buildup of this period, it would be a mistake to assume that the evangelical impulses discussed in the previous chapters disappeared. To the contrary, they did remain, albeit in altered and hybrid forms. Thus the Social Gospel represents a reconfiguration of the evangelical impulse seen in previous periods, with a modern, systematized twist in keeping with newer ideas and shifting demographics. As pseudoscientific racial ideas and categorizations needed to be reconfigured in the wake of emancipation and the Civil War, evangelism was likewise reconfigured by its advocates during this era of increasing diversification. Instead of being grounded in solely biblical or latter-day sectarian doctrine, it was merged with more contemporary and seemingly scientific social programs.[3] Carlisle and Hampton represent a dialectical merging of both religious and secular impulses, the purpose of which was not only cultural assimilation and racial uplift but self-legitimization.

Specifically, a social evolutionary doctrine based on the belief that the "totalizing" physical and psychological immersion of the subject into a desired environment was now seen as the most expedient and effective means to assimilating those who were either racially, socially, or spiritually subaltern in relation to the assumed social norms and standards of the middle-class Anglo-American reformers who advocated assimilation.[4] This methodology of social transformation was applied to many groups, including Native Americans and African Americans. The more liberal reformers of the period believed the "winning" of the frontier was not only a necessity that facilitated the growth of the American Empire but was a more "humane" alternative to the ongoing Indian wars and policies of concentration that some then advocated.[5]

In reference to the pressing "Indian question," a manifestation of the Social Gospel may be seen in the rhetoric used by national leaders when discussing the most expedient means of assimilating the indigenous population. A crystallizing piece of text in this regard is this excerpt from the *Annual Report of the Commissioner of Indian Affairs*, delivered by Commissioner Ely Parker to Congress in 1869: "The measures to which we are indebted for an improved condition of affairs are the concentration of the Indians upon suitable reservations, and the supplying them with means for engaging in agricultural and mechanical pursuits for their education and moral training. As a result, the clouds of ignorance and superstition in which many of these people were so long enveloped, have disappeared, and the light of Christian civilization seems to have dawned upon their moral darkness, and opened upon a brighter future."[6]

In Commissioner Parker's report we see the conflation discussed by Max Weber in *The Protestant Ethic and the "Spirit" of Capitalism*. Like many others at the time, Parker associates "agricultural and mechanical pursuits" with "moral training." As Weber shows, this type of formulation is, albeit in modern form, strikingly similar to that put forth by Puritan leaders two centuries earlier. Specifically Weber discusses the role of labor in Puritan theology as outlined in the teachings of Richard Baxter, a leading Puritan intellectual in England in the seventeenth century. Baxter formulated an "ethical duty of labor," or roughly what Weber calls "vocational asceticism," as an imperative to all faithful persons wishing to find salvation, both in this world and the next. In this sense modern progressives echo the fundamental relationship between faith and labor in their emphasis on industrial training as a means to both secular and heavenly salvation.[7] The boarding schools thus were conceived as "totalizing" institutions, as David Wallace Adams has termed it, in at least two senses. First, they offered "total" immersion in mainstream Anglo-American culture; second, and perhaps more important for the evangelical ethos, they offered "total" salvation, secular and spiritual.

More pertinent for this chapter is the fact that Weber's critical view of the Protestant ethic and its relationship to race relations in America was informed by his own travels and firsthand experiences in the country during the Gilded Age, and thus is of relevance to the central topics addressed in this book. As the historian Lawrence Scaff explains, Weber returned to his native Germany following an extended trip through the United States and subsequently gave a series of lectures that outlined his views on the social and political conditions he had found. His trip included stops on the frontier, in the Deep South, and in the industrial centers of the Midwest and Northeast. Weber's views of the nation encompassed many topics, including labor, industry, race relations, religion, and assimilation. These experiences, together with his historical research into evangelical Protestantism, led to his completion of *The Protestant Ethic*, which he had begun prior to his trip.[8]

In his text Weber describes a specifically modern and American version of economic enterprise. While he found ample evidence of an enthusiastic, freewheeling capitalist mentality in many of the people he met, he also focused on the effects of American capitalism on culturally subaltern populations. While Anglo-American identity was often constructed via interactions with not only the market but also cultural Otherness, such activity likewise impacted those Others. Thus Weber discusses the bureaucratization of American democracy and its effects on Native Americans living in the Indian Territory of Oklahoma near the turn of the twentieth century. Such problems were an outgrowth of market expansion to all aspects of life.

An example of this process is the General Allotment Act, which divided up the once relatively open Indian Territory into homesteads for individual settlement.[9] This act necessitated the assimilation of the indigenous population on the frontier, while simultaneously encouraging the Americanization of newer European immigrants, many of whom opted for life on the frontier by purchasing "surplus" former Indian lands, another provision of the act. Ironically, while settlement under the act may have been voluntary for European immigrants, indigenous assimilation was enforced during this era.[10]

Weber's thesis relates directly to and was informed by his awareness of the plight of indigenous Americans during the post-allotment era, as he met several on the frontier in 1904 during his journey. While there he stayed in the town of Muskogee, where he encountered the territorial leadership, most notably Robert Latham Owen. Owen was a member of the Cherokee tribe and a successful lawyer, businessman, and territorial agent, and would go on to be a senator representing Oklahoma following its elevation to statehood. He held strongly critical views on federal Indian policy, and these views influenced Weber's perceptions of American capitalism, property ownership, and race relations. Owen embraced a political ideology revolving around radical egalitarianism and self-reliance as means toward indigenous dignity and independence; this was clearly at odds with the bureaucratic treatment Native Americans received under the General Allotment Act and its aftermath. Discerning this contradiction, Weber maintained a very critical view of the supposed "universal" claims of the Puritan ethic.[11]

Regarding official governmental Indian policy during this era, Weber's "vocational aestheticism" sees a close parallel in Commissioner Parker's views. Parker disparaged indigenous spiritual beliefs as "ignorance and superstition" and was hopeful that with regimentation and training, Native youths would come to the "light of Christian civilization." Interesting are the metaphors of lightness and darkness deployed by Parker in his report. This is not dissimilar to the metaphors used by Cotton Mather, Joseph Smith, and other early Christian leaders in the country when comparing the powers of evil to those of Christ. As we have seen, in Smith's case such equations took on an almost literal racialized bent in the form of his Lamanites, while Mather chose to rhetorically associate the "pagan" Indians with those Puritan settlers possessed by Satan, an idea underwritten by pseudoscientific and aesthetic theories then current. Despite the more modern cultural context of the Gilded Age, overriding assumptions about good and evil, light and dark, industry and sloth still lingered, ultimately finding their sanction in biblical verse, pseudoscientific doctrine, and mercantile philosophy.

In practical terms, this meant establishing totalizing institutions such as boarding schools, and then the recruitment of students from the ranks of the indigenous and African American populations. Each school, whether government-funded or sectarian, generally had rigorous paramilitary training programs designed to discipline the minds and bodies of the students. Beyond this, school administrators deemed textual and visual accompaniments equally necessary. Such supplementary materials were usually written narratives and visual illustrations printed in school publications. These materials were intended to prove the efficacy of the assimilation program at each school. Pratt's Carlisle and Armstrong's Hampton are the two Gilded Age boarding schools at which we see the most prolific use of such narratives and images, and thus lend themselves to our consideration.

Pratt, Armstrong, and other school administrators used staple formulas to make their respective cases. The polarizing rhetoric and visual imagery used at Carlisle and Hampton, which tend to crudely demarcate humanity into two overarching social evolutionary categories of "savage" and "civilized," disavow any sense of what had been occurring across the continent for more than three centuries. One can only conclude that Pratt, Armstrong, and other reformers were ignorant of this history, or that they may have had some inkling of it but willfully ignored or obscured it to suit their institutional purposes. For it was in this era of the Social Gospel that reformers like Pratt and Armstrong were heavily invested in the supposed "radical" quality of their Americanizing programs. As such, the existence or efficacy of any previous efforts to Christianize the nation's indigenous populations was disavowed, either wittingly or not. Their brand of education was geared toward the newer demands of an industrializing labor market, and thus mere proselytizing for the sake of spiritual salvation was no longer sufficient in itself; further justification was required, especially when public funding was used. The indigenous students who attended the newfangled boarding schools of the Gilded Age required a "useful" education that would lead toward full industrial proletarianization, something that earlier missionaries had not accomplished.

In 1882, three years after founding the Carlisle School in Carlisle, Pennsylvania, Pratt hired a local photographer named John Choate to take before-and-after portraits of one of Carlisle's indigenous students, the Navajo Tom Torlino (figs. 35, 36). The founding of Carlisle with an act of Congress in 1879 was also part of the larger trend in American politics during the Gilded Age, in which some Washington political elites saw transformational institutions like boarding schools as politically viable and expedient means by which to assimilate what they perceived to be the nation's cultural and racial margins. This improvement was conceived in varying terms, from racial to spiritual. In this sense, these images representationally stage the Christianization of Native American youths, while likening these racial and spiritual Others to an assumed Anglicized norm.

The images of Tom Torlino, symbolic of Carlisle's transformative mission, purport to show the "savage" and thus "heathen" young man upon entering the Carlisle School, and then the "civilized" and therefore "saved" young man in the photo taken three years later. The subsequent reproduction of the images as a pair in official school publications was intended to connote Torlino's social improvement and bioracial evolution and to communicate this improvement to readers. This was an important function, as the readers were most commonly the members of Congress who allocated funding to the school. Also important for Pratt were the private donors and prominent members of the local community who otherwise may have been unnerved by the presence of such "savages" in their midst. The before-and-after portraits of Torlino are only one example of this representational trope, which became a staple of the aesthetic strategies deployed by Pratt and other boarding school leaders. With this polarized vision of Torlino's appearance, viewers were encouraged to read the images, printed side by side, as a sort of evolution from one to the other. Such a perception was critical to gaining financial and political support for the school's mission of salvation. According to Adams, such efforts on the part of Pratt and others were apparently successful, as funding for federal boarding schools increased dramatically between 1877 and 1900, despite the fact that actual graduation rates remained relatively low.[12]

Beyond the well-known ethnographic aims of these photos, they also invoke a mystical aesthetic by insisting upon the occurrence of a seemingly miraculous spiritual uplift. Choate used harder studio lighting in the "after" image to give Torlino's skin a lighter appearance. This manipulation of lighting and studio props, combined with Torlino's inevitably altered physical appearance, created a convenient political argument in visual form that Carlisle's program was an effective alternative in solving the troubling Indian question. The photos can be taken as a sign of Torlino's cultural whitewashing and racial integration, but also as a sign of his spiritual enlightenment and salvation.

Pratt seemed to sense the representational power of such images, which would become a staple at Carlisle and other indigenous boarding schools. This power included an appeal to Christian groups, as he indicated in a letter written in April 1880 to Secretary of the Interior Carl Schurz. In it he discusses his desire to recruit Navajo students like Torlino. He was eager to include them in Carlisle's population because he saw the tribe as amenable to the school's industrial training due to their prior knowledge of metalworking and other skills. Further, he tells Schurz that many Navajos would be suited to the school's famous Outing program, during which they would work and live with local families in the region, the Cumberland Valley of central Pennsylvania. As the Navajos had already been practitioners of Christianity, due in part to the work of waves of Christian missionaries, Pratt tells Schurz that the residents of Carlisle, living in a "Presbyterian Valley," as he puts it, would enthusiastically contribute to this missionary work, thereby complementing the school's religious training.[13]

If we wish to understand the Torlino images and others like them as evangelical in addition to social evolutionary, we need to consider the context of its making at Carlisle. Pratt had contradictory attitudes toward the role of religion in the processes of assimilation. As Jacqueline Fear-Segal has noted, Pratt did at times publicly criticize the work of missionaries, seeing their methods as too permissive and lacking in industrial efficiency.[14] Besides spiritual transformation, another aspect of Carlisle's program was full proletarianizing of the student for market purposes. This becomes overt in images such as figure 37, by the documentary photographer Frances Benjamin Johnston during her visit to the campus in 1901. Here Johnston gives us one of her famous classroom images, which Pratt staged for publication in school catalogues to impress donors and potential backers. The value of labor is highlighted in the composition, in the form of a large mantra pasted onto the wall. Importantly, a portrait of Pratt, overseeing his charges in absentia, is visible just below the words, and the class teacher sits at the piano just below his portrait. The seemingly compliant students sit in dutiful, almost prayer-like poses, hands obediently resting on laps, the young women apparently overawed by this display of symbolic power and entranced by the model students at the front of the room engaged in what appears to be a debate.

They seem willing participants in their indoctrination into the system of industrial labor then prevalent in the nation.

As I and other historians have noted, the docile appearance of the students in Johnston's photographs of Carlisle are as much a by-product of her technical methods as anything. Johnston used large-format cameras with large glass plate negatives. As the camera required a tripod and the plates required an exposure of multiple seconds, students needed to be instructed in their posing to have the images appear as intended.

Despite Pratt's ambivalence and his insistence on functional education above and beyond strict evangelism, the school did in fact incorporate religious instruction. While the weekdays at Carlisle were taken up by nonsectarian work training and academic classes, evenings and Sundays were a time of biblical instruction, sermonizing, and prayer. These programs were conducted by the school in conjunction with local clergy, who offered their churches as spaces for the students' moral uplift. Pratt allowed for a nondenominational chapel on campus as well as a chapter of the Young Men's Christian Association (YMCA).[15]

The word "evangelical," in the context of the Social Gospel, may be read in the traditional or literal Christian sense but also, as mentioned earlier, in a more secular sense as well. According to the precepts of the Social Gospel as enacted at schools like Carlisle, to be evangelized meant to be transformed in a totalized sense and not just spiritually. Thus we may say that Carlisle and Hampton were somewhat secularized evangelical institutions bent on making Americans out of those perceived to be less than American. This drive to make Americans, while clearly a political aim, may more precisely be said to be nationalistic, bourgeois, and yet universalizing. Throughout his career Pratt spoke of the values bestowed on Carlisle students as if they were unproblematic and indisputable in their appropriateness and applicability, as if they were biblical verse. Likewise assumed was the supposed "degeneracy" of the students in their pre-assimilation state: "The day of real progress for the Indian will begin when each Indian becomes an *individual* and an *organized unit* in himself to make the most of himself that he can. One of the greatest hindrances to the Indian in his transit from barbarism to civilization is his entire exclusion from the experiences of practical civilized life."[16]

Armstrong harbored similar ideas regarding race and assimilation. He was born in Hawaii in 1839, the son of two missionaries working with the American Missionary Association (AMA). Fear-Segal points out that Armstrong had two overriding ideas regarding race as applied to his pedagogical ambitions. First, he perceived non-Anglo races as being culturally and evolutionarily "backward," which he would have absorbed via cultural osmosis, as pseudoscientific ideas regarding race dated back centuries in both the United States and Europe. Speaking of a hierarchy that reminds one of Blumenbach's craniological categorizations, Armstrong once said the following regarding African Americans and Native Americans: "These people, who are with us and with whom we share a common fate, are a thousand years behind us in moral and mental development. Substantially the two races (Negro and Indian) are in the same condition, and the question as to what education is best for them, and how such education is to be put within their reach, is pressing itself closely upon all thinking men and women."[17]

Not only does Armstrong perceive African Americans and Native Americans as lagging millennia behind Anglo-Americans in evolutionary terms, but in this quote and elsewhere he conflates their identities. He also would add native Hawaiians to the mix, seeing all three groups as akin in this sense. It is also significant that Armstrong conflates their state of mental development with a lack of moral development, both of which he sought to remedy through a program of enforced labor at Hampton. Conveniently for him, the lack of moral development inherent in these races demanded the inclusion of this compulsory labor at the school and greatly assisted him in keeping Hampton afloat financially, as the school could not afford a large maintenance staff during its early years. Thus the "immorality" of the students fed into the financial need of the institution.[18]

Armstrong felt that given the "child-like" and "slow" students at Hampton, a curriculum that emphasized both religious and moral training as well as coursework in relatively simple and useful trades best suited their needs. Thus in documentary photographs made at the school, we see such activities emphasized. Figure 38, taken by Johnston in 1899 while on assignment at Hampton, shows very young children already being taught basic domestic skills. Johnston places the camera at eye level with the children, so that the female instructor, the doors, and the shelves in the background tower over the students. Such a composition offers a becoming metaphor for Armstrong's racial ideology, as the students are here *made* child-like and in need of moral and intellectual guidance. This image also encapsulates the type of skills Armstrong wished to emphasize at Hampton—those of a proletarian nature—given his view of the evolutionarily retarded status of all members of these races, regardless of age. The domineering presence of the teacher within the composition is typical of another aesthetic trope common to images at both Hampton and Carlisle, what I have previously called the "overseer" trope: here the students are surveilled both by the off-site future viewer of the photograph and by the "overseer" within the image. This is a simple yet important perspective, as Armstrong and his successor at Hampton, Hollis Burke Frissell, needed to remind donors of the constant guidance being given to these students with inferior racial makeup and thus poor character traits. As he put it in "Lessons from the Hawaiian Islands," "The negro and the Polynesian have many striking similarities. Of both it is true that not mere ignorance, but deficiency of character is the chief difficulty, and that to build up character is the true objective point of education."[19]

In correspondence over the years, Pratt praised Armstrong for his work in uplifting subaltern populations, a mission that would inspire Pratt to found Carlisle. In addition to his position at

Hampton, like Pratt, Armstrong was an army officer who cut his professional teeth during the Civil War. He became the founder of the Hampton Institute in 1868 and a leading member of the AMA, an evangelical abolitionist group that sought to educate and assimilate Native American and African American youths in the wake of the war.

The two men would strike up a friendship over the years, and Pratt's structuring of the curriculum at Carlisle would be heavily influenced by Armstrong's ideas at Hampton. Pratt first met Armstrong after he had been assigned to clear the frontier of remaining indigenous resistors after the Civil War, when the federal government's attention shifted to the western frontier. The Fort Laramie Treaty of 1868 provided for the establishment of tribal and intertribal reservations on which the indigenous peoples of the nation's interior were supposed to dwell. Keeping them on the designated reservations was important not only for the laying of new rail lines across the frontier, but also because of the new property relations mandated by the Fort Laramie Treaty and the later Dawes Act of 1887. Pratt and other officers were charged with enforcing the treaty and ensuring that violators of the terms would be punished, usually by imprisonment. Most such violators were sent to Fort Sill, a military prison located within the Indian Territories, or what would eventually become the state of Oklahoma. In 1875 the federal government ordered Pratt to transport the most hardened resistors to Fort Marion, Florida (the former Castillo de San Marcos in Saint Augustine), with the aim of cutting their tribal ties and diminishing their influence on the frontier.[20]

While at Fort Marion, Pratt's thinking about the Indian question began to evolve. He firmly believed that his prisoners could in fact be transformed in multiple respects from their assumed state of savagery to that of a civilized American citizen. Pratt began to repeatedly photograph the prisoners with the purpose of establishing the veracity of his new ideas and reeducation programs, in which the prisoners were taught various "industries" designed to punish but also reform them. Both practices would later become integral for his programs at Carlisle.

Thus, while he had the prisoners at the fort, Pratt had them dress in paramilitary uniform and execute military marches and drills. In addition, he had them learn various skills, such as archery and shell polishing, so that upon their release they would have the means to make a living in the mainstream of American society. Always one for publicity, Pratt hired photographers to come to the fort and photograph the prisoners. In figure 39 Pratt even posed himself, his wife, and his young children, apparently to convince viewers of his trust in the character of his newly civilized charges, who are in uniform. Interesting as well is how the prisoners have dutifully removed their caps, making their faces more visible to the camera, a tacit acknowledgment of the surveillance that was important to the maintenance of order at Fort Marion. In this instance Pratt's intended audiences would have been elected officials and bureaucrats in Washington with whom he was regularly corresponding. He hoped that in producing such images, he might eventually win their favor in the establishment of a more permanent educational institution, funded by the federal government.[21]

In his autobiography, *Battlefield and Classroom*, Pratt describes his acquaintance with Armstrong. While Pratt had considered furthering the "improvement" of his prisoners prior to making Armstrong's acquaintance, it was Armstrong's missionary work at Hampton that would come to complement his own thinking, as the program at Hampton accomplished both evangelization and proletarianization simultaneously. Ms. Mather, one of Pratt's instructors at Fort Marion, introduced the two men, and in a series of letters Pratt eventually convinced Armstrong to take on some of the prisoners at Hampton, which had been established several years earlier. Pratt relays that upon their meeting he and Armstrong "talked much about the future of these young men and the need for them to become Americanized." In a related anecdote, while reminiscing about his first few days at Hampton after arriving with the prisoners, Pratt emphasizes the institutional power backing his and Armstrong's brand of Americanization: "I remained with the prisoners at Hampton for a few days. During that time we visited Fort Monroe at Old Point, where we went through the then-strong fortifications, and also the Norfolk Navy Yard, where we were shown through one of our largest naval war vessels. *Everything impressed the white man's power upon the Indians, particularly the 20-inch gun in Fort Monroe then being tested at long-range firing and into the mouth of which a boy of eight years might crawl*" (emphasis added).[22]

Pratt was both a social reformer and a career military man. As the title of his autobiography implies, he saw a conceptual linkage between the marshal combat on the frontier and the educational processes in the classrooms of the boarding schools. Throughout the autobiography Pratt draws unsettling analogies such as the one just quoted. The industrialization of Christian assimilation during the Gilded Age was highly institutionalized, to the point of being militant, as it existed as both an alternative to and a mirror of the physical and cultural massacres that were then occurring on the frontier. It also echoed the larger desire for the establishment of a Christian American Empire both domestically and, in the next century, globally.

In order to fully understand Pratt's enthusiasm for Armstrong's program at Hampton, it will be helpful to briefly consider the founding of the institution, which was financed largely by the American Missionary Association. The AMA, which was incorporated in 1849, played the central role in chartering Hampton in 1868. As such, from its origin Hampton was conceptualized as an explicitly evangelical institution, with the spiritual training and transformation of the student imbuing the curriculum. This is stated clearly in the constitution of the AMA, which was drafted at the time of the organization's incorporation. Article II states, "The object of this Association shall be to conduct Christian missionary and educational operations, and to diffuse a knowledge of the Holy Scriptures, in our own and other countries which are destitute of them, or which present open and urgent fields of effort."[23] Article III describes the ideal candidate for membership: "Any person of evangelical sentiments*, who professes faith in the Lord Jesus Christ, who is not a slaveholder, or in the practice of other immoralities, and who contributes to the funds, may become a member of the Society; and by the payment of thirty dollars, a life member."[24]

The asterisk appearing after the term "evangelical sentiments" leads to a footnote at the bottom of the page that defines "evangelical" for the reader, presumably either an AMA member or a prospective member, and pertains directly to the style of pedagogy practiced at Hampton: "By evangelical sentiments, we understand, among others, a belief in the guilty and lost condition of all men without a Savior; the Supreme Deity, Incarnation and Atoning Sacrifice of Jesus Christ, the only Savior of the world; the necessity of regeneration by the Holy Spirit, repentance, faith, and holy obedience, in order to achieve salvation, the Immortality of the Soul; and the retributions in the judgement in the eternal punishment of the wicked, and salvation of the righteous."[25]

One may see in the AMA constitution the driving force behind the Hampton project. Support for the social and evangelical experiment undertaken at Hampton was not only broad-based geographically but also in terms of denomination. Thus moral and financial support came from many quarters, which is significant given that the founding and early years of Hampton coincided with the Reconstruction era in the South. One may therefore sense a larger symbolic mission that was not only spiritual but also political, as Hampton represented an opportunity to promote and exhibit a newly unified national agenda in the wake of the Civil War.

In fact, despite its location in the Tidewater region, many of Hampton's early supporters constituted a veritable roll call of northeastern political, social, and economic elites. This may be seen in a letter sent to Armstrong and collectively signed by a large group of contributors who, "being interested in Indian Education," requested that he travel to New York to give "an account of [his]

184   *The Social Gospel*

efforts in this direction at the rooms of the Chamber of Commerce." Among the signatories were the financier J. P. Morgan, the former New York governor and presidential candidate Samuel J. Tilden, and Whitelaw Reid, a powerful journalist, editor, and future vice presidential candidate.[26]

Pratt writes to Armstrong to inform him of the strong support coming from the AMA and leaders of a variety of Christian denominations. Referring to the good wishes from the Episcopal Church, Pratt says, "A long letter from Bp. Whipple, only expresses his strong feelings of the progress of Christ's kingdom and the opinions he has on the Indian Dept. Transfer problem. . . . I am praying for you today. If God wants it so, it will come."[27]

Such evangelical comments are common in letters between Pratt and Armstrong, as both were engaging in what they saw as obligatory works of Christian charity by founding their schools. Here Pratt mixes these evangelical references, such as "it will come," referring to "Christ's kingdom," with banal procedural concerns, such as the "transfer problem," referring to the transfer of students to and from Hampton. In another letter to Armstrong, Pratt even claims that a group of young Lakota students he was escorting to Hampton from the Dakota Territory had "pledged to speed their own salvation on your basis of applications to duty and to hard work,"[28] referring to the rigorous paramilitary curriculum at the schools.

These letters have a provocative visual echo in an 1899 photograph taken by Johnston (fig. 40) when she was hired by Armstrong's successor at Hampton, the Reverend Hollis Burke Frissell, to execute this and similar images, some of which would serve as visual documents for Hampton's didactic exhibition on racial evolution at the Universal Exposition in Paris in 1900 as well as the Pan-American exhibition in Buffalo in 1901.[29] The photo displays her characteristic composition and naturalistic lighting, which she would also use at Carlisle in 1901 on assignment for Pratt. Two Hampton students rigidly face the camera in a restrained stoic pose; they wear the familiar paramilitary uniforms and flank a taxidermied bald eagle behind a table upon which an open Bible is present. Here Johnston visualizes the agenda of the boarding school in one compositionally simple yet conceptually dense image, aligning the two students with signifiers of nationalism, worship, and natural history.

With this evangelical agenda in mind, Armstrong and the AMA successfully directed public perception of the school's mission and programs. It is therefore hardly surprising to read the following characterization of education at Hampton, written by Sarah Eden Smith in an article for the *Boston Evening Transcript* following Smith's visit to the campus in 1884: "But however poetic may be our idea of the untutored grace and beauty of the Indian maiden in her native home, I think no one could seriously hesitate to give the preference to the intelligent Christian womanhood into which so many of these young girls are growing under the guidance of Ms. Eustis and her faithful assistants."[30]

In this passage from her article on visual arts training at Hampton, Smith is referring to the pedagogy of Ms. Eustis, one of Armstrong's instructors. She deploys tropes common at the time and essential to the framing of public perception of the supposed successes of boarding school curriculum. Thus she juxtaposes "untutored grace" with "intelligent Christian womanhood," the implication being that the broadly advertised social evolution wrought by Hampton's pedagogy was indeed effective in uplifting the previously "untutored" Indian into a greater sense of Christian enlightenment. This statement is, in effect, a rhetorical analogue to the before-and-after photographs so critical to the propagation of the missions undertaken at Carlisle and Hampton.

Apparently Smith, like many others, was not well versed in the various and complex histories of Anglo-indigenous cultural and spiritual exchange. The excerpt raises questions about the writer's perception and knowledge of Native Americans more broadly at this time. One is given to wondering what idea Smith had of the students' "native home," as she describes it in the passage. Even placing distant history aside, it was increasingly apparent that during this era (the mid-1880s) most Native Americans, or at least the students at the boarding schools, had been placed onto reservations en masse, via either direct force or treaty. These reservations were commonly staffed by religious officials who were granted access to the tribes by the federal government in an effort to Christianize any remaining "heathen" Indians.[31] It is curious that Smith, and many others, would continue to insist upon a polarizing dichotomy between what Pratt termed the "blanket Indian" and the more evolved "civilized" Indian.

In light of Smith's analysis of the culture at Hampton, it is helpful to recall that like Pratt, Armstrong and his successors at Hampton sought visualizations of the efficacy of the school's mission. Images such as figure 41, a reproduced print, commonly graced the covers of issues of the *Southern Workman*, the official school newspaper. We see a young "maiden" who appears to be African American, looking knowingly out at the viewer as she literally and metaphorically ascends a staircase leading to the entrance of a neoclassical building. Such metaphors of ascent and passage, from one realm into another, were important at Carlisle and Hampton. The young girl is well dressed and inhabits a natural environment that is climatically hostile, as she is pelted by rain and windblown. She seems unconcerned, however, as she shields herself with an umbrella and gives us a glance of assurance as she is about to enter the protective structure a few steps ahead.

While the girl appears to be African American and not indigenous, it is important to recall Armstrong's racial theories. Armstrong was known for publicly stating his contention that both races were substantially alike in terms of mental inclination and overall character and that both being "child-like" posed identical problems to the reformer who wished to have them educated and assimilated. Thus we may safely assume that the images used at Hampton, which sometimes depict African Americans and sometimes Native Americans, are conceptually applicable to both groups, at least in Armstrong's eyes.[32]

This provocative image takes on an evangelical tone when one considers it in relation to a poem printed on the first page of the same issue, authored by a writer identified as Helen W. Ludlow, who was on the paper's editorial staff. The poem is entitled "On the Threshold," which refers to the scene shown on the cover. The first stanza reads:

Standing—waiting—on the threshold—
Half in hope, and half in fear—
For the Temple gates to open
Of the strange, the glad New Year.[33]

The stanza nicely complements the image. It characterizes the girl's journey, significantly, as passive rather than proactive. She "stands" and "waits" for the "gates to open" rather than opening them herself. Also, her destination is defined metaphorically, as a "Temple" with a capital "T." Such a reference in the context of Hampton, and of evangelical institutions more broadly, can best be taken as quasi-biblical and otherworldly. The Temple in this sense would be the favored New Jerusalem of American evangelical discourse as well as full assimilation into the mainstream of American social life. The reference to the "glad New Year" may be taken on two levels, one literal, the other more figurative. This particular issue was the January 1879 issue, thus the line refers to the temporal moment. However, given the image's evangelical overtones, it may also refer to spiritual time, the dawning of a new consciousness and life for the girl, or alternately the dawning of a new millennium, in which all peoples are being prepared for the Second Coming via Christian indoctrination.

Perhaps the most famous image of Hampton from this era (fig. 42), *Stairway to Treasurer's Residence: Students at Work*, was included in what would become the *Hampton Album*, republished and annotated by John Szarkowski and Lincoln Kirstein under the auspices of the Museum of Modern Art in 1966. While Szarkowski and Kirstein saw the undeniable aesthetic quality in Johnston's Hampton images, the photographs were originally intended for display in the American pavilion of the Universal Exposition in

Paris in 1900 and to illustrate the Hampton catalogue of 1899–1900.[34] Szarkowski was apparently so taken by the composition that he selected it to be on the cover of the republished catalogue.

In her now iconic image, Johnston depicts several male students diligently at work renovating an attractive staircase inside the house used as a residence by the school's treasurer Alexander Purvis. As in many of her boarding school images, the figures appear to be rigidly posed rather than caught in the midst of real action, as no blurring is visible. This clarity would have been technically difficult to accomplish otherwise because of Johnston's use of large-scale glass plates and a large-format camera.[35] Indeed the aesthetic clarity of the image is the key here, as in much of Johnston's work. It serves to make the image appear iconic (rather than indexical) by abstracting the "reality" being depicted.[36]

The "static, majestic calm which pervades" the images of the album causes one to contemplate images individually, outside of the rush of time, and dwell on the profundity and monumentality of the change seen within. In other words, these images, while intended to "document," also abstract the actuality of life at the schools in favor of a stillborn aesthetic quality that stands for assimilationist ideology more generally.[37] Johnston arranges the students in a hierarchy, from the ground floor up to the landing. In a word, elevation prevails. And perhaps further elevation awaits, as the sharp light coming from the window on the left illuminates the upper level of the staircase, which leads to the private rooms of Hampton's treasurer. In fact the body of the young man on the ground floor at center right conforms to the shape of the railing he constructs. As in figure 37, here too we might say "labor conquers all things."

And yet although Johnston's images from both institutions emphasize the role of labor in the curricula, we must consider how "labor" was being defined at Carlisle and Hampton. It is clear from repeated public pronouncements and publications that both Pratt and Armstrong wished to inculcate the Protestant work ethic into their charges and that, as Weber notes, their conception of labor included moral and spiritual uplift. As Armstrong phrased it in the text of a catalogue commemorating his time at Hampton:

> The thing to be done was clear: to train selected Negro youth who should go out and teach and lead their people, first by example, by getting land and homes; to give them not a dollar that they could earn for themselves; to teach respect for labor, to replace stupid drudgery with skilled hands; and to these ends, to build up an industrial system, for the sake not only of self-support and intelligent labor, but also for the sake of character. . . . It cannot pay in the *money* way, but it will pay in a *moral* way; especially with the freedman. It will make them men and women as nothing else will. It is the only way to make them good Christians.[38]

For Armstrong labor was not merely a skill or a means of bread-winning but a moral imperative, bringing the practitioner closer to Christ. His emphasis on "moral" payment over "money" payment is indicative of his conception of labor, at least as pertaining to Hampton students. It would make them more "moral," presumably as compared to their inherent racial characteristics as well as the culture of their "primitive" ancestors, and yet they should not expect monetary compensation. This bespeaks Armstrong's vision of a proletarianized versus a professionalized workforce being turned out by Hampton, which is logical considering his views of race.[39]

His views are also convenient from a fiduciary perspective. What figure 37 reveals, perhaps unwittingly and in addition to its obvious intent, was the presence of de facto slave labor on the Hampton campus. Under Armstrong, the school administration controlled its budgetary outlays by using students to maintain the grounds and engage in other mundane, day-to-day tasks, which they would otherwise have had to contract out for, and also melded seamlessly with the "academic" curriculum. Thus all such moralizing speech on Armstrong's part may likewise be read as rhetorical cover for Hampton's institutional hypocrisy: the very institution supposedly dedicated to the liberation of the freedman and the Native American was one at which the economic relations

The Social Gospel

between the social classes and racial groups that defined serfdom were virtually replicated. Armstrong's comment in a *Southern Workman* article from 1876 takes on a more sinister quality from this perspective: "The Indians are grown up children; we are a thousand years ahead of them in the line of progress."[40]

Johnston was originally hired by Frissell to produce a series of platinum prints on the school's campus beginning in late 1899. Correspondence between Johnston and Cara Folsom, a teacher on staff and editor of *Southern Workman*, indicates that she and her assistants were involved with doing photographic work for Hampton for several years. In addition to setting up dates for jobs to be executed, the correspondence contains extensive invoices by Johnston to Hampton, and the costs are substantial for the time. In one set of invoices Johnston lists the final price for the photographs for the Paris exposition as nearly one thousand dollars.[41] Her resulting images are wide-ranging in terms of composition and subject matter but generally show the beauty of the campus and the activities in which the students were engaged. In this sense, her job there was similar to that done for Pratt at Carlisle in 1901: to document the efficacy of the curriculum in uplifting the students and to prove that the technique of environmental immersion was effective for civilization, salvation, and the more practical goal of industrial training.

With these images and the accompanying display at Paris, Hampton's new superintendent, Frissell, collaborated with the African American educators Booker T. Washington and Thomas Julius Calloway on a project that they hoped would show to the world the progress made by black Americans in the wake of emancipation a generation earlier. That the idea of social evolution and its proof was important to Calloway, an African American attorney and education activist, is indicated in a letter to Washington, founder of the famous Tuskegee Institute in Alabama:

> To the Paris Exposition, however, thousands upon thousands of them will go and a well selected and prepared exhibit, representing

the Negro's development in his churches, his schools, his homes, his farms, his stores, his professions and pursuits in general will attract attention as did the exhibits at Atlanta and Nashville Expositions, and do a great and lasting good in convincing thinking people of the possibilities of the Negro. . . . Not only will foreigners be impressed, but hundreds of white Americans will be far more convinced by what they see there than what they see, or can see, every day in this country, but fail to give us credit for.[42]

Calloway's view of the efficacy of the exhibitions at Paris is very significant, as he was named director of the Negro Educational Exhibit for the federal government's official commission on the organization of the Paris Exposition.[43] For Calloway, Johnston's photographs were enhancements or supplements that would improve upon what "white Americans" could see in their daily lives. This supports the interpretation of Johnston's Hampton images as primarily *symbolic* in their aesthetic functioning, as in their pristine clarity and stillness they decontextualize visual bits from life at Hampton, which was anything but ideal for most students, who worked and studied under economic duress.

Despite Calloway's and Washington's apparent enthusiasm for Johnston's photographs, correspondence indicates that Calloway originally had desired that an actual physical demonstration of Hampton's teaching methods be presented at the Exposition. This possibility was denied by Frissell, who in a letter to Calloway explained that due to logistical limitations, Johnston's images would suffice: "I think it had better be understood that Hampton's work shall be presented only by its photographs, which I think are going to be extremely good."[44] Frissell believed in the aesthetic persuasiveness and the efficiency of photographs to effectively convey the ideology of boarding school education, seeing them as legitimate stand-ins for the real thing.

On a further note regarding the function and circulation of Johnston's photographs, Frissell's correspondence indicates a willingness to have them widely circulated not only in Hampton

The Social Gospel

publications and at the Exposition but in the emerging mass media throughout the United States. It seems that he wished to attain a larger following for the school, hoping to reach out beyond the ordinary boarding school constituencies of elite donors, similar to what Pratt had in mind at Carlisle. In one letter Frissell encouraged Johnston in her request to use prints of her negatives for publication in the magazine *World's Work*, which in 1900 was a new mass-printed magazine focusing on commerce, agriculture, and industry.[45] In another letter to Johnston, Frissell expresses his eagerness to circulate the prints, stating, "We wish to allow you any liberty in the use of the pictures which is not in conflict with the best interests of the school."[46]

In other letters written to Albert Shaw, who at the time was the editor of the magazine *Review of Reviews*, Frissell offered to let Shaw have prints of Johnston's negatives "free of charge" in exchange for an article on Hampton to be published in the *Review*. He urges Shaw in another letter to share images Shaw had used for the *Review* article with the editor of *The Christian at Work*, a magazine financed by the Christian at Work Association. This would seem to indicate the appeal of Johnston's images to Christian readers, who would likely have perceived moral virtues being bestowed upon the students, therefore legitimizing Hampton's evangelical underpinnings.[47]

At the Paris Exposition, Johnston had significant control over the selection and installation of the Hampton photographs, as well as that of twenty-eight other female photographers whose work was represented in the American pavilion. Johnston's photographs were housed in a section called "The Palace of Social Economy of American Negro Exhibition." Although the images made by Johnston came from a private institution, their larger symbolic function was to display the efficacy of U.S. government policy in relation to race, as well as fulfilling Frissell, Washington, and Calloway's desire to prove the ascent of the African American since emancipation to potentially skeptical international audiences. Such a perception was desired by officialdom throughout the country, in both the public and the private sector, as a sort of face-saving gesture. Race relations in the country in the wake of Reconstruction were often mired in violence and overt bigotry. To counteract these problems, both governmental and nongovernmental agencies established homogenizing institutions like Hampton and Carlisle to assimilate the indigenous and black students to the assumed "norms" of Anglo-American life. Evangelism and industrial training were commonly seen as fundamental to such efforts, and Johnston's images were used to signify their viability in practice.[48]

Frissell was eager to depict property ownership by prosperous Hampton graduates, which would indicate the success of Hampton's pedagogy. Johnston therefore included numerous photographs that displayed the apparent material largesse of some former Hampton students and juxtaposed these with photographs purporting to depict the living conditions of African Americans who had not had the benefit of Hampton's pedagogy (figs. 43, 44). In an essay he wrote for the *Southern Workman*, Frissell related his plan for the installation of Johnston's works at Paris, putting special emphasis on the before-and-after images:

> The exhibition which Hampton is preparing to send to the Paris Exposition emphasizes the importance placed by the school authorities on the training of the *Indians and Negro* in the arts that pertain to home and farm life. It will consist in a series of pictures showing the relation of the various subjects in the school's curriculum to the central one of agriculture. . . . *It is part of the plan of the exhibit to contrast the new life among the Negroes and Indians to the old, and then show how Hampton has helped to produce the change.* The old-time one room cabin and the old mule with his rope harness . . . will be contrasted with the comfortable home of the Hampton graduate. . . . The Indian tipi of the past, too, with all that it meant of nomadic life, will be contrasted with the fixed abode of the young Indian farmer. (emphasis added)[49]

When paired, these images echo the before-and-after trope deployed by Choate at Carlisle in the 1880s. The point is for the

The Social Gospel

exhibition viewer to perceive a seemingly "miraculous" social, cultural, and economic evolution between the paired images. Such a "miraculous evolution" was in keeping with the dual ideologies at Hampton: the sanctification of the student as well as his or her social evolution. Thus in the first photograph we see the "primitive" southern black, lodged in poverty, ignorance, and social isolation. In the second we see hygienic, assimilated blacks attentively looking out at the camera, inhabiting a cleansed environment of orderly exteriors and manicured yards. In both cases we see the eerie stillness for which Johnston's images are most well-known, lending them simultaneously a clear documentary quality and a sense of artifice. Given the technical limitations under which Johnston worked on this series, the photographer had to pose her subjects. Nevertheless, according to Frissell and others, Johnston's work for the Exposition was effective, as he accepted them as viable two-dimensional stand-ins for actual exhibits.[50]

Interesting as well in Frissell's commentary on the images is his apparent lack of understanding of indigenous history, a lack he shared with many whites of his generation. He invokes the "tipi versus adobe" cliché, which from a historical perspective is a false dichotomy. Indigenous peoples, ranging from the Anasazi to the Mississippian, had established permanent fixed settlements centuries before the arrival of European missionaries, for instance in Chaco Canyon and Cahokia. By the turn of the twentieth century, when Frissell and others commentated on Native history, these sites had long since been rediscovered and excavated by archaeologists. Such sites were commonly either abandoned out of environmental necessity or destroyed by Europeans wishing to erase indigenous culture. But many pre-Columbian peoples not only hunted and gathered but mastered advanced agricultural techniques in advance of being "taught" them by Europeans centuries later.

Frissell was most concerned with the perceived morality of the photographs' subjects. It was important that Johnston's subjects, especially in the "after" shots, be perceived as obedient and docile. This is indicated in letters he wrote in which he discussed both

Johnston's work and the aims of the exhibition. In one letter to Calloway, he discusses census data that he claims indicate the relative success of Hampton graduates when compared to other African Americans, and then explains the role of the exhibition in proving these contentions:

> The state of Virginia shows, as you are undoubtedly aware, a great increase in the amount of real estate owned by colored people. . . . The census report shows this increase to be one third . . . showing the increase in property in certain counties and the consequent decrease in crime. . . . If the matter could be *properly worked up* it would not only be of advantage to show in Paris, but of very great value in answering the statements that are frequently made in regard to the futility of Negro education. (emphasis added)[51]

Frissell was greatly concerned with the perception of African Americans and Native Americans as being "criminally" inclined, a widespread pseudoscientific view during the Gilded Age. For him, the Anglo-American cultural convention of property ownership was a silver bullet of sorts that proved the higher moral state of the subject, thus his need for Johnston's before-and-after property images at the Exposition. His fixation with attaching Christian morality to property ownership is elaborated in his next sentences: "It is very clearly demonstrable that where Hampton graduates have gone the character of those communities have changed greatly for the better. A report for instance of Gloucester County (Virginia) as showing the improvement in schools, churches, moral character and land holding, would be good."[52]

Again, "land holding" and "moral character" plus "improvement" in schools and churches are all apparently measurable and necessarily interwoven in Frissell's view. Questions of what exactly constitutes "moral character" are of course assumed, but given the times and what we know about both Armstrong's and Frissell's legacies at Hampton, it may be said to coincide with middle-class Anglo-American norms of the day, at least as pertaining to acquisitiveness.

Architecture too was employed at the expositions, either within images or as real space, to signify ascent and progress at the boarding school of the Gilded Age. The education historian Marinella Lentis offers a stimulating interpretation of the setup of boarding school exhibition pavilions at world's fairs during this period. Lentis argues that the architectural layout of the Carlisle pavilion at the Pan-American Exposition in Buffalo in 1901 indicates such an agenda on the part of Pratt as well as the organizers of the fair. Visitors had to walk through a large, ritualistic gateway to enter a series of two interconnected exhibition rooms, passing from a display of the "primitive" pre-assimilation indigenous culture to a display of the "civilized" effects of boarding school education. Lentis suggests that this gateway was deliberately placed to be a conspicuous yet subtle architectural and evolutionary borderline between the two rooms and between two evolutionary phases of indigenous development.[53]

Such architectural structures were often echoed in boarding school imagery and may be seen as a conceptual or aesthetic reiteration of the "passage" trope seen in figure 41, *On the Threshold*. All tropes of this sort, whether executed in imagery, in rhetoric, or in architectural spaces, were intended to convey the sense of positivistic evolutionary development supposedly occurring at the schools, which carried coded racial messages regarding the students and their perceived shortcomings as members of Other races.

While it is tempting to see this ideology as monolithic, it was by no means unchallenged in the country during the Gilded Age. The historian W. E. B. Du Bois (1868–1963) was its most prominent critic. Du Bois, a professor at Atlanta University and founder of the National Association for the Advancement of Colored People (NAACP), opposed the educational model advocated by Washington, Frissell, Calloway, and others. He focused his critique on what he called "industrial education," associating it with Washington's call for "conciliation of the South" and his "submission and silence as to civil and political rights." Du Bois was referring to the Atlanta Compromise of 1895, an agreement struck between Washington and his supporters in the black community and the white leadership of the South. The central tenet of the agreement was that African Americans would receive basic education and due process under the law and would be afforded economic opportunity, and in return they would not agitate for civil rights. In contrast, Du Bois and his followers favored political activism and insisted on civil rights in addition to economic development. Most notably, Du Bois took aim at what he saw as Washington's philosophy of "adjustment and submission": "Mr. Washington represents in Negro thought the old attitude of adjustment and submission; but adjustment at such a peculiar time as to make his programme unique. This is an age of unusual economic development, and Mr. Washington's programme naturally takes an economic cast, becoming a gospel of Work and Money to such an extent as apparently almost to completely overshadow the higher aims of life. . . . Mr. Washington's programme accepts the alleged inferiority of the Negro races."[54]

In his criticism of Washington's program, and by extension that of the evangelical boarding schools more broadly, Du Bois senses that Washington's sense of "liberation" is wrought at the price of social and political justice as well as higher economic gain. As mentioned previously, Pratt, Armstrong, Frissell, Washington, and other reformers of the era sought proletarianization over economic autonomy or higher education, despite the fact that this era enjoyed rapid technological and economic change and thus greater opportunity.

As we have seen, the evolutionary developmentalism advocated by the schools and targeted by Du Bois in his criticism was established rhetorically and aesthetically in many ways. The context of Torlino's portraits, as well as that of other boarding school images, has a long history in American visual culture. The association of spiritual salvation with a Europeanized physiology and the "proper" bearing that accompanies it has long been a visual linchpin in the evangelical ambitions of New World spiritualists, dating back to colonial Puritan settlements (figs. 3, 4). In more modern images, such as those of Johnston and Choate, we see a convergence of ideas regarding bioracial evolution as well as spiritual salvation, which served nineteenth-century American institutions in symbolically resolving racial tensions.

It should be recalled that, as in other evangelical contexts, a parallel pseudoscientific discourse was nearly always present in the aspirational contexts of evangelical boarding school rhetoric. The coinciding of these twin discourses is apparent in Armstrong's claim that "the Indians are grown up children; we are a thousand years ahead of them."[55] It was also a significant perception in the minds of school visitors, some of whom published their impressions widely. To illustrate, Helen W. Ludlow, the Hampton employee and editor of the *Southern Workman* who wrote the poem "On the Threshold," visited Carlisle and then wrote an article regarding her perception of the school for *Harper's New Monthly Magazine*. While that poem indicates Ludlow's faith in the social and racial evolution offered at Hampton, the article, written a couple of years later, offers further insight into her thinking on assimilation and its significance. At the outset Ludlow writes the following about Indian education: "There will be many, no doubt, who will smile at the title of this article, much as if it had read 'Education for Buffaloes and Wild Turkeys.' Such, however, will be likely to read it, as others will from a more sympathetic stand-point. For it is evident that, from one standpoint or another, public interest is excited upon the Indian question now as perhaps never before."[56]

While it is clear from the tone of the passage that Ludlow is attempting to infuse humor into what was at the time a very serious political topic, her likening of Native Americans to nonhuman species is significant in lieu of the linkage between boarding school education and pseudoscience, and as such should not be taken for granted as a joke. It was common in pseudoscientific thought throughout the nineteenth century to construe non-Caucasians as lower on an evolutionary scale, as is obvious in the craniological texts written by Morton and Nott. Armstrong's comment on

Indians hints at this, although he does not openly refer to Native Americans as subhuman.

Ludlow's authorial intent seems to be to shock the reader. Her article, beyond this opening reference to the "degraded" state of the Indian prior to education, is peppered with before-and-after illustrations (figs. 35, 36). Again, images such as these are intended to document the miraculous changes that have been wrought by Pratt and Armstrong, especially when considering the perceived near subhuman state of the Indian prior to admittance, as "race" and "species" were sometimes confused or conflated. The conflation of these categories could serve a function. If members of a different race were also seen as marginally human, their transformation could be packaged as all the more shocking. As Ludlow puts it later in her article, "the salvation of the race" was brought on by the "exigencies of the new era" as well as the "vision" of Armstrong at Hampton. She then credits the "gospel of work and self-help" as being essential for "all human development, and therefore as good for negroes as for Sandwich-Islanders," and she asks, "Why should it not try the same for the Indian?"[57]

Like other observers of Indian prisoners and boarding school students, she seems caught between empathy for their plight and disdain for their not-quite-human status. An alternative way to perceive such rhetoric and imagery, however, would be to think of it in the context of phrenology, which was still thriving in the country. One may say that phrenology offered a scientized metaphysics under the veneer of empiricism. It (supposedly) allowed one to discern the unseen—another person's mental state—based on superficial appearances. Initially imported from Europe through the teachings of Spurzheim, Combe, and others, phrenology found eager audiences in America and saw its heyday as a serious pseudoscience during the ante-bellum era in the United States.[58]

The surge in the popularity of phrenology may be attributed to a number of factors. Foremost among these was a need to legitimize slavery, as Morton and Nott sought to do before emancipation, by casting nonwhite races as mentally and morally inferior to the white race. Following the Civil War, there was an increasing need to gain perceptual mastery in the nation's growing industrializing cities. Phrenological knowledge and its advocates sought to allay the anxieties brought on within the middle class as a result of these changing demographic conditions.[59]

Due to these newer social conditions in the United States, the brothers Orson and Lorenzo Fowler, Nelson Sizer, Samuel R. Wells, and others succeeded in transforming phrenology into an entrepreneurial undertaking following the war. Their texts were copiously illustrated with various human "types" and often likened these human types to animal species. Some even contained comparative phrenological charts, which were imbued with a biosocial evolutionary logic.

For example, in the preface to his book *New Physiognomy* of 1875, Wells laments what he sees as science's relative ignorance regarding the wonders of the human brain, while positing his brand of phrenology as a means to unlocking its secrets: "We can comprehend something of matter, its properties and uses, but almost nothing of the mind itself, save that it occupies and uses the body for a time and then drops it to return to the God who gave it. . . . For more than twenty years we have been engaged in the study of man, and in 'character reading' . . . enabling us to classify the different forms of body, brain, and face and to reduce to *method* the process by which character may be determined."[60]

Like most postwar phrenological hucksters, Wells attempted to make his particular interpretation of phrenology sound more "scientific" or "systematic" than any attempted previously. Interesting as well in this passage is Wells's nod to religious faith, acknowledging God as the giver of the mind. This is another indication of the intellectual interdependencies of pseudoscience and faith after the Civil War.

In proving the legitimacy of his method, Wells offers many illustrations intended to establish correspondences between character and physiology. In his introduction he presents the reader with a visual comparison, to be read phrenologically. It is a sketch of the American legislator Daniel Webster shown bust-length and in profile, juxtaposed with the bust of what Wells labels an "idiot." Wells writes, "We cannot possibly conceive of a Webster with the meaningless face and small, backward sloping head of an idiot."[61] Such side-by-side comparative readings aesthetically echo the before-and-after portraits of the boarding schools. A cultural exemplar is shown together with a member of a despised cultural underclass. Pratt and Armstrong's "miracle" was the taking of the despised and forcibly elevating them to approximations of middle-class exemplars. So while phrenology may have peaked in terms of its perceived scientific legitimacy *before* the war and emancipation, its comparative intellectual and aesthetic structures remained largely in place after the war, albeit in altered form.

Phrenological thought, as well as its pseudo-empirical imagery, takes on a more sinister tone when hierarchies of both race and species were applied. Thus in many phrenological texts and illustrations, a confusion between "race" and "species" is evident. Phrenologists perceived a progressive evolution in various animal species and human races, based on the sloping of the front of the skull, identified by Wells as being of utmost importance for phrenological analysis. The slope of the skull was taken as an indicator of the size and angle of the frontal lobe of the brain within, thus indicating intelligence. In "lower" animals, such as reptiles, the slope is the most extreme; in four-legged mammals it is less severe, and in the human races even less so. The implication is that nonwhite races, in addition to containing congenitally unfit types such as the "idiot," bear a closer relationship to lower animal species because their facial slope is more severe than that of the Caucasian. The legitimacy of this contention has its origins in Blumenbach's and Morton's systematic measurements of human skulls.[62]

This discussion may be easily tied back into my discussion of the establishment of the evangelical boarding schools. Oddly, evangelism became one potential antidote to the lack of racial fitness perceived in many groups. As I discussed in my first

The Social Gospel

book, *The Art of Americanization at the Carlisle Indian School*, the linkage between pseudoscience and the philanthropic rhetoric of the boarding schools is borne out in a series of phrenological busts commissioned by Pratt and the Smithsonian Institution and executed by sculptors Clark Mills and Joseph Palmer (fig. 45). The busts were intended to establish the congenital criminality of the indigenous military prisoners at Fort Marion, Florida, who were to inspire Pratt to later recruit his first generation of students. Their criminal inclinations were to be seen empirically in their skull shape and proportion, and Pratt would claim that environmental immersion was the only "cure" for this degeneracy.[63]

The commissioning of the busts was motivated not only by Pratt's need to establish the exigency for reform in the prisoners but also by the ethnographic collecting of the Smithsonian. With this in mind, Pratt carried on an extended correspondence with Spencer F. Baird, who at the time was the secretary of the Smithsonian and who wished to have busts made from the plaster casts so as to construct figures for the Smithsonian's ethnographic dioramas, displays that would become a cornerstone of the epistemology of natural history. The specifically phrenological quality of the busts are revealed by Mills's artistry as well as Baird's desire to have "accurate" likenesses for his display, the Hall of Native Peoples.[64]

By his own account, Mills was trained by an Italian sculptor who at the time was living in Mills's hometown of Charleston, South Carolina. In fact Mills found his calling in the fine arts after seeing a phrenologist in Charleston who recommended that he pursue such a career. In addition to this account of the origins of his craft, Mills was also influenced by George Combe's well-known antebellum aesthetic tract, *Phrenology Applied to Painting and Sculpture*. Combe's ideas were welcomed by many American artists of the time, as it was perceived that they offered a scientifically accurate method for depicting the heads of various persons and groups in artworks.[65] Mills eventually came to national recognition with his monumental equestrian statue of Andrew Jackson, placed on display in Lafayette Square in Washington.

In his correspondences with Baird, Mills describes his Native subjects from a bluntly phrenological perspective: "We have completed all the Indian casts. . . . They are undoubtedly the most important collection of Indian heads in the world, and when they have become extinct, as which fate is inevitable, posterity will see a facsimile of a race of men that once over ran this great country not only their physiognomies but phrenological development also."[66]

Mills echoes Baird's own view of the inevitability of the demise of indigenous cultures in America, and thus the need to preserve their likeness for posterity. But Mills goes beyond these general aims in his invocation of phrenological knowledge. Pratt's own belief in environmental immersion seemingly rejects the essentializing tenets of phrenology, yet pseudoscientific categories in this case had a use value in that the masks and busts lent Pratt's aims the veneer of "scientific" legitimacy. Mills would continue his phrenological assessment of the prisoners in another letter to Baird two weeks later:

> When I began taking the casts of the Indians I found the size of the brain fully up to the average of the white race—I thought all that was necessary for them was education, but as I advanced I found that one set of organs were more fully developed than others. . . . Distructiveness & Secretiveness [regions of the brain are] large, the first having to kill their food, second having to obtain by stealth and strategy. . . . Locality large never get lost—Eventuality—large, never forgets an event. . . . It seems those largely developed organs having been cultivated over so many generations have become permanent, they are transmitted to posterity.[67]

Mills's laundry list—Destructiveness, Locality, and Secretiveness—were invented by phrenologists and were intended to correspond to particular character traits. Thus if one had strong "Locality," as indicated by the prominence of that "organ" in the brain, one remembered directions well and never got lost, as Mills indicates. Mills finds Destructiveness and Secretiveness are strong in the specimens, corresponding to commonly held Anglo stereotypes of

Native Americans as being both violent, criminal, and stealthy, as Fowler found in his phrenological assessment of his Indian chief.

While Mills's grounding was in phrenology, one must also consider the specifics of the artistic exchange involving him, Pratt, and Baird, as it constituted one of the empirical foundations of Carlisle. I'm referring to Mills's ethnographic life masks of Pratt's prisoners for Baird's Hall of Native Peoples. Baird and other ethnologists of the time shared the belief that the "pristine" state of the Native would soon disappear forever due to frontier expansion, and thus specimens needed to be preserved for posterity.[68]

Beyond this general ethnographic and historical desire, both Baird and Pratt wished to scientifically demonstrate the natures of the prisoners, thereby bolstering Pratt's argument that they were in need of transformation. With this in mind, Baird requested that in addition to the masks, Pratt compile a detailed synoptic table outlining the physiological descriptions as well as tribal affiliation of each of the sixty-four prisoners. Further, Baird asked that each prisoner's criminal record be included in the data. Baird published this data in the 1878 edition of the *Proceedings of the National Museum*, emphasizing the importance of the shape of each subject's head in ascertaining his cultural attributes and personal proclivities.[69]

In this context, the urgency of the boarding school mission more broadly is put into stark relief. In the specific case of Hampton, that institution's evangelical education became all the more evident, as evangelical belief, despite the seeming tempering factors of modern social sciences, remained steadfast in its emphasis on salvation through Christ. The fact that Frissell even felt the need to make an argument against criminal tendencies on the part of African Americans indicates the pressure he sensed in the surrounding society. At one point he even traveled in criminological circles, wishing to educate himself on the issue. Frissell's interest in the idea of a "Negro criminality," then current in criminology, was heightened at the moment Johnston's photographs were being

made at Hampton; perhaps he understood her work as a coun-
terdiscourse in the medium in relation to the more widespread
use of photography in police work.[70]

Important to note in this discussion of race, science, and
evangelism in Gilded Age America is that the scientific racism
proffered by Mills, Wells, Sizer, and the Fowlers was by no means
unchallenged. Perhaps the most notable—and progressive—voice
in this counterargument was that of the anthropologist Franz
Boas (1858–1942). While Boas's views on questions of race and
culture were by no means completely egalitarian, they are for
the time quite liberal and represent a significant departure from
the normative assumptions of scientific racism and evangelical
assimilationism. Boas was himself an immigrant to the country
and served as curator at the Museum of Natural History in New
York, curator at the Smithsonian, and professor at Columbia
University. He is moreover commonly seen as having defined an
American "national character" for the field.[71]

During his career he closely studied the material cultures
and physiological characteristics of indigenous American tribes.
However, Boas eschewed any biological or congenital determinism
in his classificatory systems of human societies. Rather he saw
distinctions between "races" as arising from more circumstantial
and environmental factors, and he attributed differences in skull
size to mating habits, environmental adaptations, or even events
in the life of individual subjects. Further, Boas took the vantage
point and preconceptions of the scientist into account as possibly
influencing ethnological perceptions. For him, biblical references
were therefore completely irrelevant. Likewise he believed cultural attributes such as religion and mythology were products of
accretion and contact with "foreign elements" over time rather
than something autonomous and "organic."[72]

To sum up, Boas rejected racial and cultural essentialism, as
well as the implicit or explicit hierarchies that accompany such
essentialism, in favor of cultural relativism. Such an assertion
would seem obvious in the case of the Native American students

at the boarding schools, whose worldviews were often syncretic combinations of Christian beliefs and traditional spiritualism. From Boas's perspective, the viability of the dualities proposed by assimilationist philosophy, such as "Christian versus pagan" or "saved versus damned" or "civilized versus savage," breaks down.

While Pratt and Armstrong had an extremely complex and wide-reaching set of ideas regarding salvation, race, education, and American identity, there were competing schools of thought at the time, as well as negative responses by some of their students and others in the indigenous communities affected by their ambitions. It is clear that Pratt and Armstrong did their best to impose both mental and physical controls on their prisoners and students. These controls were intended to assimilate them into the "mainstream" Anglo-American world, if mostly at a proletarian economic level. From the outset, Pratt had his prisoners at Fort Marion don paramilitary clothing, engage in drills, and guard themselves, in addition to the external surveillance imposed by prison and school staff as well as the myriad photographers hired to document their transformation. In short, he imposed not only external controls but *internal* psychic controls on each student, or in critical theoretical terms, a Foucauldian self-awareness.[73]

Records indicate that Pratt's efforts at Fort Marion and later at Carlisle produced very mixed results. It was not until 1889 that Pratt could boast a single graduate from Carlisle, and by the turn of the twentieth century, twenty years after Carlisle had been founded, only 209 out of nearly 4,000 students who had attended the school actually graduated, and most held only a grammar-school level of proficiency in academic subjects. Of those who did not graduate, many returned to their reservations and lived out lives in segregation and relative obscurity. Others, like Carlisle students Luther Standing Bear and Carlos Montezuma, left the school to strike out on their own in the white world. Still others encountered delinquency, illness, and even death while at the school. For example, David Wallace Adams has written that in 1881, Armstrong reported that roughly 20 percent of the original prisoners brought to Hampton by Pratt had either died at the school or shortly thereafter.[74]

Some primary sources pertaining directly to individual students do remain in the form of letters, magazine articles, and autobiographies. From these we can see that the perceptions of assimilation, race, and Christian identity varied. Ota Kte was one of the original students who arrived at Carlisle with Pratt in October 1879. As the son of the Sioux chief Standing Bear, he was deemed an important find for Pratt in his quest to convert the next generation of leaders from within the tribes. In his autobiography, *My People the Sioux*, Ota Kte ("Plenty Kill" in English) relays the story of how the newly arrived students had the most basic aspect of their identity taken away almost immediately after arrival at Carlisle: their name. Pratt deemed indigenous names unacceptable, so he and his staff forced the children to choose an Anglicized, usually biblical name from a list written on a blackboard. Ota Kte selected the name Luther and thus became "Luther Standing Bear," adopting his father's name as a surname per Western tradition.[75]

Standing Bear's autobiography is one of the most extensive existing documents written by a former student describing life at the first generation of government off-reservation boarding schools. His assessment of Pratt's pedagogy and of life at the school is ambivalent, as he sees the complexities of his experience from multiple perspectives. For example, with reference to Pratt's vaunted training programs, which attempted to mix academic and industrial pedagogy, Standing Bear takes a skeptical view:

> Now there was one thing I really wanted, and that was to have all my time in school, instead of working as a tinsmith half of the day. I could not see that the trade was going to benefit me any, as the Government was already giving the Indians all the tinware they wanted. But Captain Pratt said that a trade was a good thing for a boy to learn. Then I asked if I could not go into the carpenter shop and learn that trade. . . . Captain Pratt did not agree with me. I had made a big round tin ball for the top of the flag pole,

and the people from Washington had seen [it] . . . and my work
was considered good. . . . What worried me was the thought that
I might not be able to work the trade after I returned home.[76]

This is a revealing passage. Although Standing Bear at times
strikes a nostalgic tone when discussing his years at Carlisle, he
does not shy away from critique. The "industrial training" was
the cornerstone of Pratt's curriculum and a large part of his sales
pitch for funding from the government and private donors. The
assumption donors made, often based on the photographs and
heavily edited school publications, was that the training was
relevant and would provide students with a means for self-support
after leaving the school. Thus even if actual graduation rates were
low for years, Pratt and his backers could take solace in the idea
that the students would at least be gaining something from their
time at the school. As Standing Bear asserts, however, this was
not true for him and many other students. In fact after leaving
Carlisle without a diploma, he worked as a sales clerk at John
Wanamaker's department store in Philadelphia, then returned to
live on his reservation and worked as a schoolteacher for a time.
He became a "Wild West" performer in Los Angeles later in life,
a choice Pratt abhorred. In his narrative Standing Bear gives us
the longer term consequences of the education he received at
Carlisle, as *My People the Sioux* was published in 1928, much
later in his life.[77]

Interestingly the tie between pseudoscience and assimilation
comes up in the book as well. Standing Bear mentions that on a
diplomatic mission to Washington with his father and Pratt, the
three met with a curator (possibly Spencer F. Baird) who attempted
to persuade Luther to serve as an ethnographic model for a bust
portrait at the Smithsonian, a fate that befell the prisoners of Fort
Marion a few years earlier:

On occasion to this visit to Washington . . . Captain Pratt said he
would take me through the Smithsonian Institution. . . . Captain
Pratt told me to tell my father that the man wanted to make a bust

of me as the first Indian boy to enter Carlisle School. He said it
would be finished in marble, like many others in the building. . . .
The man explained that first my face would be greased . . . then
tubes would be put into my nostrils to breathe through, after
which plaster of paris would be put all over my face and head,
and left there to harden. Then it would be broken off very careful,
so as not spoil the impression of my head.[78]

Standing Bear here describes almost exactly the process to which
the Fort Marion prisoners were subjected. The passage also indicates
the ulterior motives in this "diplomatic" visit, and not surprisingly
Standing Bear tells us that his father refused to allow Pratt to have
the impression made, finding the idea "shocking," in Luther's
words.[79] Pratt wished to have more ethnographic evidence of
the state of his students. While there are no explicit references to
phrenology in Standing Bear's account of the incident, it is possible
that Pratt and Baird had this in mind. If Pratt was suspicious
of pseudoscience and dedicated to social reform, one wonders
what exactly he hoped to gain by subjecting Standing Bear to
this treatment.

Another boarding school student, Chauncey Yellow Robe, has
also left behind a significant archive of personal documents pertaining to his years at the school. Yellow Robe displays an orientation
toward his experience somewhat different from Standing Bear's,
as seen in his extensive correspondence with school officials and
fellow alumni. He offers a positive take on his experiences at the
school and its mission of Christian evangelism in this letter to
Moses Friedman, one of Pratt's successors as superintendent:

I thank you for your kind Christmas greeting. . . . I entered
Carlisle as a student in the fall of 1883 with long hair, feather,
blanket, and painted face and above all not knowing a word of
English. You probably have seen one of my photos it may be
there yet on the wall for curiosity. I do not regret having been
transformed from savagery to an independent American citizen.
Through my experience I believe that there is only one way to

educate the Indian—is to take him away from his environment on the reservation and give him ample opportunity in the thickest atmosphere of civilization.[80]

Yellow Robe supports Pratt's version of assimilation, almost to a tee. His description of himself upon arrival at the school—"long hair, feather, blanket, and painted face"—is almost a recital of Pratt's characterizations of what he termed "blanket Indians." For Pratt, such "blanket Indians" represented not only savagery but also the failure of Indian education, as such Indians were at the most primitive stage of their evolution (both social and spiritual) and represented the potential threat of regression to such a primitive state. As such, the "blanket Indian" was a convenient rhetorical device he could use in writings and speeches, and it became a verbal analogue to the "before" photographic portrait.

Yellow Robe's reference to his "before" photograph indicates his awareness of the intended conceptual function of the image. He mentions it to Friedman as if it serves as lingering and valid "proof" of his own "savagery" upon arriving at Carlisle. Clearly the photographic sessions with Choate, Johnston, and other boarding school photographers had a significant impact on him psychologically, as nearly thirty years later he recalled the image being made and displayed an understanding of the representational codes of the medium as appropriated by his Anglo-American middle-class overseers. His alienation from his former self is likewise evident in his choice of the word "curiosity" in describing the photograph. For some students, and this is important to remember, their newly assimilated identities were fully internalized and not necessarily viewed with irony or resentment. It is therefore a mistake to assume that all students were passive agents in their own assimilation, even though Pratt tended to view them that way.

That Yellow Robe was highly thought of by Pratt and later Carlisle administrators and served as a model for the pedagogical outcomes they desired is further evidenced by the fact that his before-and-after images were used by Pratt in 1895 on the cover of the school's catalogue (fig. 46). The cover, by the Philadelphia engraving firm Grosscup & West, gives us what had become a widely copied and repeated visual trope in boarding school imagery. On the left is the "primitive" Yellow Robe in the tondo encircled by pieces of animal hair or feathers. Below that is the picturesque lifestyle of the unassimilated Indian: tipi, untamed land, wild animals, complete with a "blanket Indian" sitting in front. On the right is the assimilated Yellow Robe, confidently gazing off to the side, with cropped hair and wearing the prerequisite Anglo-American fashions. Below the new and improved Yellow Robe is the signifier of civility: the frame house with manicured grounds surrounding it. The artist places an assimilated couple, perhaps former students, strolling in front of their property. In the background is a nod to the evangelical aspirations of the school: a church with steeple and cross. This particular catalogue was significant for Pratt not only because of Yellow Robe's appearance on the cover but also because it features illustrations by a Carlisle student who had been studying photography at the time, John Leslie. Thus Pratt was able to showcase two of his model students, one serving as a signifier of the assimilation process and the other contributing directly to the making of the document.

With Carlisle and Hampton we see the merging of social Darwinian immersion with Christian evangelical salvation forming the basis of the assimilationist education offered. While their legacies, inflected by pseudoscientific social evolutionary thought, are ambivalent at best, in the coming decades of the twentieth century we see fluctuations and backlashes against the boarding school method. Likewise we see the reassertion of pedagogical methods, such as the bell curve, that carry the specter of racist pseudoscience in the guise of the statistical assessment of students as well as the institutions charged with their education.

Epilogue

For centuries, dominant cultural, political, scientific, and religious institutions in the United States have attempted—with varying degrees of success—to define and control subaltern populations via an array of institutionalized techniques, with the aid of various ideas, concepts, and aesthetic tropes. Thus we have seen the use of chromatic metaphors in text and image deployed in the service of the establishment and maintenance of both spiritual and pseudoscientific hierarchies. From Blumenbach's Enlightenment-era craniological categories of the "five races," it was only a small step to essentializing various groups as "white," "black," "red," and so forth, with all that these metaphors either implied or stated explicitly. In addition to the use of chromatic metaphor, such metaphors and categories were then fixed into hierarchies of racial evolution, as seen in the writing of Samuel Chapman Armstrong, with his conflation of the evolutionary traits of indigenous Hawaiians and African Americans. Such a sense of stunted evolution was a core concept in both scientific and evangelical racism, as it gave Armstrong and other Anglo-American reformers the ammunition needed to legitimize the assimilationist agenda of Hampton and other schools. It also gave Joseph Smith the ammunition he needed to inspire generations of enthusiastic followers to target darker-skinned groups in Mormon missionary work, an instruction codified in Mormonism's founding scripture.

Both the chromatic metaphoric and racial evolutionary tropes dovetailed with evangelical millennial concerns regarding the Second Coming. This apocalyptic apprehension lent a heightened urgency to the evangelical work of many Protestant denominations, as the explicitly stated Christological covenant demanded the "charitable" salvation of subaltern souls. Conveniently such millenarian leanings also easily fit in with the newly emergent bourgeois mercantile work ethic. All of the principal evangelical and pseudoscientific concepts could be channeled into a concern with the proletarianization and/or enslavement of non-Europeans, as seen in the writings of Cotton Mather, Smith, Armstrong, Pratt, Morton, and others.

One needs to be cautious, however, in assigning the epithet "trope" to these processes in a simplistic fashion. Such tropes have always had real-world consequences for those who deploy them and for those who were their target, and they continue to do so today. This is evidenced by the fact that the cultural heritage of assimilationism is ambivalent at best. If one seeks statistical outcomes as a measure of the viability of the Carlisle School, for instance, it has been widely documented that the historic graduation rates during its first twenty years of existence were quite low, with fewer than 10 percent of the total enrolled students ever finishing the program. In addition to this problem, student illness, delinquency, and death were constant companions to Pratt during his tenure at the school.[1] Pratt would resign as superintendent in 1904, and Carlisle was closed by Congress in 1918. In contrast, Armstrong's Hampton has survived and is today a thriving university, albeit with less explicitly evangelical aims. Its private philanthropic funding structure, historically supported by a cadre of highly committed donors, has allowed it to sidestep the political vagaries of federal assimilation policy.

Further, it is tempting in hindsight to look askance at the evangelical movements discussed in this study. The proclamations made by their advocates, together with the visual imagery produced by the artists affiliated with them, might strike one as quaint, provincial, or outmoded from the perspective of our increasingly globalized, multicultural society of the twenty-first century. The evangelical obsession with concepts like nationalism, progress, and salvation, married to very particular and academicized conceptions of beauty and taste, read as relics of a bygone era, with its now defunct and superseded "national character."

However, even a cursory glance at American cultural history in the twentieth century shows that despite the dated appearance and sense of many of the images and ideas discussed in this book, both evangelism and racial pseudoscientific cultural trends nevertheless have survived, albeit in altered forms. While Franz Boas's cultural relativism attempted to overturn racial scientific assumptions around the turn of the twentieth century, thereby challenging its hegemonic claims, newer waves of pseudoscientific racism would appear along with newer brands of Christian radicalism. Pseudoscience was never far from the mainstream of scientific and medical thought, and even persisted among more "progressive" reformers of the twentieth century. To cite just one example, even the liberal Boas himself at times forwarded pseudoscientific ideas about Natives. In a famous letter to Pratt, Boas, who was involved in organizing the government's Ethnological Exhibition at the Chicago World's Fair, sought to explain the "distribution of types of man" via the use of anthropometric measurements and lay figures in the exhibition's dioramas, desiring to get these measurements from the school's students.[2]

One also sees the rise of the eugenics movement in the United States and western Europe in the early twentieth century.[3] As I discuss in my first book, eugenic anthropometric measurements were used on boarding school students in order to explain their "capacities," perhaps most famously on the Olympic athlete and Carlisle graduate Jim Thorpe in 1912. Thorpe's exceptional athleticism was explained via visual exhibition and the statistical aggregation of his physical measurements, not unlike the strategy used by Morton and his polygenist colleagues decades earlier. Such statistically based methods, whether physiological or mental, were used to parse and hierarchize students of all races in the

United States throughout much of the twentieth century and may be seen as an extension of the pseudoscientific logic of craniometry.[4]

Indeed, throughout the first half of that century, anthropometry, eugenics, intelligence testing, and other racially inflected "sciences" would impact not only the cultural landscape in America but, more important, actual public policy toward immigrants and minorities. For example, physiological and intelligence data collected by eugenicists such as Henry Goddard and Harry H. Laughlin were taken as a pretext on which to enforce immigration quotas and bans as well as the execution of mass sterilization programs. Much of this activity was fueled by irrational fears of immigrants "overtaking" the nation. Beginning in the 1920s and going through the 1960s such fears were further fueled by the racial theorists Lothrop Stoddard and Carleton S. Coon, both of whom saw alarming migration patterns at play that would threaten the colonial-era white supremacist model. Both appealed to an empirical basis for their ideas by reifying the simplistic Blumenbach-Morton array of racial categorizations.[5]

In spiritual terms, the rise of Pentecostalism, Protestant Fundamentalism, and Neoconservative evangelism indicates that while the nation has diversified religiously over the past century, the ideas of older Christian evangelists have survived, often in response to perceived modern threats like demographic shifts, Darwinism, secularization, and diversification. Pentecostalism and Fundamentalism in particular sought to regain an emotionally grounded and "charismatic" form of faith and worship in the face of modern secularization, often employing bizarre, unconventional rituals in the expression of a supposedly superior faith.[6] In contrast to Pentecostalism's eccentricities, some Christian denominations have sought more mainstream legitimacy for extreme views. Thus throughout the twentieth century in the United States debate persisted over the scientific legitimacy of evolutionary theory, although it is largely accepted in mainstream science. Fundamentalists especially consider the

Bible to be the literal word of God and have consistently favored the teaching of "young earth" creationism in public schools, a notion that parallels the views of polygenism in the early nineteenth century.[7]

In terms of specific evangelical imagery, the art historian Robert Gambone has pointed out that evangelical iconography survived in American culture throughout the first half of the twentieth century, appearing not only in popular contexts but also in the work of fine artists such as John Steuart Curry, Thomas Hart Benton, and many others. To take just one example, Curry gives us an overtly biblical reference in a contemporary scene with his *Mississippi Noah*, where he mines popular American prints and classical works of French painting in the service of an apocalyptic depiction of current environmental catastrophe and race in America during the Depression. He depicts an evangelized African American family, helpless in a flood, using prayer as a source of salvation, while no logistical or federal assistance is in view.[8] The appearance of biblical and evangelical imagery is not surprising in the mid- and even late twentieth century, as evidenced by the earlier discussion of the prominence of such motifs in the work of Mormon artists Arnold Friberg and Del Parson.

The emergence of eugenics and the campy, mass-mediated fundamentalism of the first half of the twentieth century would set the stage for further continuances and evolutions in the second half. While the overtly white supremacist rhetoric and symbolism of the Gilded Age was for the most part jettisoned from mainstream cultural and political contexts, these ideas nevertheless have persisted, albeit in sublimated form for much of the post–Civil Rights period. It is clear from even a cursory glance at the political upheavals and racial tensions of the millennium that these problems were only below the surface during the preceding decades.

With all of these examples in mind, it is important to remember that the episodes outlined in this book are not merely historical curiosities belonging to a less enlightened era. They are our own, as the contestation of identity, political authority, and cultural prerogatives is ongoing. As such, it would be a mistake to assume, as some have done, that the nation has entered a safely "postracial" era in which all such problems are relics of the past. It is incumbent on all of us as citizens to remain alert and engaged, should we wish this grand experiment of ours to survive for the benefit of the many.

Notes

Introduction

1. This project, which is an intellectual outgrowth of my first book, *The Art of Americanization at the Carlisle Indian School*, seizes upon the basic principles of that work and seeks to explore them in newer—albeit closely related—intellectual contexts. In that book I examined the role of pseudoscientific imagery in the processes of "Americanization" during the Gilded Age. What I found was that institutions, ranging from the federal government to the art world and private philanthropic and commercial interests, all shared a concern with the assimilation of various subaltern cultural groups, or groups perceived as existing outside of assumed cultural, social, and aesthetic norms. These norms were in turn defined by the very Anglo-American reformers who supported such assimilation, and so were logically circular in nature. Such assimilation was seen by its advocates as a humane alternative to incarceration or genocide and was a preemptive measure against resistance or revolt. While the first book focused on the depiction of Native Americans in such a context, one could also extend the analysis to include African Americans, the working classes, and what were then newer immigrants from southern and eastern Europe. To the bourgeois Anglo-American mind, all of these groups were often conflated in terms of their perceived deficiencies and thus were seen as candidates for enforced assimilation. On the conflation of various "subaltern" groups in America, such as Jewish and Slavic immigrants and Native Americans, see also Trachtenberg, *Shades of Hiawatha*. On the aesthetic slippage inherent in the perception of "subaltern" groups, see Boime, *The Art of Exclusion*.

2. The term "blanket Indian" was coined by Richard Henry Pratt, founder of the assimilationist Carlisle Indian School. Pratt intended the term to be a derogatory swipe at what he saw as the "primitive," unarticulated state of indigenous cultures in this country. By referring to Native Americans collectively as "blanket Indians," he could forge the perception that they were all interchangeable and equally in need of his brand of assimilationist education.

3. The term "messianic" used here and in the title of the book refers to the support of institutional projects intended to transform and assimilate Otherness in America as

well as to the more biblical sense of the term, which refers to the imminent coming of a new era brought about by Christ's return to this world during the Final Judgment. The concept of salvation, also introduced in this paragraph, refers to the redeeming of the assumed "heathen" souls of the indigenous Others targeted for assimilation. Spiritual salvation, along with mental and physiological transformation, was a cornerstone of Anglo-American assimilation projects, especially in the nineteenth century. This sense of salvation was of course driven by commonly held American Protestant views of eschatology. Eschatology, broadly speaking, refers to the study of the end of time: death, judgment, and the coming next world. For the Protestants sects under consideration here, this entailed the Second Coming of Christ and the wiping away of this world in favor of a coming golden age.

4. By "millenarian" I refer to religious movements that tend to view America as a sort of spiritual New Jerusalem and social utopia, an idea common in Puritan literature, for instance. In this view the New World is a staging place for personal and social salvation and evangelization in lieu of an often assumed Second Coming of Christ. Thus the Puritan historian Cotton Mather's characterization of the Massachusetts Bay Colony as a "City of Gold," a reference intended to highlight the radical potential for the colony as well as a retrospective reference to the coming world of Christ as characterized in the Gospel of Matthew as a divine city with streets paved with gold.

5. See Evans, *The Social Gospel in American Religion*; Ahlstrom, *A Religious History*.

6. Evans, *The Social Gospel*, introduction.

7. Recent scholars, including Ibram X. Kendi in *Stamped from the Beginning*, have addressed the complex interrelationship between evangelical discourse and race in America. However, the current literature is lacking in terms of applying this perceived relationship to the enforced assimilation of racial subaltern groups, and their subsequent visualization.

8. See Kelley, "The Rest of Us," 273; also Wolfe, *Traces of History*.

9. Trachtenberg, *Shades of Hiawatha*, xiv–xvi.

10. Richard Henry Pratt to Samuel C. Armstrong, August 6, 1878, Samuel Chapman Armstrong Papers.

11. Genesis 17:1–10 (NKJV); see Cotton Mather's sermon *Theopolis Americana*.

12. Eliot, *The Christian Commonwealth*.

13. See Richard Mather, "Commentary on Ephesians" cited in Kendi, *Stamped from the Beginning*; also Baxter, *A Christian Directory*.

14. The term "market Christianity" was first suggested to me in a discussion with Moris Stern, a friend and colleague who teaches in the philosophy department of Brooklyn College, CUNY. See Weber, *The Protestant Ethic*, 256–57.

15. Weber, *The Protestant Ethic*, 8–28.

16. Calvin, *The Institutes of the Christian Religion*, 125; Weber, *The Protestant Ethic*, 76–78. Weber also links this ethic to Luther's notion of "calling" (28–36). In America he sees the development of the spirit of capitalism in the writings of Benjamin Franklin (11–27). According to Weber, Franklin manages to make an ethic out of what in prior times would have been considered avarice.

17. Marx, "A Contribution to the Critique of Political Economy," 158–61. Tying this discussion of evangelical activity and imagery back into the aforementioned economic agendas shared by many Christians during this time, we must recall that one of the cornerstones of evangelical activity was the inculcation of a market-based ethos in the minds of their target audiences. A model for understanding the mania for evangelical conversion through much of American history is provided by the German philosopher and economist Karl Marx (1818–83) in his well-known text *The German Ideology*, written with Friedrich Engels. In an effort to understand the historical genesis and evolution of capitalism, Marx divides capitalist societies into two fundamental parts: the "base" and the "superstructure." He argues that within capitalism the base is formed by all of the *actual* implements of material production. Thus it would consist of machines, tools, the bodies of workers, buildings, private property, and so forth. He goes on to claim that the superstructure consists of all of those things that, while not directly related to production, nonetheless *reinforce* relations of production between the various social classes. Thus he sees religion, politics, art, law, and education as constituting the superstructure. From this perspective visual images are a perfect ideological accompaniment in the establishment of a new and ever-changing economic and social order. Marx sums up these superstructural elements as "ideological" and those of the base as "productive." According to him, the seemingly superfluous ideological aspects of capitalist society are actually critical in "legitimizing" the relations of production between varying groups within that society. Therefore the elites of capitalism deploy religious belief and practice in an effort to preempt resistance to their economic designs on the part of the "masses," the majority of the population, which owns little or no wealth or property.

18. Weber, *The Protestant Ethic*, 11–27.

19. Weber, *The Protestant Ethic*, 8–28; Franklin, *The Autobiography*, 141–45.

20. Nott discusses this idea at length in his pseudoscientific book *Types of Mankind*, which I discuss in chapter 2.

21. In terms of the publicizing of evangelical activities, the American Tract Society stands out. Formed in the 1820s, during the height of the Second Great Awakening, the ATS was dedicated to publishing and disseminating Christian evangelical ideas through the printed word. For more on the ATS, see Morgan, *Protestants and Pictures*, 19–29.

22. Notable among the apocalyptic preachers in America during the antebellum era was William Miller (1782–1849). His followers, known as "Millerites," believed his claim that through a sort of mystical numerological calculation, the world would come to an end and Christ would return to earth in the year 1843. While the Millerite movement (later named Seventh-Day Adventism) would focus more on self-salvation that the evangelization of others, this kind of millennial thinking was widespread in the United States during this and other eras, albeit usually lacking this degree of numeric accuracy. See Miller, *William Miller's Apology and Defense*.

23. Trachtenberg, *Shades of Hiawatha*, xiv–xvi.

24. Shohat, *Unthinking Eurocentrism*.

25. The issue raised here is similar to that raised by Erwin Panofsky in his discussion of the representation of classical myths during the Middle Ages and Renaissance.

When the artists of any era deploy "retrospective" characterizations of past events—whether real or mythic—they are so doing in a renewed context and taking into account the demands and expectations of that context. Further, they are *receiving* the stories necessary to create such imagery through a variety of edited and translated sources that have evolved over time, beginning with the original source. Thus while these images purport to render "accurate" visions of past events, they do so with the exigencies of their historical present(s) in mind. See Erwin Panofsky, "Iconography and Iconology: An Introduction to the Study of Renaissance Art," in Preziosi, *The Art of Art History*, 220–35.

26. Morgan and Promey, *The Visual Culture of American Religions*, 2–3.

27. Morgan, *Protestants and Pictures*, 8–11. See especially Morgan's discussion of the graphic transmissibility of Protestant imagery in the United States in the nineteenth century. Newer technologies, such as lithography, halftone, and photography, only served to reinforce the perceived legitimacy of such images by lending them a perceptually "democratic" aura due to the proliferation of these mediums.

1. Puritanism and Fidelity

1. Audi, *The Cambridge Dictionary of Philosophy*, 452–53. Luther conceived of consubstantiation as the parallel presence of the flesh and blood of Christ with the physical bread and wine during the Christian Eucharist. This contrasts with the older Catholic view of transubstantiation, which argues that the flesh and blood literally inhabit and become one with the bread and wine during the Eucharist. Luther's *theologia crucis* (theology of the cross) argues that Christ's suffering and divinity are the only way to salvation and that human faculties like reason and activities like spiritual works are futile and a belief in them may even lead to arrogance and thus damnation. His "Two Kingdoms" theory posits that God rules the earth through secular governments and laws and rules heaven through "gospel and grace," or the divinity of Christ, which is something humans may never fully achieve. He saw the Catholic Church as a false representative of Christ in this world.

2. For more on early Puritan history in England and the Marian Exile in relation to Calvinism, see Solt, *Church and State in Early Modern England*.

3. Indeed the controversy over the role of works and faith would become a central sticking point in Puritan theological debates in New England. Mainstream Puritan leaders such as Increase Mather supported an emphasis on works, while others, including the renegade Anne Hutchinson and the minister John Cotton, believed faith was the primary means to salvation. Hutchinson's position was eventually called Antinomianism; she and her supporters were persecuted during a series of trials and banished from the colony.

4. Audi, *The Cambridge Dictionary of Philosophy*, 99; Craven, *Colonial American Portraiture*, 3–4.

5. Craven, *Colonial American Portraiture*, 6–7.

6. Calvin, *The Institutes of the Christian Religion*, book 1, chapters 10–11.

7. Craven, *Colonial American Portraiture*, 17–26.

8. Craven, *Colonial American Portraiture*, xvi–xvii.

9. See John Cotton, "God's Promise to His Plantation," in Heimert and Delbanco, *The Puritans in America*, 75–80. For more on Descartes, see his *Discourse on the Method*.

10. Audi, *The Cambridge Dictionary of Philosophy*, 193–96.

11. Bercovitch, *Puritan Origins*, 9–10.

12. Bercovitch, *Puritan Origins*, 9–10.

13. Winthrop, "A Model of Christian Charity," in Heimert and Delbanco, *The Puritans in America*, 82.

14. Winthrop, "A Model of Christian Charity," 83.

15. Winthrop, "Reasons to Be Considered for Justifying the Undertakers of the Intended Plantation in New England and for Encouraging Such Whose Hearts God Shall Move to Join with Them in It," in Heimert and Delbanco, *The Puritans in America*, 72.

16. Mather, *Magnalia Christi Americana*, 23.

17. Mather, *Magnalia Christi Americana*, introduction, section 3.

18. Mather, "Reserved Memorials," in Heimert and Delbanco, *The Puritans in America*, 324.

19. Mather, "Reserved Memorials," 324–25.

20. Winthrop, "A Model of Christian Charity," 88.

21. Bercovitch, *The Rites of Assent*, 36–37.

22. Mather, *Theopolis Americana*.

23. Mather, *Theopolis Americana*.

24. Mather, *Theopolis Americana*.

25. Craven, *Colonial American Portraiture*, 38–39.

26. Craven, *Colonial American Portraiture*, 39; Miller et al., *American Encounters*, 67–70.

27. Craven, *Colonial American Portraiture*, 40–46.

28. Craven, *Colonial American Portraiture*, 50.

29. Miller, et al., *American Encounters*, 71–73.

30. Szasz, *Indian Education*, 104.

31. "Massachusetts Bay Charter," in Van Steeg and Hofstadter, *Great Issues*, 80.

32. Shurtleff, *Records of the Governor and Company*, 24.

33. Shurtleff, *Records of the Governor and Company*, 386. Please note that for this quote, despite the eccentricities in orthography, syntax, and grammar, I have chosen to transcribe the Early Modern English used by the original writer.

34. Shurtleff, *Records of the Governor and Company*, 392, 396–97. Also Martha Clark, email to author, July 11, 2016. Clark is the curator at the Massachusetts State Archives.

35. Thieme and Becker, *Allgemeines Lexikon der Bildenden Kunstler*, 105.

36. de Certeau, *The Writing of History*, xxv–xxvi.

37. "Massachusetts Bay Charter," in Van Steeg and Hofstadter, *Great Issues*, 75.

38. Bercovitch, *Rites of Assent*, 9; also Mather, *Magnalia Christi Americana*, introduction.

39. Bercovitch, *Puritan Origins*, 1–4.

40. Mather, *The Wonders of the Invisible World*, in Heimert and Delbanco, *The Puritans in America*, 339–40.

41. Mather, *Wonders*, 340.

42. Mather, *Wonders*, 340.

43. Heimert and Delbanco, *The Puritans in America*, 337–39.

44. Mather, *Memorable Providences*, introduction.

45. Kendi, *Stamped from the Beginning*, 15–18.

46. Kendi, *Stamped from the Beginning*, 21.

47. Kendi, *Stamped from the Beginning*, 18–20, 45.

48. Arber, *A list*, 15.

49. Cave, *The Pequot War*, 5–10.

50. Underhill, *Newes from America*, 1–2.

51. Underhill, *Newes from America*, 19.

52. Underhill, *Newes from America*, 32.

53. Brigham, *Paul Revere's Engravings*, 207–8.

54. Green, *A Vision of Hell*, 2–4. For more on Green, see Rohrer, *Jacob Green's Revolution*.

55. Brigham, *Paul Revere's Engravings*, 207–8.

56. *Bickerstaff's Boston almanack*, n.p. The writer identifies himself at the end as "Isaac Bickerstaff," which was a humorous pseudonym common in printing at the time. The name was originated by the British writer Jonathan Swift earlier in the eighteenth century.

57. *Bickerstaff's Boston almanack*, n.p.

58. Mather, *Memorable Providences*, introduction.

59. Heimert and Delbanco, *The Puritans in America*, 275–76, 337–39.

60. Szasz, *Indian Education*, 101–2.

61. Irwin, *Coming Down from Above*, 116–22.

62. Eliot, *A Brief Narrative*, 6, 19.

63. Eliot, *A Brief Narrative*, 19–20.

64. Eliot, *A Brief Narrative*, 21.

65. Eliot, *The Christian Commonwealth*, 1–2.

66. Irwin, *Coming Down from Above*, 117–18.

67. Buttre, *Catalogue of Engravings*, n.p.

68. Craven, *Colonial American Portraiture*, 50.

69. Irwin, *Coming Down from Above*, 121–22, 117.

70. Winthrop, "Reasons to Be Considered," 71.

71. For more on the artist, see Morisset, *La vie et l'oeuvre du Frère Luc.*

72. Bickham, *Savages within the Empire*, 21–26.

73. Bickham, *Savages within the Empire*, 25–26, 211, 219; also Pratt, *American Indians in British Art*, 33–34.

74. Bickham, *Savages within the Empire*, 25–26; Pratt, *American Indians in British Art*, 36–38.

75. Pratt, *American Indians in British Art*, 33.

2. Quakerism, Skulls, and Sanctity

1. Fox, *George Fox*, 50–51.

2. Foucault, *History of Madness*, 465–67.

3. Fox, *George Fox*, 26.

4. Fox, *George Fox*, 26.

5. Dowd, *A Spirited Resistance*, 31.

6. For more detail on Penn's biography, see Fantel, *William Penn*.

7. Penn, *William Penn's First Charter to the People of Pennsylvania*, n.p.

8. William Penn to Kings of the Indians of Pennsylvania, October 18, 1681, William Penn Papers.

9. Penn, *Primitive Christianity*, 5.

10. Penn, *Primitive Christianity*, 6.

11. Penn, *Primitive Christianity*, 8.

12. Woodward, *American Nations*, 97–100; Silver, *Our Savage Neighbors*, 202–8.

13. Silver, *Our Savage Neighbors*, 195–99, 202–8.

14. Silver, *Our Savage Neighbors*, 195–99, 202–8.

15. Brinton, "Benjamin West's Painting," 118.

16. Abrams, *The Valiant Hero*, 13–15.

17. Abrams, *The Valiant Hero*, 31–32.

18. Pohl, *Framing America*, 75–78; John Galt, "The Life and Studies of Benjamin West," in McCoubrey, *American Art*, 35–39; see also West to John Adams, November 6, 1783; West to Taylor, March 26, 1805; West to Sir William, June 15, 1810, Reel D10, Benjamin West Papers.

19. West, qtd. in Tobin, *Picturing Imperial Power*, 62–63.

20. West to anonymous, n.d., Reel P25, Benjamin West Papers.

21. Shohat, *Unthinking Eurocentrism*, 83–92. Shohat discusses the relationship between Robinson Crusoe and his indigenous friend Friday in Daniel Defoe's novel as embodying this type of relationship between colonizer and colonized.

22. Tobin, *Picturing Imperial Power*, 57–61.

23. Tobin, *Picturing Imperial Power*, 60; Abrams, *The Valiant Hero*, 192–95.

24. Penn, "Deed between William Penn and the Delaware Indians."

25. Tobin, *Picturing Imperial Power*, 61.

26. Tobin, *Picturing Imperial Power*, 66–67.

27. See, for example, Joseph Doan to Thomas Penn, March 29, 1735, Walking Purchase Records.

28. Tobin, *Picturing Imperial Power*, 57–61.

29. Benjamin West to William West, July 12, 1775, Reel 4233, Benjamin West Papers.

30. Tobin, *Picturing Imperial Power*, 72.

31. Williams, *America's First Hospital*, 127–29; History of Pennsylvania Hospital, "Famous Painting."

32. Jefferson, "Notes on Virginia," in *The Life and Selected Writings*, 173–267.

33. See Sellers, *Charles Willson Peale*.

34. Galt, "The Life and Studies of Benjamin West," 39.

35. Benjamin West to W. Darton, February 2, 1805, qtd. in Landis, "Benjamin West and the Royal Academy," 247–48; Galt, "The Life and Studies of Benjamin West," 38–39.

36. Mather, *Memorable Providences*, introduction.

37. Mather, *The Angel of Bethesda*, 5–7, 130–32.

38. Gamwell and Tomes, *Madness in America*, 18–20.

39. Rush, *Medical inquiries and observations*, 357–67. On the founding of the Pennsylvania Hospital and the involvement of Franklin and Dr. Thomas Bond (also a Quaker), see Grob, *The Mad among Us*, 18–21. Here I would like to thank Professor Julius Rubin, who in conversation with me pointed out that although the Pennsylvania Hospital was technically a secular institution (and not specifically Quaker), it was nonetheless informed by the principle of the moral management and governance of its patients. This principle was first institutionalized in America by the Reverend Thomas Scattergood, a Quaker minster who founded the Friends Asylum Hospital in Frankford, Pennsylvania, in 1813. This institution was intended to offer humane treatment for those "deprived of the use of their reason." For more on the founding of the Friends Hospital, see National Parks Service, "National Landmark Historical Nomination."

40. Foucault, *History of Madness*, 465–67, 471–72.

41. See Williams, *America's First Hospital*, 1–16, 43, 54–55, 64–65; Gamwell and Tomes, *Madness in America*, 18–20.

42. Josiah Hewer to Benjamin West, September 1, 1800, Reel P24, Benjamin West Papers.

43. Benjamin West to Josiah Hewer, July 8, 1801, Reel P24, Benjamin West Papers.

44. West to Hewer, July 8, 1801.

45. Foucault, *Madness and Civilization*, 38–64.

46. Gamwell and Tomes, *Madness in America*, 26–29.

47. Samuel Coates to Benjamin West, 1810, Reel P24, Benjamin West Papers.

48. Coates, *Description*, 3.

49. Coates, *Description*, 10–11.

50. See, for example, Hicks, *Memoirs*.

51. Edward Hicks to Samuel West, February 1841, Edward Hicks Papers.

52. Ford, *Edward Hicks*, 16–20; Mather and Miller, *Edward Hicks*, 15–16.

53. Mather and Miller, *Edward Hicks*, 16; Ford, *Edward Hicks*, 19–22.

54. John Comly to Isaac and Samuel Hicks, June 15, 1817, Reel 4151, Edward Hicks Papers.

55. Ford, *Edward Hicks*, 25.

56. Hicks, *Memoirs*, 91–92.

57. Hicks, *Memoirs*, 89–91.

58. Ford, *Edward Hicks*, 37–46.

59. Scholars have differed on the gender of the child. Ford, *Edward Hicks*, perceives it as female; Mather and Miller, *Edward Hicks*, interpret it as male.

60. Mather and Miller, *Edward Hicks*, 21.

61. Ford, *Edward Hicks*, 55.

62. Ford, *Edward Hicks*, 48; Weekley, *The Kingdoms of Edward Hicks*, 53.

63. Ford, *Edward Hicks*, 48, 54.

64. Ford, *Edward Hicks*, 46–48.

65. Hicks, *Memoirs*, 14–15.

66. Hicks, *Memoirs*, 85–91.

67. Hicks, *Memoirs*, 110–11.

68. Weekley, *The Kingdoms of Edward Hicks*, 21, 51.

69. Hippocrates and Heracleitus, *Nature of Man*, 61–96.

70. Hicks, *Memoirs*, 39.

71. Hicks, *Memoirs*, 39.

72. Hicks, *Memoirs*, 268–69.

73. Weekely, *The Kingdoms of Edward Hicks*, 53.

74. Weekely, *The Kingdoms of Edward Hicks*, 58–59.

75. Pomeroy, *Alexander Anderson*, 3:2427–31.

76. Mather and Miller, *Edward Hicks*, 77.

77. Hicks, *Memoirs*, 350.

78. Pomeroy, *Alexander Anderson*, 1:xxiii–lxxi.

79. For more on Anderson, see Pomeroy, *Alexander Anderson*, vol. 1.

80. Ford, *Edward Hicks*, 143; see Cuvier, *Essay on the Theory of the Earth*. In this text Cuvier refers to a succession of "revolutions" or floods in primordial times that precipitated the subsequent appearance of humans and other species in later times. He makes no reference to a divine cause for such "revolutions," yet his views contradict those of most evolutionists of the nineteenth century, who see evolution as a gradual process of adaptations. Cuvier's views, at least conceptually, parallel those most evangelical Christians of the era. For instance, Cuvier at one point cites the Book of Genesis and its account of the Flood of Noah in the construction of his catastrophist argument.

81. Wood, *A Biographical Memoir*, n.p.

82. Wood, *A Biographical Memoir*, n.p.

83. Fabian, *The Skull Collectors*, 93.

84. For more on the history and philosophy of phrenology, see Mauro, *The Art of Americanization*, 18–26.

85. Spurzheim, *Outline of Phrenology*, 20–22; Combe, *The Constitution of Man*, 3–28; Mauro, *The Art of Americanization*, 23.

86. Blumenbach, "On the Natural Variety of Mankind," 200–213.

87. Blumenbach, "On the Natural Variety of Mankind," 201–2; Genesis 3:1–24 (NKJV); Johann Joachim Winckelmann, "The History of Ancient Art," in Fernie, *Art History and Its Methods*, 74.

88. Blumenbach, "On the Natural Variety of Mankind," 201–2; Genesis 3:1–24 (NKJV); Winckelmann, "The History of Ancient Art," 74; also Jeremiah 6:15 (NKJV).

89. Morton, *Crania Americana*, 5.

90. George Combe, "Phrenological Remarks on the Relations between the Natural Talents and Dispositions of Nations, and the Development of their Brains," in Morton, *Crania Americana*, 269–72.

91. Combe, "Phrenological Remarks," 271; Morton, *Crania Americana*, preface.

92. Fabian, *The Skull Collectors*, 98–100.

93. Fabian, *The Skull Collectors*, 16.

94. Fabian, *The Skull Collectors*, 14.

95. Morton to Combe, April 5, 1839, Samuel Morton Papers, Historical Society of Pennsylvania.

96. Combe to Morton, April 14, 1838, Samuel Morton Papers, American Philosophical Society.

97. George Catlin, "Letter from the Mouth of the Yellowstone River," in McCoubrey, *American Art*, 95.

98. Morton, *Crania Americana*, preface.

99. Bisbee and Colesar, *John Collins Artist*, 13–20.

100. Morton, *Crania Americana*, introduction.

101. Morton, journal entry, January 1834, Samuel Morton Papers, American Philosophical Society.

102. Josiah Nott to Samuel Morton, October 15, 1844, Samuel Morton Papers, Historical Society of Pennsylvania.

103. George R. Gliddon, preface, in Nott, *Types of Mankind*, xi.

104. Louis Agassiz, "Sketch of the Natural Provinces of the Animal World and Their Relation to the Different Types of Man," in Nott, *Types of Mankind*, lxviii.

105. James Aitken Meigs, "The Cranial Characteristics of the Races of Men," in Nott and Gliddon, *Indigenous Races of the Earth*, 213; also Morton, *Crania Aegytiaca*, 66.

106. Agassiz, "Sketch of the Natural Provinces," lxxvi.

107. Nott, *Types of Mankind*, 85–86.

108. Nott, *Types of Mankind*, 62.

3. Mormonism, Light and Dark

1. Joseph Smith to John Wentworth, March 1, 1842, in Smith, "Gospel Classics."

2. See Hunter, *Archaeology and the Book of Mormon*, 29–33. Hunter argues that the Aztec deity Quetzalcoatl, which he refers to as the "White Bearded God," is actually a reference to Christ's visitation to the Americas. As such, the iconographic presence of the famous feathered serpent on Aztec temples is a depiction of Christ.

3. Smith to Wentworth, March 1, 1842.

4. For example, Kidd, *The Great Awakening*, on the genesis of "awakenings" in American society. Also see Kruczek-Aaron, *Everyday Religion*, for an assessment of the material culture of Protestants in America during the Second Great Awakening.

5. Reeve, *Religion of a Different Color*, 1–5.

6. Smith, *The Personal Writings*, 433, original journal entry March 14, 1838.

7. Brown, *The Word in the World*, 2.

8. Brown, *The Word in the World*, 2–3.

9. Brown, *The Word in the World*, 42–44.

10. Smith, *Book of Mormon*, introduction. The term "reformed Egyptian" is referenced in the *Book of Mormon* at Mormon 9:32.

11. Smith, *Book of Mormon*, introduction

12. Smith, *Book of Mormon*, introduction.

13. Winthrop, "A Model of Christian Charity," 91.

14. Boyd Packer, "The Arts and the Spirit of the Lord," speech, Brigham Young University, Provo, Utah, February 1, 1976.

15. Packer, "The Arts and the Spirit of the Lord."

16. Packer, "The Arts and the Spirit of the Lord."

17. Smith, "The Life and Ministry of Joseph Smith," xxii–25.

18. Smith, *Pearl*, 1:10.

19. Smith, "The Life and Ministry," xxii–25.

20. Smith, "Life and Ministry," xxvi–25; Smith, *Pearl*, 1:17.

21. Jackson, "Del Parson."

22. Smith, *Pearl*, 1:27–29.

23. Critchley, "Why I Love Mormonism."

24. Smith, "Persecution," in "The Testimony."

25. Smith, *Pearl*, 1:30–35.

26. Smith, *Pearl*, 1:36–54.

27. Oman, "Christensen, Carl Christian Anton."

28. Boime, *The Art of Exclusion*, 1–2.

29. Smith, *Book of Mormon*, introduction.

30. Smith, *Book of Mormon*, 1 Samuel 28:3–6; Smith, "The Life and Ministry of Joseph Smith," xxii–25.

31. Colbert, "Spiritual Currents."

32. Colbert, "Spiritual Currents," 536–57; Fuller, *Spiritual but Not Religious*, 15, 17.

33. Smith, *Book of Mormon*, 1 Nephi 2:4.

34. Smith, "Life and Ministry," xxii–25.

35. Smith, *Book of Mormon*, 1 Nephi 17:13.

36. Smith, *Book of Mormon*, 1 Nephi 18:2.

37. Smith, *Book of Mormon*, 1 Nephi 18:23–25.

38. Swanson, "The Book of Mormon Art."

39. Smith, *Book of Mormon*, 2 Nephi 5:21.

40. For details of the story of the "saved" Lamanite Samuel, see Helaman 13–16 in the *Book of Mormon*.

41. Oliver Cowdery et al., introduction, in *The Book of Mormon*.

42. Smith, *Book of Mormon*, 4 Nephi 1:17.

43. Oliver Cowdery to Hyram Smith, March 3, 1831, in Smith, *The Personal Writings*, 230.

44. Smith, *Book of Mormon*, Alma 53:10–22.

45. Smith, *Book of Mormon*, 1 Nephi 2:16.

46. Packer, "The Arts and the Spirit of the Lord."

47. Saunders, "The Art and Social Conditions."

48. Smith, *Book of Mormon*, 3 Nephi 11.

49. For example, see Galton, *Inquiries into Human Faculty*. On Hofmann, see Swanson Jones, Froelke, and Froelke, "Heinrich Hofmann"; Swanson Jones, "Heinrich Hofmann."

50. Weber, *The Protestant Ethic*, 8–28.

51. Swanson Jones, "Heinrich Hofmann."

52. Winckelmann, "The History of Ancient Art," 68–76.

53. For more on the history of the Düsseldorf Academy, see Atkinson, "Düsseldorf"; Vaughn, *German Romantic Painting*.

54. Stott, "Alexander Ross's Anglo-Israelist Monument."

55. Lombroso, *Crime*, xiv.

56. Fowler, *The Practical Phrenologist*.

57. See, for example, Fowler's discussion of his "Indian Chief" in *The Practical Phrenologist*, 87–88.

58. For more on Catlin, see Truettner et al., *The West as America*.

59. Untitled, *Pittsburgh Post-Gazette*, August 14, 1834.

60. For more on Smith's death and the subsequent history of LDS, see Brooke, *The Refiner's Fire*; Bushman, *Joseph Smith*.

61. Blackhawk, *Violence over the Land*, 230, 244.

62. "Fight between the Mormons and the Indians," *Morning Courier* (Louisville KY), June 21, 1850.

63. Blackhawk, *Violence over the Land*, 238.

64. Blackhawk, *Violence over the Land*; "News from the West—The Mormons and Emigrants," *Morning Post* (Pittsburgh PA), August 6, 1850.

65. Blackhawk, *Violence over the Land*, 257–64.

4. The Social Gospel

1. See, for example, Duncan, *Civilizing Rituals*.

2. Ahlstrom, *A Religious History*, 763–84.

3. The most well-known champions of the social gospel during this era were Richard T. Ely and Walter Rauschenbusch. For primary sources by both men, see Handy, *The Social Gospel in America*.

4. For more on totalizing institutions such as the boarding schools, see Adams, *Education for Extinction*.

5. Both Pratt and Armstrong represent the more "liberal" wing of opinion with respect to the Indian question. Environmental immersion, while culturally genocidal, was at least not literally genocidal, a viewpoint advocated by some at the time. Further, the transformations that were assumed to occur as a result of a successful immersion were seen by them as a Christian imperative, signaling the triumph of a philanthropic Christian ethic in public policy.

6. Parker, *Annual Report*; Pruscha, *Documents*, 133–34.

7. Weber, *The Protestant Ethic*, 105–8. Significantly, Weber here links Puritanism, Calvinism, and Quakerism for their shared emphasis on the asceticism of one's calling in life as a means of salvation. See also Adams, *Education for Extinction*.

8. Scaff, *Max Weber in America*, 182–85.

9. In *Max Weber in America*, Scaff discusses the bureaucratic sprawl of the Dawes-Bixby Commission, which was the subagency within the Department of Interior charged with the actual division of the Territory. The Commission grew rapidly to employ hundreds of people in this mission.

10. Scaff, *Max Weber in America*, 82, 185–91.

11. Scaff, *Max Weber in America*, 85–87.

12. Adams, *Education for Extinction*, 26–27.

13. Richard Henry Pratt to Carl Schurz, April 8, 1880, Richard Henry Pratt Papers.

14. Fear-Segal, *White Man's Club*, 170.

15. Witmer, *The Indian Industrial School Carlisle*, 28.

16. Pratt, "The Carlisle Idea," n.p.

17. Fear-Segal, *White Man's Club*, 103; Armstrong, untitled.

18. Fear-Segal, *White Man's Club*, 107, 109, 113–14.

19. Fear-Segal, *White Man's Club*, 108; Armstrong, "Lessons from the Hawaiian Islands."

20. Mauro, *The Art of Americanization*, 37–38; Pratt, *Battlefield and Classroom*, 105. The Dawes Act was passed by Congress under the leadership of Senator Henry Dawes of Massachusetts. It was designed to allot small parcels of land to specific individuals living on reservations. It represents an effort to break the hunting and gathering lifestyle of the Plains tribes in favor of conventional agriculture. The Fort Laramie Treaty was intended to immobilize the indigenous population on the reservations, and the Dawes Act was intended to inculcate Anglo-American property values. It also represents an assault on the indigenous tradition of shared communal property. For the texts of both the treaty and the act, see Pruscha, *Documents*, 109–13, 170–73.

21. Pratt, *Battlefield and Classroom*, 116–35, 167–79; Mauro, *Art of Americanization*, 39.

22. Pratt, *Battlefield and Classroom*, 192.

23. American Missionary Association, "Constitution."

24. American Missionary Association, "Constitution."

25. American Missionary Association, "Constitution."

26. Various to Samuel C. Armstrong, December 26, 1878, Samuel Chapman Armstrong Papers.

27. Pratt to Armstrong, August 6, 1878, Samuel Chapman Armstrong Papers.

28. Pratt to Armstrong, November 4, 1878, Samuel Chapman Armstrong Papers.

29. Johnston to Cara Folsom, May 16, 1901, Frances Benjamin Johnston Collection; Hollis B. Frissell to Frances B. Johnston, February 9, 1900; March 11, 1901, Hollis Burke Frissell Letter Books.

30. Smith, "A Summer Experiment II."

31. Ulysses S. Grant to Congress, Washington DC, December 5, 1870, in Pruscha, *Documents*, 134.

32. Armstrong, untitled, 139.

33. Ludlow, "On the Threshold," 2.

34. See Szarkowski and Kirstein, *The Hampton Album*; Browne, *Catalogue of the Hampton Normal and Agricultural Institute*.

35. Museum of Modern Art, "The Hampton Album," press release, December 14, 1965.

36. Museum of Modern Art, "The Hampton Album."

37. Museum of Modern Art, "The Hampton Album."

38. Armstrong, *Twenty-Two Years' Work*, 6.

39. Fear-Segal, *White Man's Club*, 109; Armstrong, *Indian Education*, 4.

40. Armstrong, untitled, in *Southern Workman* 5, no. 7 (1876): n.p., quoted in Fear-Segal, *White Man's Club*, 109.

41. Frances Benjamin Johnston, invoice for "Photographs for Paris Exposition," n.d., Frances Benjamin Johnston Collection; Johnston to Folsom, May 16, 1901; May 26, 1901; October 6, 1904; October 21, 1904; October 25, 1904, Frances Benjamin Johnston Collection.

42. Thomas J. Calloway to Booker T. Washington, October 4, 1899, quoted in Harlan and Smock, *The Booker T. Washington Papers*, 226–27.

43. Hollis Burke Frissell to Thomas J. Calloway, December 14, 1899, Hollis Burke Frissell Letter Books.

44. Frissell to Calloway, December 14, 1899.

45. Frissell to Johnston, March 11, 1901, Hollis Burke Frissell Letter Books.

46. Frissell to Johnston, February 9, 1900, Hollis Burke Frissell Letter Books.

47. Frissell to Shaw, January 30, 1900; June 2, 1900, Hollis Burke Frissell Letter Books.

48. Mauro, *The Art of Americanization*, 105–6; Berch, *The Woman behind the Lens*, 39; Smith, *American Archives*, 172–76; Przylyski, "American Visions."

49. Frissell, untitled.

50. Mauro, *The Art of Americanization*, 106–7.

51. Frissell to Calloway, December 23, 1899, Frissell Letter Books.

52. Frissell to Calloway, December 23, 1899.

53. Lentis, *Colonized through Art*, 257–60.

54. Du Bois, *The Souls of Black Folks*, chap. 3.

55. Fear-Segal, *White Man's Club*, 109.

56. Ludlow, "Indian Education," 659.

57. Ludlow, "Indian Education," 660.

58. Davies, *Phrenology*; also see Mauro, *The Art of Americanization*, 18–26.

59. For a summary of phrenology's social functions, see Colbert, *A Measure of Perfection*.

60. Wells, *New Physiognomy*, iii–iv.

61. Wells, *New Physiognomy*, xviii.

62. Morton, *Crania Americana*, introduction.

63. The prisoners' perceived inherent criminality was best summed up in letters written by Mills to Spencer F. Baird, in which the artist delivers a litany of phrenological traits possessed by them and visible in their skull structure. See, for instance, Mills to Spencer F. Baird, July 15, 1877; July 31, 1877, Spencer F. Baird Papers.

64. See Baird to Pratt, May 21, 1877, Spencer F. Baird Papers.

65. Colbert, "Clark Mills"; Mauro, *The Art of Americanization*, 34.

66. Mills to Baird, July 15, 1877, Spencer F. Baird Papers.

67. Mills to Baird, July 31, 1877, Spencer F. Baird Papers.

68. Spencer F. Baird to Richard Henry Pratt, May 21, 1877, Richard Henry Pratt Papers.

69. National Museum of Natural History, *Proceedings*, 201, 211.

70. Frissell to Walter F. Wilcox, December 1899, Frissell Letter Books.

71. Stocking, *The Shaping of American Anthropology*, 1–23; Moore, *Visions of Culture*, 30–41.

72. Stocking, *The Shaping of American Anthropology*, 1–23.

73. Foucault, *Discipline and Punish*, 170–94.

74. Adams, *Education for Extinction*, 63, 124–35.

75. Standing Bear, *My People the Sioux*, 137–38; Barb Landis, "The Names," in Fear-Segal and Rose, *Carlisle Indian Industrial School*, 91.

76. Standing Bear, *My People the Sioux*, 175–76.

77. Standing Bear, *My People the Sioux*, 175–204; Pratt, *Battlefield and Classroom*, 303–4.

78. Standing Bear, *My People the Sioux*, 169.

79. Standing Bear, *My People the Sioux*, 169.

80. Chauncey Yellow Robe to Moses Friedman, December 20, 1910, file 1327, RG 75, Records of the Bureau of Indian Affairs.

Epilogue

1. Adams, *Education for Extinction*, 63. See also Churchill, *Kill the Indian, Save the Man*.

2. Franz Boas to Richard Henry Pratt, June 8, 1891, Richard Henry Pratt Papers.

3. Ordover, *American Eugenics*.

4. Mauro, *The Art of Americanization*; Wheeler, *Jim Thorpe*.

5. Stoddard, *The Rising Tide of Color*; Coon, *The Races of Europe*; Jackson and Weidman, *Race, Racism, and Science*.

6. Synan, *The Holiness-Pentecostal Tradition*, 187–219.

7. Stephens and Giberson, *The Anointed*, 1–20. The young earth theory posits that, per creationist narratives, the planet is only about 6,000 to 10,000 years old. This contrasts with mainstream geological thought, which posits that the earth is roughly 4.5 billion years old, based on the dating of rocks.

8. Gambone, *Art and Popular Religion*, 1–40.

Bibliography

Archival and Unpublished Sources

Benjamin West Papers. Archives of American Art, Smithsonian Institution, Washington DC.

Coates and Reynell Family Papers. Historical Society of Pennsylvania, Philadelphia.

Edward Hicks Papers. Archives of American Art, Washington DC.

Frances Benjamin Johnston Collection. Hampton University Archives, Hampton University, Hampton, Virginia.

Frances Benjamin Johnston Papers. Library of Congress, Washington DC.

Hollis Burke Frissell Letter Books. Hampton University Archives, Hampton University, Hampton, Virginia.

Records of the Bureau of Indian Affairs. National Archives and Records Administration, Washington DC.

Richard Henry Pratt Papers. Western Americana Collection, Beinecke Library, Yale University.

Samuel Chapman Armstrong Papers. Hampton University Archives, Hampton University, Hampton, Virginia.

Samuel Morton Papers. American Philosophical Society, Philadelphia, Pennsylvania.

Samuel Morton Papers. Historical Society of Pennsylvania, Philadelphia.

Scriptures and Study (online archive). The Church of Jesus Christ of Latter-day Saints, Salt Lake City, Utah.

Spencer F. Baird Papers. Smithsonian Institution Archives, Washington DC.

Stott, Annette. "Alexander Ross's Anglo-Israelist Monument: A Material Response to Spiritual Crisis." Unpublished paper, accessed July 2016. Microsoft Word file.

Walking Purchase Records. Haverford College, Haverford, Pennsylvania.

William Penn Papers. Haverford College, Haverford, Pennsylvania.

Published Sources

Abrams, Ann Uhry. *The Valiant Hero: Benjamin West and Grand-Style History Painting.* Washington DC: Smithsonian Institution Press, 1985.

Adams, David Wallace. *Education for Extinction: American Indians and the Boarding School Experience, 1875–1928.* Lawrence: University Press of Kansas, 1995.

Ahlstrom, Sydney. *A Religious History of the American People.* 2nd ed. New Haven CT: Yale University Press, 2004.

American Missionary Association. "Constitution of the American Missionary Association." *American Missionary* 33, no. 10 (October 1879): 317–18.

Ambinder, Marc. "Falwell Suggests Gays to Blame for Attacks." *ABC News,* September 14, 2001. http://abcnews.go.com/Politics/story?id=121322&page=1.

Arber, Edward. *A list, based on the registers of the stationer.* Birmingham, UK: Private printing, n.d.

Armstrong, Samuel C. *Indian Education at Hampton Normal and Agricultural Institute, Hampton, Virginia.* New York: George Nesbitt, 1881.

———. "Lessons from the Hawaiian Islands." *Journal of Christian Philosophy* 3 (January 1884): n.p.

———. *Twenty-Two Years' Work of the Hampton Normal and Agricultural Institute.* Hampton VA: Normal School Press, 1893.

———. Untitled. In *Proceedings of the Department of Superintendence.* Circulars of Information 3. Washington DC: Bureau of Education, 1883, 139.

Atkinson, J. Beavington. "Düsseldorf: Its Old School and Its New Academy." *Art Journal* 6 (1880): 97–100.

Audi, Robert, ed. *The Cambridge Dictionary of Philosophy.* Cambridge, UK: Cambridge University Press, 1995.

Baxter, Richard. *A Christian Directory: or, a sum of practical theologie, and cases of conscience.* London: Simmons, 1673.

Berch, Bettina. *The Woman behind the Lens.* Charlottesville: University of Virginia Press, 2000.

Bercovitch, Sacvan. *The Puritan Origins of the American Self.* New Haven CT: Yale University Press, 1975.

———. *The Rites of Assent: Transformations in the Symbolic Construction of America.* New York: Routledge, 1992.

Bickerstaff's Boston almanack. Boston: Mein & Fleeming, 1767.

Bickham, Troy O. *Savages within the Empire: Representations of American Indians in 18th Century Britain.* New York: Oxford University Press, 2005.

Bisbee, Henry H., and Rebecca Bisbee Colesar. *John Collins Artist, 1814–1902.* Burlington NJ: Burlington County Historical Society, 1979.

Blackhawk, Ned. *Violence over the Land: Indians and Empires in the Early American West.* Cambridge MA: Harvard University Press, 2006.

Blumenbach, Johann Friedrich. De Generis Humani Varietate Nativa. Gottingen: Vandenhoek and Ruprecht, 1795.

———. "On the Natural Variety of Mankind." In *Slavery, Abolition, and Emancipation: Writings in the British Romantic Period,* vol. 8: *Theories of Race,* edited by Peter J. Kitson. London: Pickering & Chalto, 1999.

Boime, Albert. *The Art of Exclusion: Representing Blacks in the Nineteenth Century.* Washington DC: Smithsonian Institution Press, 1990.

Brigham, Clarence. *Paul Revere's Engravings*. Worcester MA: American Antiquarian Society, 1954.

Brinton, Ellen Starr. "Benjamin West's Painting of Penn's Treaty with the Indians." *Bulletin of Friends Historical Association* 30, no. 2 (1941): 99–189.

Brooke, John L. *The Refiner's Fire: The Masking of Mormon Cosmology: 1644–1844*. Cambridge, UK: Cambridge University Press, 1994.

Brown, Candy Gunther. *The Word in the World: Evangelical Writing, Publishing, and Reading in America, 1789–1880*. Chapel Hill: University of North Carolina Press, 2004.

Browne, Hugh M., et al. *Catalogue of the Hampton Normal and Agricultural Institute, Hampton, Virginia, for the Academic Year 1899–1900*. Hampton VA: Hampton Institute Press, 1900.

Bushman, Richard Lyman. *Joseph Smith: Rough Stone Rolling*. New York: Knopf, 2005.

Buttre, J. C. *Catalogue of Engravings*. New York: J. C. Buttre, 1894.

Calvin, John. *The Institutes of the Christian Religion*. 1536. Translated by Henry Beveridge. Grand Rapids MI: Christian Classics Ethereal Library, 2002.

Cave, Alfred. *The Pequot War*. Amherst MA: Amherst College Press, 1996.

Churchill, Ward. *Kill the Indian, Save the Man: The Genocidal Impact of American Indian Residential Schools*. San Francisco: City Light Books, 2004.

Coates, Samuel. *Description of The Picture Christ Healing the Sick in The Temple, Painted by Benjamin West, Esq. President of The Royal Academy, And Presented by the Author To The Pennsylvania Hospital*. Philadelphia: S. W. Conrad, 1817.

Colbert, Charles. "Clark Mills and the Phrenologist." *Art Bulletin* 70, no. 1 (March 1988): 134–37.

———. *A Measure of Perfection: Phrenology and the Fine Arts in America*. Chapel Hill: University of North Carolina Press, 1996.

———. "Spiritual Currents and Manifest Destiny in the Art of Hiram Powers." *Art Bulletin* 82, no. 3 (September 2000): 529–43.

Combe, George. *The Constitution of Man*. Hartford CT: S. Andrus & Sons, 1842.

Coon, Carleton S. *The Races of Europe*. New York: Macmillan, 1939.

Craven, Wayne. *Colonial American Portraiture*. Cambridge, UK: Cambridge University Press, 1986.

Critchley, Simon. "Why I Love Mormonism." *New York Times*, September 16, 2012. http://opinionator.blogs.nytimes.com/2012/09/16/why-i-love-mormonism/.

Cuvier, Georges. *Essay on the Theory of the Earth*. Translated by Robert Jameson. New York: Kirk & Mercein, 1813.

Davies, John. *Phrenology: Fad and Science*. New Haven CT: Yale University Press, 1956.

de Certeau, Michel. *The Writing of History*. Translated by Tim Conley. New York: Columbia University Press, 1992.

Descartes, Rene. *Discourse on the Method*. 1637. Edited and translated by George Heffernan. South Bend IN: University of Notre Dame Press, 1994.

Dowd, Gregory Evans. *A Spirited Resistance: The North American Indian Struggle for Unity, 1745–1815*. Baltimore MD: Johns Hopkins University Press, 1993.

Du Bois, W. E. B. *The Souls of Black Folk*. New York: Penguin Books, 1996. PDF ebook.

Duncan, Carol. *Civilizing Rituals: Inside Public Art Museums*. New York: Routledge, 1995.

Eliot, John. *A Brief Narrative of the Propagation of the Gospel among the Indians of New England.* 1670. Boston: John K. Wiggin & William Parsons Lunt, 1868.

———. *The Christian Commonwealth.* London: Livewell Chapman, 1659.

Evans, Christopher Hodge. *The Social Gospel in American Religion: A History.* New York: NYU Press, 2017.

Fabian, Ann. *The Skull Collectors: Race, Science, and America's Unburied Dead.* Chicago: University of Chicago Press, 2010.

Fantel, Hans. *William Penn: Apostle of Dissent.* New York: William Morrow, 1974.

Fear-Segal, Jacqueline. *White Man's Club: Schools, Race, and the Struggle of Indian Acculturation.* Lincoln: University of Nebraska Press, 2007.

Fear-Segal, Jacqueline, and Susan D. Rose, eds. *Carlisle Indian Industrial School: Indigenous Histories, Memories, and Reclamations.* Lincoln: University of Nebraska Press, 2016.

Fernie, Eric, ed. *Art History and Its Methods: A Critical Anthology.* London: Phaidon, 1995.

"Fight between the Mormons and the Indians." *Morning Courier* (Louisville KY), June 21, 1850.

Ford, Alice. *Edward Hicks: His Life and Art.* New York: Abbeville Press, 1985.

Foucault, Michel. *Discipline and Punish: The Birth of the Prison.* Translated by Alan Sheridan. New York: Vintage Books, 1977.

———. *History of Madness.* Translated by Jonathan Murphy and Jean Khalfa. London: Routledge, 1972.

———. *Madness and Civilization: A History of Insanity in the Age of Reason.* Translated by Richard Howard. New York: Random House, 1955.

Fowler, Orson. *The Practical Phrenologist.* Boston: O. S. Fowler, 1869.

Fox, George. *George Fox: An Autobiography.* Edited by Rufus Jones. Philadelphia: Friends United Press, 1908.

Franklin, Benjamin. *The Autobiography of Benjamin Franklin.* Edited by Leonard W. Larabee et al. 2nd ed. New Haven CT: Yale University Press, 2003.

Frissell, Hollis B. Untitled. *Southern Workman* 29, no. 1 (1900): 8.

Fuller, Robert. *Spiritual but Not Religious: Understanding Unchurched America.* New York: Oxford University Press, 2001.

Galton, Francis. *Inquiries into Human Faculty and Its Development.* London: Macmillan, 1883.

Gambone, Robert L. *Art and Popular Religion in Evangelical America, 1915–1940.* Knoxville: University of Tennessee Press, 1989.

Gamwell, Lynn, and Nancy Tomes. *Madness in America: Cultural and Medical Perceptions of Mental Illness before 1914.* Ithaca NY: Cornell University Press, 1995.

Green, Jacob. *A Vision of Hell.* Boston: John Boyle, 1773.

Green, Steven K. *Inventing a Christian America: The Myth of the Religious Founding.* New York: Oxford University Press, 2015.

Grob, Gerald. *The Mad among Us.* New York: Free Press, 1994.

Handy, Robert T., ed. *The Social Gospel in America, 1870–1920.* New York: Oxford University Press, 1966.

Harlan, Louis R., and Raymond W. Smock, eds. *The Booker T. Washington Papers.* Vol. 5. Urbana: University of Illinois Press, 1972.

Heimert, Alan, and Andrew Delbanco, eds. *The Puritans in America: A Narrative Anthology*. Cambridge MA: Harvard University Press, 1985.

Hicks, Edward. *Memoirs of the Life and Religious Labors of Edward Hicks, Late of Newtown, Bucks County, Pennsylvania, Written by Himself*. Philadelphia: Merrihew & Thompson, 1851.

Hippocrates and Heracleitus. *Nature of Man. Regimen in Health. Humours. Aphorisms. Regimen 1–3. Dreams. Heracleitus: On the Universe*. Translated by W. H. S. Jones. Loeb Classical Library 150. Cambridge MA: Harvard University Press, 1931.

History of Pennsylvania Hospital. "Famous Painting: Christ Healing the Sick in the Temple (1817)." Penn Medicine, last modified 2015. http://www.uphs.upenn.edu /paharc/timeline/1801/tline12.html.

Hofstadter, Richard, ed. *Great Issues in American History*. Vol. 2: *From the Revolution to the Civil War, 1765–1865*. New York: Vintage Books, 1958.

Hunter, Milton R. *Archaeology and the Book of Mormon*. Salt Lake City UT: Deseret Book, 1956.

Irwin, Lee. *Coming Down from Above: Prophecy, Resistance, and Renewal in Native American Religions*. Norman: University of Oklahoma Press, 2008.

Jackson, Dave. "Del Parson: The Artist." *Desert Saints Magazine* 5, no. 4 (2005): 12–13.

Jackson, John P., and Nadine Weidman. *Race, Racism, and Science: Social Impact and Interaction*. Piscataway NJ: Rutgers University Press, 2005.

Jefferson, Thomas. *The Life and Selected Writings of Thomas Jefferson*. Edited by Adrienne Koch and William Peden. New York: Modern Library, 1998.

Kamenka, Eugene, ed. and trans. *The Portable Karl Marx*. New York: Penguin Books, 1983.

Kelley, Robin D. G. "The Rest of Us: Rethinking Settler and Native." *American Quarterly* 69, no. 2 (2017): 267–76.

Kendi, Ibram X. *Stamped from the Beginning: The Definitive History of Racist Ideas in America*. New York: Nation Books, 2016.

Kidd, Thomas. *The Great Awakening: The Roots of Evangelical Christianity in Colonial America*. New Haven CT: Yale University Press, 2007.

Kruczek-Aaron, Hadley. *Everyday Religion: An Archaeology of Protestant Belief and Practice in the Nineteenth Century*. Gainesville: University of Florida Press, 2015.

Landis, Charles I. "Benjamin West and the Royal Academy." *Pennsylvania Magazine of History and Biography* 50, no. 3. (1926): 241–53.

LeBron, Christopher. *The Color of Our Shame: Race and Justice in Our Time*. New York: Oxford University Press, 2013.

Lentis, Marinella. *Colonized through Art: American Indian Schools and Art Education, 1889–1915*. Lincoln: University of Nebraska Press, 2017.

Lombroso, Cesare. *Crime: Its Causes and Remedies*. Translated by Henry P. Horton. Boston: Little, Brown, 1911.

Ludlow, Helen W. "Indian Education at Hampton and Carlisle." *Harper's New Monthly Magazine*, April 1881, 659–75.

———. "On the Threshold." *Southern Workman* 8, no. 1 (1879): 2.

Luther, Martin. *95 Theses, with the Pertinent Documents from the History of the Reformation.* Edited and translated by Kurt Aland. St. Louis MO: Concordia, 1967.

Marr, Kendra. "Donald Trump, Birther?" *Politico*, March 17, 2011. http://www.politico.com/story/2011/03/donald-trump-birther-051473.

Marx, Karl. "A Contribution to the Critique of Political Economy." 1859. In *The Portable Karl Marx*, edited and translated by Eugene Kamenka. New York: Penguin Books, 1983.

Marx, Karl, and Friedrich Engels. *The German Ideology.* 1845. Amherst NY: Prometheus Books, 1998.

Mather, Cotton. *The Angel of Bethesda.* Edited by Gordon Jones. Barre MA: American Antiquarian Society, 1972.

———. *Magnalia Christi Americana.* 1702. Hartford CT: Silus Andrus, 1820.

———. *Memorable Providences, Relating to Witchcrafts and Possessions.* 1689. University of Missouri–Kansas City. http://law2.umkc.edu/faculty/projects/ftrials/salem/ASA_MATH.HTM.

———. *Theopolis Americana.* 1709. National Humanities Center. http://nationalhumanitiescenter.org/pds/becomingamer/economies/text2/theopolisamericana.pdf.

Mather, Eleanor Price, and Dorothy Canning Miller. *Edward Hicks: His "Peaceable Kingdoms" and Other Paintings.* East Brunswick NJ: Associated University Presses, 1983.

Mauro, Hayes Peter. *The Art of Americanization at the Carlisle Indian School.* Albuquerque: University of New Mexico Press, 2011.

McCoubrey, John, ed. *American Art 1700–1960: Sources and Documents.* Englewood Cliffs NJ: Prentice-Hall, 1965.

Miller, Angela, et al. *American Encounters: Art, History, and Cultural Identity.* Upper Saddle River NJ: Pearson/Prentice Hall, 2008.

Miller, William. *William Miller's Apology and Defence.* Boston: Joshua V. Himes, 1845.

Moore, Jerry D. *Visions of Culture: An Introduction to Anthropological Theories and Theorists.* 4th ed. New York: Altamira Press, 2012.

Moquin, Wayne, and Charles van Doren, eds. *Great Documents in American Indian History.* New York: Praeger, 1973.

Morgan, David. *Protestants and Pictures: Religion, Visual Culture, and the Age of American Mass Production.* New York: Oxford University Press, 1999.

Morgan, David, and Sally Promey, eds. *The Visual Culture of American Religions.* Berkeley: University of California Press, 2001.

Morisset, Gérard. *La vie et l'oeuvre du Frère Luc.* Quebec: Edité par Médium, 1944.

Morton, Samuel. *Catalog of Skulls of Man and The Inferior Animals.* Philadelphia: Merrihew & Thompson, 1851.

———. *Crania Aegytiaca.* Philadelphia: John Penington, 1844.

———. *Crania Americana; or, A comparative view of the skulls of various aboriginal nations of North and South America. To which is prefixed an essay on the varieties of the human species.* Philadelphia: J. Dobson, 1839.

Murray, Charles, and Richard Herrnstein. *The Bell Curve: Intelligence and Class Structure in American Life.* New York: Free Press, 1994.

National Museum of Natural History. *Proceedings of the National Museum.* Vol. 1. Washington DC: Government Printing Office, 1878.

National Parks Service. "National Landmark Historical Nomination: Friends Hospital." 1998. https://www.nps.gov/nhl/find/statelists/pa/FriendsHospital.pdf.

The New King James Version Study Bible. 2nd ed. Edited by Earl D. Radmacher, Ronald B. Allen, and H. Wayne House. Nashville TN: Thomas Nelson, 1982.

"News from the West—The Mormons and Emigrants." *Morning Post* (Pittsburgh PA), August 6, 1850.

Nott, Josiah. *Types of Mankind: Or, Ethnological Researches Based upon the Ancient Monuments, Paintings, Sculptures, and Crania of Races, and upon their Natural, Geographic, Philological, and Biblical History.* Philadelphia: Lippincott, Gambo, 1854.

Nott, Josiah, and George R. Gliddon. *Indigenous Races of the Earth.* Philadelphia: J. B. Lippincott, 1857.

Oman, Richard G. "Christensen, Carl Christian Anton." In *Utah History Encyclopedia*, edited by Allan Kent Powell. Utah Education Network, 2016. http://www.uen.org/utah_history_encyclopedia/c/CHRISTENSEN_CARL.html.

Ordover, Nancy. *American Eugenics: Race, Queer Anatomy, and the Science of Nationalism.* Minneapolis: University of Minnesota Press, 2003.

Parker, Ely. *Annual Report of the Commissioner of Indian Affairs, for the Year 1869.* University of Wisconsin–Madison Libraries, Digital Collections. http://digicoll.library.wisc.edu/cgi-bin/History/History-idx?type=header&id=History.AnnRep69.

Penn, William. "Deed between William Penn and the Delaware Indians, July 15–August 1 1682." Historical Society of Pennsylvania, Digital Library. https://digitallibrary.hsp.org/index.php/Detail/objects/2523.

———. *Primitive Christianity.* 1696. Salem MA: George F. Reid, 1844.

———. *William Penn's First Charter to the People of Pennsylvania, April 25, 1682.* Edited by Albert Cook Myers. Philadelphia: William Moland's Sons, 1925.

Pohl, Frances K. *Framing America: A Social History of American Art.* 3rd ed. New York: Thames & Hudson, 2012.

Pomeroy, Jane. *Alexander Anderson: Wood Engraver and Illustrator.* Vols. 1–3. New York: American Antiquarian Society, 2005.

Pratt, Richard Henry. *Battlefield and Classroom: Four Decades with the American Indian, 1867–1904.* Edited by Robert M. Utley. Norman: University of Oklahoma Press, 2003.

———. "The Carlisle Idea." In annual illustrated school catalogue. Carlisle PA: Carlisle Indian Industrial School, 1902.

Pratt, Stephanie. *American Indians in British Art, 1700–1840*. Norman: University of Oklahoma Press, 2005.

Preziosi, Donald, ed. *The Art of Art History: A Critical Anthology*. New York: Oxford University Press, 2009.

Pruscha, Franics, ed. *Documents of United States Indian Policy*. 3rd ed. Lincoln: University of Nebraska Press, 2000.

Przylyski, Jeannenne. "American Visions at the Paris Exposition, 1900: Another Look at Frances Benjamin Johnston's Hampton Photographs." *Art Journal* 57, no. 3 (1998): 60–68.

Radmacher, Earl D., ed. *New King James Version Study Bible*. 2nd ed. Nashville: Thomas Nelson. 2007.

Reeve, W. Paul. *Religion of a Different Color: Race and the Mormon Struggle for Whiteness*. New York: Oxford University Press, 2015.

Rohrer, Scott. *Jacob Green's Revolution: Radical Religion and Reform in a Revolutionary Age*. University Park: Pennsylvania State University Press, 2014.

Rush, Benjamin. *Medical inquiries and observations upon the diseases of the mind*. Philadelphia: Kimber & Richardson, 1812.

Saunders, David. "The Art and Social Conditions of John Walter Scott (1907–1987)." *Illustration* 14 (Summer 2012): 4–47.

Scaff, Lawrence. *Max Weber in America*. Princeton NJ: Princeton University Press, 2011.

Sellers, Charles Coleman. *Charles Willson Peale*. New York: Scribner, 1969.

Shohat, Ella. *Unthinking Eurocentrism: Multiculturalism and the Media*. New York: Routledge, 1994.

Shurtleff, Nathaniel B., ed. *Records of the Governor and Company of the Massachusetts Bay in New England*. Vol. 1: *1629–1641*. Boston: William White, 1853.

Silver, Peter. *Our Savage Neighbors: How Indian War Transformed Early America*. New York: W. W. Norton, 2008.

Smith, Joseph. *Book of Mormon: Another Testament of Jesus Christ*. Palmyra NY: E. B. Grandin, 1830. Reprint, Salt Lake City UT: Church of Jesus Christ of Latter-day Saints, 2007.

———. "Gospel Classics." Church of Jesus Christ of Latter-day Saints, July 2002. https://www.lds.org/ensign/2002/07/the-wentworth-letter?lang=eng.

———. "The Life and Ministry of Joseph Smith." In "Teachings of the Presidents of the Church: Joseph Smith." Church of Jesus Christ of Latter-day Saints, 2011. https://www.lds.org/manual/teachings-joseph-smith?lang=eng.

———. *The Pearl of Great Price*. Liverpool, UK: F. D. Richards, 1851.

———. *The Personal Writings of Joseph Smith*. Edited by Dean C. Jessee. Salt Lake City UT: Deseret Book, 1984.

———. "The Testimony of the Prophet Joseph Smith." Church of Jesus Christ of Latter-day Saints. Accessed October 2016. https://www.lds.org/scriptures/bofm /js?lang=eng.

Smith, Sarah Eden. "A Summer Experiment II: Art among the Indians." *Boston Evening Transcript*, June 2, 1884, 5.

Smith, Shawn Michelle. *American Archives: Gender, Race, and Class in Visual Culture*. Princeton NJ: Princeton University Press, 1999.

Solt, Leo. *Church and State in Early Modern England, 1509–1640*. Oxford: Oxford University Press, 1990.

Spurzheim, Johann Gaspar. *Outline of Phrenology*. London: Treuttel, Wurtz, and Richter, 1829.

Standing Bear, Luther. *My People the Sioux*. Boston: Houghton Mifflin, 1928.

Stephens, Randall R., and Karl W. Giberson. *The Anointed*. Cambridge MA: Harvard University Press, 2011.

Stocking, George, ed. *The Shaping of American Anthropology 1883–1911*. New York: Basic Books, 1974.

Stoddard, Lothrop. *The Rising Tide of Color against White World-Supremacy*. New York: Charles Scribner's Sons, 1920.

Swanson, Vern. "The Book of Mormon Art of Arnold Friberg, Painter of Scripture." *Journal of Book of Mormon Studies* 10, no. 1 (2001): 26–35, 79.

Swanson Jones, Angela. "Heinrich Hofmann: Painter of Christ." In *Sacred Gifts: The Religious Art of Carl Bloch, Heinrich Hofmann, and Frans Schwartz*, 47–65. Provo UT: Brigham Young University Press, 2014.

Swanson Jones, Angela, Hans Froelke, and Ruth Froelke. "Heinrich Hofmann: The Famous Religious Paintings of an Unknown Artist." *Fine Art Connoisseur*, July–August 2011, n.p.

Synan, Vinson. *The Holiness-Pentecostal Tradition: Charismatic Movements in the Twentieth Century*. Grand Rapids MI: William B. Eerdmans, 1997.

Szarkowski, John, and Lincoln Kirstein. *The Hampton Album*. New York: Museum of Modern Art, 1966.

Szasz, Margaret Connell. *Indian Education in the American Colonies, 1607–1783*. Lincoln: University of Nebraska Press, 1988.

Thieme, Ulrich, and Felix Becker, eds. *Allgemeines Lexikon der Bildenden Kunstler*. Vol. 13. Leipzig: Verlag von E. A. Seemann, 1920.

Tobin, Beth Fowkes. *Picturing Imperial Power: Colonial Subjects in Eighteenth Century British Painting*. Durham NC: Duke University Press, 1999.

Trachtenberg, Alan. *Shades of Hiawatha: Staging Indians, Making Americans, 1880–1930*. New York: Hill & Wang, 2004.

Truettner, William. *Painting Indians and Building Empires in North America, 1710–1840*. Berkeley: University of California Press, 2010.

Truettner, William, et al. *The West as America: Reinterpreting Images of the Frontier*. Washington DC: Smithsonian Institution Press, 1991.

Underhill, John. *Newes from America*. London: Peter Cole, 1638.

Van Steeg, Clarence, and Richard Hofstadter, eds. *Great Issues in American History*. Vol. 1: *From Settlement to Revolution, 1584–1776*. New York: Vintage, 1969.

Vaughn, William. *German Romantic Painting*. 2nd ed. New Haven CT: Yale University Press, 1994.

Weber, Max. *The Protestant Ethic and the "Spirit" of Capitalism*. Edited and translated by Peter Baehr and Gordon C. Wells. New York: Penguin Books, 2002.

Weekley, Carolyn J. *The Kingdoms of Edward Hicks*. Williamsburg VA: Colonial Williamsburg Foundation, 1999.

Wells, Samuel. *New Physiognomy*. New York: Samuel R. Wells, 1875.

Wheeler, Robert. *Jim Thorpe: The World's Greatest Athlete*. Norman: University of Oklahoma Press, 1981.

Williams, William H. *America's First Hospital: The Pennsylvania Hospital, 1751–1841*. Wayne PA: Haverford House, 1976.

Witmer, Linda. *The Indian Industrial School Carlisle, Pennsylvania 1879–1918*. Carlisle PA: Cumberland County Historical Society, 2002.

Wolfe, Patrick. *Traces of History: Elementary Structure of Race*. London: Verso Books, 2016.

Wood, George B. *A Biographical Memoir of Samuel George Morton, M.D.* Philadelphia: T. K. & P. G. Collins, 1853.

Woodward, Colin. *American Nations: A History of the Eleven Rival Regional Cultures of North America*. New York: Viking Press, 2011.

Index

Abraham (biblical character), 6

Abrams, Ann Uhry, 75, 79

Adam (biblical character), 9, 38, 111, 112

Adams, David Wallace, 172, 176, 207–8

aesthetic(s): assimilation and, 1; beauty and, 112; Christian, 137; economics and, 9, 13; Greek, 155, 156, 160, 162; in hierarchies, 154; imagery and, 5, 57, 96, 99, 115, 161, 176, 180, 188, 189, 202; Jesus Christ and, 157; Mormon, 132–33, 137, 138–39, 142; mystical realm and, 59; in narrative, 125; Native Americans and, 46; norms of, 219n1; polarization and, 40, 81–82; Puritan, 16, 29; race issues and, 157, 162; secular, 48; "subaltern" populations and, 213; symbolism and, 192; vocational, 173

African Americans: assimilation of, 171, 174, 219n1; conflated with other races, 213, 219n1; in imagery, 187, 191–92, 193, 194–96, 217; as Other, 29; perceptions about, 205; in professions, 191; property ownership and, 196; pseudoscience and, 12, 160; Puritans and, 44, 45; rights of, 197–98; Samuel Chapman Armstrong on, 179, 190; Samuel Morton and, 118; slavery and, 12; in Social Gospel movement, 3, 13

Agassiz, Louis, 118, 120–22

Ahlstrom, Sydney, 170

Albany Congress, 79–80

Algonquian tribe, 58

AMA (American Missionary Association), 179, 181, 183–84, 185, 186

Americanization: Anglicization and, 4; Christianity and, 4, 123; of European immigrants, 173; imagery supporting, 4; by institutions, 175, 178, 182–83, 219n1

American Missionary Association (AMA), 179, 181, 183–84, 185, 186

The American Portrait Gallery (Buttre), 55

American race, 111–12, 113, 122

American Tract Society (ATS), 106, 221n21

anachronisms in art, 79, 81, 82–83, 94

Anderson, Alexander, 106, 107

The Angel of Bethesda (Mather), 87

Anglicans and Anglicanism: authoritarianism of, 23, 24, 64; as dogmatic, 8, 98; Native Americans and, 60; as pretentious, 71; Puritanism and, 21, 28; Samuel Morton and, 109; as threat, 42, 43

Anglicization, 3–4, 6, 175

Anglo-Americans: cultural identity of, 172; education of, 169; as norm, 1–2, 12, 171, 194, 207, 219n1; Other and, 5, 12; pseudoscience and, 6–7, 12, 196, 213; Puritanism and, 55; race issues and, 115, 123, 127, 161, 179; religious beliefs and, 66, 157, 219n3; tensions among, 107; in text and imagery, 56, 78; westward movement of, 162, 163

Anglo-Indian relations, 40, 77, 93, 107, 167–68

Anglo-Israelite history, 126, 157, 160

The Animal Kingdom (Cuvier), 108

animals: humans and, 104, 105, 120–21, 201,

imagery in, 125–26, 129, 132–33, 138–39, 142–43, 145, 147–48, 149, 153–54; narrative of, 136, 144, 145–49, 157; race issues in, 126, 142, 149–50, 165; text in, 129, 135, 142, 153, 163; translations of, 141
Borghese Gladiator (sculpture), 85
Boston Evening Transcript, 186
Bountiful (promised land), 163
bows and arrows, 37–38
Boyle, John, 48, 53
branches, symbolic, 77, 100, 101
bridge, symbolic, 100–101
A Brief Memoir of the Life of William Penn (Wakefield), 101
brightness, 82, 93–94, 141
Burns, Thomas F., 158
busts (sculpture), 203, 209–10
Buttre, John Chester, 54–55, 57; *The American Portrait Gallery*, 55

Cahokia, 195
California (Powers), 145
Calloway, Thomas Julius, 191–92, 193
Calvin, John, 8–9, 20, 21–23, 32, 58, 220n16; *The Institutes of the Christian Religion*, 22
Calvinism, 16, 33, 62, 230n7
cannibalism, 40, 114
capitalism, 4, 7, 8, 9–10, 13, 23, 172, 173, 220n16, 221n17
Carlisle Indian School: beginnings of, 181–82; catalogue of, 211–12; evangelism and, 167, 178; imagery and, 1, 17, 174, 175–78, 180, 187; labor issues and, 177–78, 189–90; legacy of, 207–8, 212, 214; personal name policy of, 208; phrenology and, 205; purpose of, 194; representation in exposition of, 197; students on, 208–11; text and, 174, 199
Catalog of Skulls of Man and the Inferior Animals (Morton), 122
Catholics and Catholicism: lay public and, 130; Martin Luther and, 20–21, 222n1; in New France, 58–59; as Other, 41; Puritanism and, 21, 22, 23, 25, 28, 42; Quakers and Quakerism and, 71, 98; as threat, 43
Catlin, George, 57, 114–15, 161–62
Caucasian race, 111–13, 115–16, 157

Cave, Alfred, 47
Certeau, Michel de, 39
certitudo salutis, 8, 9, 21
Chaco Canyon, 195
character: moral, 196; national, 206, 215; pseudoscience and, 104, 110, 118, 180, 201–2, 204; Samuel Chapman Armstrong on, 190
charity: boarding schools as, 185; messianism and, 2, 9; profit and, 10; Puritanism and, 26–27, 31, 52, 58, 61; Quakerism and, 87, 89, 90–91
Charles II, King, 68
charters: company, 35–37, 40, 51, 52; governmental, 68–70
Cherokee tribe, 173
Chicago World's Fair, 215
Choate, John, 199; *Tom Torlino, a Navajo . . .*, 175, 176, 198, 200
Christ. *See* Jesus Christ
Christ at 33 (Hofmann), 153–54
Christensen, C. C. A., 57, 133–34, 138, 140–41; *The Hill Cumorah*, 141–42, 143; *Joseph Smith Preaching to the Indians*, 161–62
Christensen, Trevor, 133
Christ Healing the Sick in the Temple (West), 83, 86, 89, 90–91, 92–93
The Christian at Work, 193
Christianity: Americanization and, 4, 123; assimilation and, 4, 183, 219n3, 220n7; Catholic compared to Protestant, 28, 43, 72; colonialism and, 19; evangelical, 3, 128; market, 7–8, 23, 220n14, 221n17; Native Americans and, 11, 39, 54, 58, 60, 177; primitive, 14, 28–29, 66, 71, 93; pseudoscience and, 3; race issues and, 10; rationality and, 24; science and, 118, 119. *See also* Anglicans and Anglicanism; Catholics and Catholicism; evangelism; Jesus Christ; Mormonism; Mormons; Protestantism; Puritans and Puritanism; Quakers and Quakerism; Social Gospel movement
Christianization, 4, 13, 17, 42, 175
Christian triumphalism, 5, 54, 61
Christian Union (Sinclair), 116–17
Church of England, 21, 28. *See also* Anglicans and Anglicanism

Church of Jesus Christ of Latter-day Saints.
See Mormonism; Mormons
"city on a hill," 26, 132, 165
Civil War, 155, 158, 164–65, 170, 184
clothing in imagery, 33, 79, 81–82, 100, 153
Coates, Samuel, 92–94
cogito, 24
Colbert, Charles, 144–45
Collins, John, 108, 116
colonialism, 13, 19, 63, 77–78
color: as metaphor, 142, 182, 213; and race, 17,
    111–12, 142, 162, 213–14. *See also* brightness;
    darkness; lightness; whiteness
Combe, George, 109, 110–11, 113–15, 159;
    *Phrenology Applied to Painting and
    Sculpture*, 203
Comly, John, 97
communion, 15, 63, 77, 92, 134, 137
composition in art, 47, 56–57, 76, 78, 84,
    99–100, 180, 189, 191
Conestoga tribe, 74
congressional acts, 175, 214, 231n20
The Constitution of Man (Spurzheim), 109–10
consubstantiation, 20, 222n1
conversion, 53–54, 60, 128, 149–50, 164
Coon, Carleton S., 216
Cornelius, Peter von, 155
Cotton, John, 222n3
covenants, 2–3, 6, 11, 27, 38, 42, 54, 58, 66
Cowdery, Oliver, 144, 145, 150
Crania Americana (Morton), 110–11, 116, 117,
    119, 120
craniology, 2, 108, 160, 202–3, 213
craniometry, 111, 156, 215–16
Craven, Wayne, 22, 23, 33–34, 57
criminality, 159, 203, 205, 232n63
criminology, 157–58, 205–6
Critchley, Simon, 139
Crown, English, 51, 80, 88. *See also* Great Britain
Curry, John Steuart: *Mississippi Noah*, 217
Cuvier, Georges, 106, 107–8; *The Animal
    Kingdom*, 108; *Essay on the Theory of the
    Earth*, 227n80

Daniel (biblical character), 106–7
darkness: metaphors of, 174; morality and,
    171; Mormonism and, 127, 145, 149–50, 160;
    Native Americans and, 44, 50; physiology

and, 48; Quakerism and, 99; race issues
    and, 45; spirituality and, 47, 48
Darwin, Charles, 108; *Descent of Man*, 170.
    See also social Darwinism
Dawes, Henry, 231n20
Dawes Act (1887), 173, 181, 231n20
Dawes-Bixby Commission, 230n9
Debating Class, Carlisle Indian School
    (Johnston), 177–78, 190
deeds, land, 80–81
Defoe, Daniel: *Robinson Crusoe*, 225n21
"degeneracy," 12, 88, 111, 178, 203
De Generis Humani Varietate Nativa
    (Blumenbach), 111–13
deliverance, 136, 146, 148
demographic shifts, 51, 168–69, 170, 201, 216
demonic possession: insanity and, 88; Mather
    family on, 41, 43, 44; Native Americans
    and, 16, 19–20, 53, 86; Other and, 29
demonic world, invisibility of, 41, 45, 48, 53
demons in text and imagery, 48–49, 50–51
Department of the Interior, 230n9
Depression, 217
Descartes, René: *Discourses*, 24; *Meditations*, 24
Descent of Man (Darwin), 170
destructiveness, 159–60
devil. *See* Satan
didacticism, 13, 63, 77–78, 152, 185
Discourses (Descartes), 24
divination, 143–45
divine providence, 28, 31, 32, 70
doctrine: of antinomianism, 25; economics and,
    8; Martin Luther and, 20; Mormon, 125–26,
    128–29, 133, 134, 136, 138, 142; pseudoscien-
    tific, 12; Quaker, 95, 99; rationalism and,
    24; of Second Coming, 5; in Social Gospel
    movement, 170–71; of *sola fide*, 20, 25, 71
Dowd, Gregory Evans, 66–67
Du Bois, W. E. B., 197–98
Durand, Asher B., 55; *Progress*, 78–79
Durer, Albert, 154
Düsseldorf Academy, 155

economics: affecting portraiture, 32–33;
    African Americans and, 198; evangelism
    and, 7–8, 9–10, 13, 135–36, 221n17; in
    Gilded Age, 168, 169, 170; proletarianism
    and, 207; Quaker, 67; slavery and, 118

education, 1, 108, 109, 155, 169, 171, 197, 219n2. *See also* boarding schools; Carlisle Indian School; Hampton Institute

Eliot, John, 6, 52–58

Elizabeth I, Queen, 21

Ely, Richard T., 230n3

emancipation, 158, 170, 193

empiricism: Cotton Mather and, 41; in criminology, 158, 203; increased reliance on, 24; metaphysics and, 40, 110; Mormonism and, 132, 134; pseudoscientific, 7, 12, 200, 202, 216; scientific, 5, 30; slavery and, 121; Social Gospel movement and, 170, 205; supernatural and, 51

Endicott, John, 36–37, 223n33

Engels, Friedrich: *The German Ideology*, 221n17

England. *See* Great Britain

English Reformation, 64

Enlightenment, 4, 24, 51, 65, 84–85, 87, 88, 110, 156, 213

entrepreneurialism, 123

epistemology, 14, 133, 156–57, 170, 203

eschatology, 3, 219n3

Essay on the Theory of the Earth (Cuvier), 227n80

Ethiopian race, 111–12, 113, 118, 121

ethnography, 85, 203, 205, 209–10

Eucharist, 100, 222n1

eugenics, 215–16, 217

Eustis, Ms., 186

"evangelical" as term, 130, 178, 184

evangelism: assumptions of, 72; boarding schools and, 17, 167–68, 182, 183–84, 193, 202–3, 205, 206, 210, 212; economics and, 9–10, 135–36; expositions and, 194; imagery and, 1, 2, 5, 13–14, 54–55, 56–57, 58–59, 98, 177–78, 187–88; Mormon, 127, 128, 130; Native Americans and, 67, 70, 117; pseudoscience and, 7, 198–99; Puritans and, 40, 52–53; race issues and, 127, 167; salvation and, 2–3, 11–12; science and, 108; Second Coming and, 214; secular aspects of, 178–79; Social Gospel movement and, 2–3, 170; survival of, 214–16; text and, 48, 53, 188; "the Word" and, 129–30; work ethic and, 172

Evans, Christopher, 3

Eve (biblical character), 38, 111, 112

evolution: biological, 170; catastrophic,

108, 227n80; racial, 176, 179–80, 185, 199, 213–14; social, 170–71, 174, 176, 186, 191, 195, 199, 211; spiritual, 211

E.W.: *On the Threshold*, 187, 197

expositions, 188–89, 191–96, 197

Fabian, Ann, 114

face masks, 209–10

faith: charismatic, 216; imagery and, 58–59; inner, 66, 71; labor and, 171–72; market Christianity and, 7–8; outer, 66; primitive Christianity and, 14, 28–29, 71, 93; salvation and, 20, 25, 27, 47, 222n3; works and, 21, 25, 99, 222n3

Faithorne, William, 51

Fear-Segal, Jacqueline, 177, 179

Final Judgment, 3, 219n3

"First Day" clothing, 100

Flood of Noah, 45, 49, 108, 122, 227n80

Folsom, Cara, 191

Ford, Alice, 100, 107–8

Fort Laramie Treaty (1868), 181, 231n20

Fort Marion FL, 181–82, 203, 207–8

Fort Sill OK, 181

Foucault, Michel, 88–89; *Madness and Civilization*, 65

Fowler, Lorenzo, 159, 201

Fowler, Orson S., 159, 201, 205

Fox, Christopher, 65

Fox, George, 14, 16, 64–67, 68, 71, 89, 93; *Autobiography*, 64

France, 59–60, 61

Franklin, Benjamin, 10, 73, 76, 83, 88, 220n16

Freake, John, 33

Freake family, 32–34

French and Indian War, 73–74

Friberg, Arnold, 138, 148, 217; *Lehi and His People Arrive in the Promised Land*, 147–48; *Nephi and Laman*, 151–52; *The Prayer at Valley Forge*, 148; *Samuel, the Lamanite Prophesies*, 149; *Two Thousand Stripling Warriors*, 150–51

Friday (fictional character), 225n21

Friedman, Moses, 210

Friends Asylum Hospital, 226n39

Frissell, Hollis Burke, 180, 185, 191, 192–96, 198, 205–6

fundamentalism, 216–17

Galen (Greek physician), 103
Gall, Franz Joseph, 109
Galle, Theodore, 38–40
Galt, John, 75, 76, 85
Galton, Francis, 158
General Allotment Act, 173, 181, 231n20
genocide, 230n5
geology, 107–8, 217, 227n80, 233n7
George III, King, 76
The German Ideology (Marx and Engels), 221n17
Gertel, J. A., 54–55
Gilded Age: assumptions during, 174; background of, 168–70; boarding schools reflecting, 5, 11, 17, 56, 174–75, 197; evangelism and, 167; foreshadowing of, 56; ideology of, challenged, 198, 206; ideology of, continuing, 217; Native Americans and, 165, 167; pseudoscience and, 196; race issues and, 167; Social Gospel and, 2, 17, 167
Glanvill, Joseph: *Saducismus Triumphatus*, 50–51
Gliddon, George, 12, 118; *Types of Mankind*, 119–20, 160–61
God: in *Book of Mormon*, 17, 125, 130–32, 143, 145, 146, 148–49, 150, 151–52; covenants with, 6, 42, 54; evidence of, 22; fundamentalist views of, 216–17; Jews and, 94; John Calvin and, 22; Joseph Smith and, 127, 129, 136–37, 140, 143; Martin Luther and, 20–21, 222n1; in Mormonism, 133, 139, 163; pseudoscience and, 112, 201; Puritans and, 26, 31–32, 34–35, 41–42, 43–44, 45, 48, 87; Quakers and, 65, 70–72, 104, 110, 113, 121; René Descartes and, 24; slavery and, 45; "the Word" and, 130; worldly success and, 16, 22, 31–32, 33
Goddard, Henry, 216
golden plates in Mormonism, 131, 140–41, 143–45
Golden Rule, 32
A Graduate's House (Johnston), 194
graven images, 22, 63
Great Britain: in French and Indian War, 73; French Empire and, 59–60; imagery influenced by, 23, 34, 57; Marian Exile in, 21; mercantile culture of, 23; Native

Americans and, 46, 47, 54, 60–61; Puritans and, 35; Quakers and, 64, 89. *See also* Crown, English
The Greek Slave (Powers), 144
Green, Jacob: *A Vision of Hell*, 48
Gunther Brown, Candy, 129–30

Ham (biblical character), 17, 45
Hampton Album (Johnston), 188–89
Hampton Institute: catalogue of, 189; evangelism and, 167, 182, 205; founding of, 181, 183–84; imagery and, 17, 174, 180, 185–86, 187–89, 191; labor issues and, 179–80, 182, 189–91; legacy of, 196, 208, 212, 214; purpose of, 194; representation in exposition of, 185, 191–93, 194–95; supporters of, 184–85; text and, 174, 186, 188, 193, 200
Harper's New Monthly Magazine, 199
Hawaiians, native, 179, 180, 213
Hawthorne, Nathanial: *The Scarlet Letter*, 56
Hearne, Richard, 46
Heath, Charles, 101
Helaman (prophet), 151
Hellmouth (Revere), 48–49
Hendrick (Mohawk leader), 60–61
Hewer, Josiah, 90
Hicks, Edward: aims of, 16, 63, 105, 122–23; on animals, 104; background of, 96–97; beliefs of, 71, 102–5; finances of, 97; on humans, 104–5; influences on, 101, 105–8, 122; *Memoirs*, 98–99, 101, 102, 103–4, 106–7; occupations of, 97–98; *Peaceable Kingdom*, 66, 95–96, 98–102, 105; Quaker ideals depicted by, 65, 70; on Quakers, 95
Hicks, Elias, 98–99
Hicks, Isaac, 97
Hicks, Samuel, 97
Hicksites, 98, 102
hierarchization, 123, 213, 215–16
The Hill Cumorah (Christensen), 141–42, 143
Hippocrates: *On the Nature of Man*, 103
Hofmann, Heinrich, 138, 156; *Christ at 33*, 153–55
Holy of Holies, 94, 95
Holy Spirit, 116–17
Howells, Adele Cannon, 148
humorism theory, 102–4, 110

Laval, François de, 59

LDS (Latter-day Saints). *See* Mormonism; Mormons

Lehi (prophet), 144, 145, 146–47, 148

Lehi and His People Arrive in the Promised Land (Friberg), 147–48

Lemuel (son of Lehi), 148

Lenape tribe: Benjamin West on, 76–77; French and Indian War and, 73; in imagery, 76, 79, 81–82, 84, 86, 89–90, 93, 95, 101; as Other, 122; Quakers and, 16, 67, 69; Thomas Penn and, 79–81; William Penn and, 70, 72, 77–78

Lentis, Marinella, 197

leopards, 100, 105

Leslie, John, 212

liberalism, 3, 8, 22, 167, 171, 230n5

lightness: Mormonism and, 127, 137, 142, 143, 145, 146–47, 149; Native Americans and, 41, 47; Social Gospel and, 171, 174

lions, 100, 101, 105, 106, 117

literature, 30, 55–56, 138, 149, 169, 220n4. *See also* text

lithography, 56, 108–11, 116–17

Lombroso, Cesare, 158

Luc, Frère, 58–59

Ludlow, Helen W., 188, 199–200; "On the Threshold," 188, 199

Luther, Martin, 8, 20–21, 32, 220n16, 222n1; "The Ninety-Five Theses," 20

Madness and Civilization (Foucault), 65

magazines, 56, 152, 193, 199

Magnalia Christi Americana (C. Mather), 27–28, 38, 40, 42

Malay race, 111–12

Manifest Destiny, 157

Marian Exile, 21

mark of Ham, 17, 45

Marx, Karl: *The German Ideology*, 221n17

Marxism, 9–10, 221n17

Mary, Queen, 21

Massachusetts Bay Colony, 6, 19, 31–32, 33, 40, 58, 220n4

Massachusetts Bay Company (MBC), 35–38, 39, 40, 51, 52

Massachusett tribe, 56

Mather, Cotton: *The Angel of Bethesda*, 87;

beliefs of, 174; influences on, 31–32, 50–51; legacy of, 48; *Magnalia Christi Americana*, 27–28, 38, 40, 42; *Memorable Providences, Relating to Witchcrafts and Possessions*, 43–44, 51, 86–87; millenarianism of, 31, 220n4; Native Americans and, 45–46, 58; New Jerusalem and, 6, 16; on Puritan materialism, 67; race issues and, 29–30, 44–45; sermons of, 32; supernatural and, 41–43, 50–52; *The Wonders of the Invisible World*, 41–42, 45; writings of, 23, 27–29, 214

Mather, Increase, 43, 222n3

Mather, Richard, 7

Mauro, Hayes Peter: *The Art of Americanization at the Carlisle Indian School*, 203

Max Weber in America (Scaff), 230n9

MBC (Massachusetts Bay Company), 35–38, 39, 40, 51, 52

Medical Inquiries and Observations upon the Diseases of the Mind (Rush), 88

Meditations (Descartes), 24

Meigs, James Aitken, 121

Memoirs (Hicks), 98–99, 101, 102, 103–4, 106–7

Memorable Providences, Relating to Witchcrafts and Possessions (C. Mather), 43–44, 51, 86–87

memory, 15, 55, 93

mercantilism, 7–9, 22, 23, 33, 35, 66–67, 77, 83–84, 128, 214

messianism, 2, 94, 128, 219n3

metaphysics, 24, 31, 40, 50, 110, 132, 154, 200

migrants and migration, 73, 126, 146, 157, 163–64, 168–69, 216

millenarianism, 2, 214, 220n4. *See also* apocalypticism; New Jerusalem; Second Coming

Miller, William, 128, 221n22

Millerites, 221n22

Mills, Clark, 203–4, 205, 232n63; *Zotom (Kiowa)*, 203

miracles, 24, 25, 103, 202

Mississippi Noah (Curry), 217

Mohawk tribe, 60–61

Mongolian race, 111–12

monogenism, 113, 117

Montezuma, Carlos, 207

morality, 87, 91, 195, 196

More, Henry: *Saducismus Triumphatus*, 50–51

Morgan, David, 55, 137; *The Visual Culture of American Religions*, 14–15

Morgan, J. P., 185

Mormon (prophet-historian), 131, 140

Mormonism: compared to Puritanism, 126–27; diversification within, 125; evangelism and, 127; imagery and, 14, 15, 134–35, 137–38, 153–54, 161, 217; Israelites and, 126–27; literalism in, 132; mainstream Christianity and, 128–29, 160; millenarianism of, 2; overview of, 16–17; pseudoscience and, 213; race issues and, 45, 126, 142, 149, 160, 162; Second Great Awakening and, 125, 129; text and, 129–30; westward movement and, 126, 128, 163–64

"Mormon Panorama," 140, 161

Mormons: beliefs of, 126–27, 130, 131, 139, 153; federal government and, 164–65; Native Americans and, 159, 161, 162–64; as Other, 128–29, 134; Utah settlement by, 164–65

Morning Courier, 163

Morning Post, 164

Moroni (Mormon prophet), 127, 140–41, 143

Morton, Samuel: background of, 108–9; *Catalog of Skulls of Man and the Inferior Animals*, 122; *Crania Americana*, 110–11, 116, 117, 119, 120, 122; craniometry by, 113–16, 159; influence of, 120, 202, 215, 216; influences on, 109–10, 111; Quaker ideals depicted by, 65; race issues and, 12, 16, 64, 117–19, 121, 200–201

Moses (biblical character), 94

My People the Sioux (Standing Bear), 208–9

NAACP (National Association for the Advancement of Colored People), 197

national character, American, 206, 215

National Gallery (London), 83, 90

Native Americans: assimilation of, 171, 173; Benjamin West and, 85–86, 89; Christianity and, 58; as descendants of Lamanites, 149–50, 159; evangelism and, 11, 53, 56–58, 167–68, 178; Franz Boas on, 206–7, 215; in imagery, Mormon, 161–62; in imagery, Puritan, 35–36, 37–40, 46–48, 49–50, 56–57, 59, 60–61; in imagery, Quaker, 78, 79,

81–82, 85–86, 89–90, 93, 101, 107, 117; in imagery, Social Gospel movement, 175–76, 177–78, 180, 182, 185–86, 189; Joseph Smith and, 127–28; as knowledgeable, 195; land issues and, 173; Mormons and, 125, 126, 159–60, 163–64; names of, 208; negotiations by, 60; as prisoners, 181–83; pseudoscience and, 5, 6–7, 12, 118, 120, 204–5, 215; Puritanism and, 27–28, 29, 43–46, 53–54; Quakers and, 63–64, 67, 70, 72, 79–80, 82, 89–90, 102, 106–7, 118; Social Gospel movement and, 173–74, 178–80, 186, 191, 196, 199–200; as "subaltern," 1, 89–90; "vanishing," 115; in wars, 46–48, 54, 73–74; as workers, 13

naturalism, 22, 155, 170

Nauvoo IL, 126, 146, 162

Nauvoo Legion, 162–63, 164

Navajo tribe, 175, 177

Nazarenes (artist group), 155

Neagle, John, 117

Negro, Eagle, Indian (Johnston), 185–86

Nephi (prophet), 145, 147, 148, 151–52

Nephi and Laman (Friberg), 151–52

Nephites, 127, 134, 142, 149, 150–52, 153, 157, 162, 165

New American Atlas (Tanner), 100

New England, 28, 31–32, 41–42, 67

Newes from America (Underhill), 46–48

New France, 19, 58–59

New Jerusalem: America as, 3, 6, 16, 31, 41–42, 126, 220n4; Cotton Mather and, 27; Temple as, 188; threats to, 16. *See also* apocalyptism; millenarianism; Second Coming

New Physiognomy (Wells), 201

newspapers, 56, 163, 187

Newton, Isaac: *Optiks*, 45–46

New World: Mormon perception of, 127, 138; Puritan perception of, 28, 50, 52, 220n4; Quaker perception of, 70, 95, 99, 102

"The Ninety-Five Theses" (Luther), 20

Noah (biblical character), 45, 49, 108, 122, 227n80

Nott, Josiah, 12, 118, 121–22, 199; *Types of Mankind*, 119–20, 160–61

numerology, 221n22

Nutimus (Lenape Indian), 81

222n3; in imagery, 217; indulgences and, 20; inner spirituality and, 71; Joseph Smith and, 128; Martin Luther and, 222n1; profit and, 7; pseudoscience and, 6–7; Quakerism and, 89–90, 99–100; race and, 45, 113, 122, 142, 143, 149–50, 165, 168, 200; Second Coming and, 12, 219n3, 220n4; wealth and, 10; by work, 8, 172, 175

Samuel (Lamanite prophet), 149

Samuel, the Lamanite Prophesies (Friberg), 149

Sartain, John, 55

Satan, 41–44, 47, 48, 58, 86, 174

Scaff, Lawrence: *Max Weber in America*, 230n9

The Scarlet Letter (Hawthorne), 56

Scattergood, Thomas, 226n39

School of Athens (Raphael), 86

Schurz, Carl, 176–77

Scott, John, 138, 152; *Jesus Christ Visits the Americas*, 152–53

sculpture, 144–45, 156–57, 160–61

Second Coming, 3, 5, 9, 157, 188, 214, 219n3, 220n4. *See also* apocalypticism; millenarianism; New Jerusalem

Second Great Awakening: deliverance and, 136; duration of, 128; floods and, 108; imagery and, 116–17; Mormonism and, 125, 126, 129, 135–36; Puritanism and, 20, 55, 56

secularism: in the American West, 144; boarding schools and, 170, 172, 178; divine will and, 32, 222n1; in imagery, 48, 154; modern, 216; Puritanism and, 36, 51

Seventh-Day Adventism, 128, 221n22

Sharpe, Samuel, 36, 37

Shaw, Albert, 193

Shohat, Ella, 77–78

Simon, Jean, 60

Sinclair, Thomas, 108, 116–17; and Big Elk portrait, 117; *Christian Union*, 116–17

Sizer, Nelson, 201

skulls: collection of, 114–15; criminality associated with, 158, 203, 232n63; in imagery, 34; racial categories based on, 111, 113–14, 115–16, 121–22, 160; size and shape of, 7, 110–11, 159, 202, 206

slavery: focus on, 214; in imagery, 107, 117, 144; Joseph Smith and, 160; justifications for, 7, 45, 117–18, 119–20, 121, 200–201;

mixed attitudes toward, 11–12, 107, 118–19; Quakerism and, 123; student labor as, 179, 190–91

Smith, Hyrum, 150, 163

Smith, Joseph: background of, 96, 134–36; beliefs of, 132, 174; *The Book of Mormon* and, 17, 125–26, 130–31, 140, 143–47, 148, 149, 151–52, 153, 165; death of, 163; fears of, 129; in imagery, 57, 141–42, 161, 162; imagery used by, 138; as Mormon leader, 16–17, 150; Native Americans and, 127–28, 150; *The Pearl of Great Price*, 134, 141; personal migration of, 146; as "prophetic figure," 14; racial theories of, 123, 213; reactions to, 128, 262–63; slavery and, 160; visions of, 139–40; Wentworth letter of, 126, 127; writings of, 214

Smith, Sara Eden, 186–87

Smith, Thomas, 34–35

Smithsonian Institution, 203, 209–10

social Darwinism, 2, 17, 212

Social Gospel movement: capitalism and, 13; evangelism during, 167–68, 170–71, 178; imagery of, 15, 56; as liberal, 3; Native Americans and, 165; overview of, 2; proletarianization and, 175; promoters of, 230n3; salvation and, 11

Society for the Propagation of the Gospel in Foreign Parts (SPG), 60, 61

Society of Friends. *See* Quakers and Quakerism

sola fide (justification by faith), 20, 21, 25

Southern Workman, 187, 191, 194, 199

species, animal: anthropomorphization of, 107; harmony among, 100, 101, 105, 107; human races conflated with, 111, 113, 120–21, 199, 200, 202; humans compared to, 105, 201; Noah's flood and, 108

species, human, 111, 113, 159

SPG (Society for the Propagation of the Gospel in Foreign Parts), 60, 61

spiritualism, 96, 108, 144, 157, 160, 207

Spurzheim, Johann Gaspar: *The Constitution of Man*, 109–10

Stairway to Treasurer's Residence: Students at Work (Johnston), 188–89

Stamped from the Beginning (Kendi), 220n7

Standing Bear (Sioux chief, father of Luther), 208–10

Standing Bear, Luther, 207; *My People the Sioux*, 208–10

sterilization, 216

Stern, Morris, 220n14

Stoddard, Lothrop, 216

stones, divining, 143–44

Stott, Annette, 157

Straet, Jan van der, 38

streets paved with gold, 31, 132, 136, 220n4

subaltern groups, 1, 3–4, 5, 13, 171, 172, 213, 219n1, 220n7

subaltern populations, uplift of: by boarding schools, 178, 180, 186, 187, 191, 197, 202; imagery performing, 69; institutional, 1; pseudoscience and, 3, 12; racial, 6, 176; work ethic and, 10, 189–90

superstition, 51, 145, 173

Swift, Jonathan, 224n56

Szarkowski, John, 188–89

Szasz, Margaret Connell, 52

Tanner, Henry Schenk: *New American Atlas*, 100

Teaching of the Presidents of the Church, 134

technology, 47, 98, 156, 158, 168, 198, 222n27

Temple of Jerusalem, 94

Ten Commandments, 94

Teutonic appearance, 152, 153–54, 156

text: Anglo-Americans in, 56, 78; before-and-after, 186, 202; boarding schools and, 11, 174, 186, 188, 193, 199, 200; in *Book of Mormon*, 129, 135, 142, 153, 163; demons in, 48–49, 50–51; in hierarchies, 213. *See also* literature

theologia crucis (theology of the cross), 20, 222n1

Thorpe, Jim, 215

Tilden, Samuel J., 185

tipis, 44, 87, 194, 195, 212

Tobin, Beth Fowkes, 67, 77, 78, 79, 81, 89–90

Tom Torlino, a Navajo . . . (Choate), 198, 200

Torlino, Tom, 175–77, 198, 200

training: industrial, 172, 177, 191, 194, 209; moral, 171, 180; paramilitary, 174, 185–86; religious and spiritual, 180, 183

transformation: all-encompassing, 200, 230n5; mental, 219n3; physiological, 2, 219n3; prisoners in need of, 205; racial, 2,

175; social, 171; spiritual, 1–2, 12, 103, 142, 144, 175, 183, 219n3

transubstantiation, 222n1

treasure, spiritual and material, 144–45

treaties, 16, 73, 76–78, 82, 99, 101, 181, 231n20

Tribes of Israel, 126–27, 157

Twining, David, 96

Two Kingdoms theory, 20, 32, 222n1

Two Thousand Stripling Warriors (Friberg), 150–51

Types of Mankind (Nott and Gliddon), 119–20, 160–61

Underhill, John: *Newes from America*, 46–48

Universal Exposition (Paris, 1900). *See* Paris Exposition (1900)

Utah Territory, 126, 141, 144, 163–65

Ute tribe, 163, 164

utopia, social, 220n4

Vane, Henry, 47

Verelst, John, 60–61

Vespucci, Amerigo, 39–40

A Vision of Hell (Green), 48

visions and visitations, 136–37, 139–40, 143, 144, 152

The Visual Culture of American Religions (Morgan and Promey), 14–15

vocational aestheticism, 8, 173

vocational asceticism, 172

Wabanaki Confederacy, 73–74

Wakefield, Priscilla: *A Brief Memoir of the Life of William Penn*, 101

Walking Purchase (1737), 79–81

Washington, Booker T., 191–92, 193, 197–98

Washington, George, 148

Weaver, M. S., 117

Weber, Max: on Benjamin Franklin, 10; capitalism and, 7, 8, 9, 13, 23; Native Americans and, 10–11, 172–73; *The Protestant Ethic and the "Spirit" of Capitalism*, 9–10, 171–72, 230n7; theology and, 23; and work ethic, 21, 189–90, 220n16

Webster, Daniel, 202

Weekley, Carolyn, 102

Wells, Samuel R.: *New Physiognomy*, 201

Wentworth letter, 126, 127

West, Benjamin: anachronisms in art of, 79,

West, Benjamin (*continued*)
82–83; background of, 74–76; *Christ Healing the Sick in the Temple*, 83, 86, 89, 90–91, 92–93; on historic events, 76–77; interests of, 85–86; *Penn's Treaty with the Indians*, 67–68, 74–75, 76, 78–79, 81–84, 85–86, 92–93; Quaker ideals depicted by, 16, 63–64, 65, 69–70, 72; Samuel Coates on, 92–93
West, William, 82
Westall, Richard, 101
Whipple, Bishop, 185
"White Bearded God." *See* Quetzalcoatl
whiteness, 29–30, 46, 111–12, 129, 137, 142, 143, 213
white supremacy, 216, 217
wigwams. *See* tipis
Wi-jun-jon (Assiniboine leader), 115
wilderness, 165; Mormons and, 146, 162; Puritans and, 28, 40, 44, 54, 58, 136; Quakers and, 78, 95
Winckelmann, Johann Joachim, 112, 155–56
Winthrop, John: background of, 25; beliefs of, 14, 26–27, 29–31, 54, 58; sermons of, 24–27, 132; writings of, 23–24
witchcraft, 27, 41–44, 50–52, 86
wolves, 61, 100, 105
The Wonders of the Invisible World (C. Mather), 41–42, 45
"the Word," 129–30
work ethic, 8, 10, 21–22, 171–72, 173, 189–90, 214
works: by assimilation, 9; of charity, 26–27, 185; faith and, 21, 25, 99, 222n3; as futile, 222n1; in Mormonism, 130; in Quakerism, 91–92, 93, 99
World's Work, 193

Yellow Robe, Chauncey, 210–12
Yom Kippur, 94
Young, Brigham, 138, 163
"young earth" creationism, 217, 233n7

Zarahemla (ancient city), 149
Zion, 126, 132, 163
Zotom (Kiowa) (Palmer and Mills), 203

CPSIA information can be obtained
at www.ICGtesting.com
Printed in the USA
LVHW092019260719
625490LV00004B/31/P